English Translation and
Classical Reception

Classical Receptions

Series Editor: Maria Wyke, University College London

The ancient world did not end with the sack of Rome in the fifth century AD. Its literature, politics, and culture have been adopted, contested, used and abused, from the middle ages to the present day, by both individuals and states. The Classical Receptions Series presents new contributions by leading scholars to the investigation of how the ancient world continues to shape our own.

Published

Classics and the Uses of Reception
Edited by Charles Martindale and Richard F. Thomas

Ancient Rome and Modern America
Margaret Malamud

Antiquity and Modernity
Neville Morley

Sex: Vice and Love from Antiquity to Modernity
Alastair J. L. Blanshard

English Translation and Classical Reception:
Towards a New Literary History
Stuart Gillespie

English Translation and Classical Reception

Towards a New Literary History

Stuart Gillespie

WILEY-BLACKWELL

A John Wiley & Sons, Ltd., Publication

This edition first published 2011
© 2011 Stuart Gillespie

Blackwell Publishing was acquired by John Wiley & Sons in February 2007. Blackwell's publishing program has been merged with Wiley's global Scientific, Technical, and Medical business to form Wiley-Blackwell.

Registered Office
John Wiley & Sons Ltd, The Atrium, Southern Gate, Chichester, West Sussex, PO19 8SQ, United Kingdom

Editorial Offices
350 Main Street, Malden, MA 02148-5020, USA
9600 Garsington Road, Oxford, OX4 2DQ, UK
The Atrium, Southern Gate, Chichester, West Sussex, PO19 8SQ, UK

For details of our global editorial offices, for customer services, and for information about how to apply for permission to reuse the copyright material in this book please see our website at www.wiley.com/wiley-blackwell.

The right of Stuart Gillespie to be identified as the author of this work has been asserted in accordance with the UK Copyright, Designs and Patents Act 1988.

Library of Congress Cataloging-in-Publication Data

Gillespie, Stuart, 1958-
    English translation and classical reception : towards a new literary history / Stuart Gillespie.
        p. cm. – (Classical receptions)
    Includes bibliographical references and index.
    ISBN 978-1-4051-9901-8 (hardcover : alk. paper)   1. Classical literature–Translations into English–History and criticism.   2. Classical literature–Appreciation–Great Britain–History.
    3. English literature–Classical influences.   4. Translating and interpreting–Great Britain–History.
    I. Title.
    PR133.G55 2011
    820.9'142–dc22
                                                                    2010042236

A catalogue record for this book is available from the British Library.

This book is published in the following electronic formats: ePDF [ISBN 9781444396485]; Wiley Online Library [ISBN 9781444396508]; ePub [ISBN 9781444396492]

Set in 10/13 pt Galliard by Toppan Best-set Premedia Limited
Printed and bound in Malaysia by Vivar Printing Sdn Bhd

1   2011

Contents

Preface

This is not a history of English translation of ancient Greek and Latin literary works, which is one component of a large-scale task that has occupied me for some years in another context. Nor is it a history of the reception of such works by English writers – another currently ongoing enterprise under other auspices. In spite of its chronological arrangement, this book is not a history of any kind, apart from the outline Chapter 1 provides by way of orientation. Instead, it is about the shape and the implications of a historical phenomenon which is in the process of being rediscovered. It first addresses more familiar parts of the English translating tradition sometimes by period and sometimes in terms of individual works, then goes on to attend to a number of unpublished, suppressed and otherwise little-known translations – albeit some of them composed by major English writers. Both the more and the less familiar sites I visit suggest, or so I propose, new ways of mapping nearby neighbourhoods. Although many of the texts I look at have received little or no previous attention, my revisionist approach is not unique in this respect. For example, those who have happened to work more intensively than myself on early modern women writers have very often found themselves contemplating unpublished translations (translation, sometimes from Latin and Greek, was one of the things writing women did), and translation has been one of the genres that has shown us we need to reorient our literary histories to accommodate women writers.

Thus the individual case studies which follow, whether they deal with writers and translators who are well known, anonymous, or at some point between those extremes, are intended to suggest the need for reconsiderations of literary history. In other chapters I engage more directly with current orthodoxies, especially what I tend to see as insular, monoglot versions of English literary history, and argue that rethinking looks to be necessary once we understand how extensive a part classical translation has played in it over time, as anglophone writers have responded to ancient writings. One orthodoxy, for example, is the oft-assumed native generation and subsequent self-propulsion of the English literary tradition itself. Another is the supposition that the English poetic canon excludes classical poetry. Finally, I aim to offer new observations about the reception of the Greek and Latin works involved, well beyond merely pointing to the existence of translations additional to those already familiar to us. In pursuing these aims mainly through historical verse translation, with prose making much rarer appearances, I follow where English translators seem to lead. It is for similar reasons of accommodation to the historical record that the seventeenth and eighteenth centuries are this book's centre of gravity.

In making these ten or eleven short and non-exhaustive forays into the available material, I hope I may encourage others to follow. My conviction is that scholars and teachers of classical literature and English literature have much to learn from each other, and have been sadly impeded in this by what looks like the irresistible development of strongly subject-specific norms. This book reflects the hope that productive dialogues can happen not only between the writers involved in the kind of transactions I look at, but also between those who study their work – that is, between disciplines. At a local and personal level I have felt myself to be taking part in such dialogues for some time now, and for a large portion of my professional career I have looked after a journal, *Translation and Literature*, the continued success of which depends on the willingness of contributors and readers to engage in similar exchanges. This book will have succeeded if it encourages more such conversation to take place.

At the same time I am aware that I need to beg various kinds of indulgence from those with scholarly expertise in classical literature, expertise to which I can lay claim only patchily. My hope is that the price for this indulgence has been paid through my efforts to show my more immediate colleagues in English literary studies the importance to them of ancient Latin and Greek literary culture.

Stuart Gillespie
Glasgow, UK/Washington, DC, 2010

Acknowledgements

As well as more specific debts acknowledged here and in footnotes, it is a pleasure to record thanks more widely for conversations over the years to Robert Cummings and Donald Mackenzie in Glasgow, and equally to another old friend slightly further afield, David Hopkins. All have made suggestions which have improved parts of this book. Chapter 3 on Renaissance translation could not have been written but for the mutually sustaining work carried out with my co-editors Gordon Braden and Robert Cummings for the Renaissance volume of the *Oxford History of Literary Translation in English* (Volume 2, 2010). Papers given at the University of Oxford and the University of South Carolina and hosted by Bart van Es, David Norbrook and Tony Jarrells helped me refine my ideas on early modern tropes for translation. Chapter 4 on Plutarch and Shakespeare had airings at Clare Hall, Cambridge, at Penn and at the Folger Shakespeare Library: my thanks to Elinor Shaffer, Joseph Farrell, Carol Brobeck and my audiences. Earlier versions of Chapter 7 were read under the sympathetic eyes of two old comrades: Glyn Pursglove at Swansea and Leon Burnett at Essex University. Chapter 8 on eighteenth-century translation could not have come about without the assistance of the library staffs at the Beinecke Rare Book and Manuscripts Library, the Houghton Library and, over many years, the Bodleian Library, University of Oxford. For Chapter 9 on Wordsworth I owe special thanks to the National Library of Scotland for facilitating access to manuscripts; helpful suggestions on its content came from Tim Saunders. The present version of Chapter 11 has benefited from Iain Galbraith's comments. No one but myself is responsible for remaining errors.

For the well-timed award of a fellowship which enabled me to bring my work together, I thank the Board of the Folger Shakespeare Memorial Library, Washington, DC, and for assistance on the ground, its Registrar, Erik Castillo.

Some parts of this book have appeared in previous forms. For permission to revise them here, acknowledgements are due as follows. For Chapter 5, a version of which first appeared as 'Horace's Ode 3.29: Dryden's "Masterpiece in English"' in *Horace Made New: Horatian Influences on British Writing from the Renaissance*

to the Twentieth Century, edited by Charles Martindale and David Hopkins, ©
1993 Cambridge University Press. Reprinted with permission. For Chapter 6, a
version of which first appeared in *Translation and Literature*, 8 (1999), to
Edinburgh University Press. For Chapter 11, a version of which first appeared in
Ted Hughes and the Classics, edited by Roger Rees (2009), to Oxford University
Press.

The author and publisher gratefully acknowledge the permission granted to
reproduce other copyright material in this book: 'A Bed of Leaves' from *Collected
Poems* by Michael Longley, published by Jonathan Cape. Used by permission of
The Random House Group Ltd and Wake Forest University Press. 'The Storm
from HOMER, *Odyssey*, Book V' from *Collected Poems* by Ted Hughes, published
by Faber and Faber Ltd.

Every effort has been made to trace copyright holders and to obtain their permission for the use of copyright material. The publisher apologizes for any errors
or omissions in the above list and would be grateful if notified of any corrections
that should be incorporated in future reprints or editions of this book.

Note on Texts

In quoting from printed English texts the antique use of 'u' for 'v', and vice versa, has been silently reversed; so too the use of 'i' for 'j' and decorative italic for roman font. Readers should be warned, however, that it would have been highly questionable to normalize spelling and punctuation in quoting unedited manuscripts; that Chaucer is quoted in the original Middle English; and that old-spelling texts of later (seventeenth- and eighteenth-century) printed works are often quoted in preference to modernized ones. This last policy has seemed appropriate because it would be jarring to place large quantities of unmodernized manuscript verse alongside quotations from printed texts prepared on quite different principles.

1

Making the Classics Belong: A Historical Introduction

One of the oddities of the way the academic disciplines of English Literature and Classical Studies have developed, especially given early connections between them, is that translation history, an area which could in principle be of equal interest to each field, has been largely ignored by both.[1] The book you are now reading is a sign of change and has affiliations on both sides: it is published within a series falling under a 'Classical Studies' rubric, while looming large in its immediate background is the ongoing *Oxford History of Literary Translation in English*, the first full-scale history of English literary translation and a publishing project of Oxford University Press's Literature (not Classics, not Modern Languages) department. But these are very late omens and much remains to be done. Just as we are becoming used to reception moving towards the forefront of the study of ancient literatures,[2] my view is that translation should move towards the forefront of the study of reception. The increasingly monoglot nature of the Anglo-American academic world might provide some excuse for the neglect of translations within the study of English literature, but it cannot do the same for Classics.

What follows in this chapter is a historical sketch designed to provide an overall context for the discussions of individual periods and works that follow. But its further purpose is to suggest in brief compass the scale and centrality of translation from ancient Latin and Greek works in the literature of the anglophone world over the centuries. Its scale and centrality are the reasons why, as I argue from

1. A strong connective link around the time of the beginnings of English teaching in the mid-eighteenth century was the study of rhetoric. See Rhodes (2004), 189–208; Crawford (1998). A recent call for full incorporation of the analysis of translations into Classical Studies is Armstrong (2007).
2. Literally so in the case of Charles Martindale's *Cambridge Companion to Virgil*, 1997, and even more pronouncedly in certain other recent Cambridge Companions when the proportions are weighed.

English Translation and Classical Reception: Towards a New Literary History, First Edition. Stuart Gillespie.

various angles below, a change in the way we write the history of this literature is needed. As things currently stand, 'translation' is not a heading with a lot of entries below it in literary historians' indexes. Within the current *Oxford English Literary History*, for example, the first volume to be published, on the period 1350–1547, offers four index entries on 'translation' to a 600-page study. The work of Chaucer, who was thought of even by his contemporary Deschamps as a 'grand translateur', falls entirely within this period. The *Cambridge Guide to Literature in English* has no entry for 'translation', though there are entries for 'tragedy', 'epic' and even 'imitation'.[3]

The activity of translation had, of course, been at the centre of western culture well before the arrival of the earliest forms of the English language. Translation was fundamental to Roman literature: it is taken for granted as much in modern as in ancient times that Latin letters grew expressly out of translations from works in the Greek epic and dramatic tradition. Livius Andronicus (*c.* 284–204 BCE), sometimes claimed as the 'father of Roman literature', introduced Greek writing to the Romans by translating the *Odyssey* into the Italian Saturnian metre and adapting Greek tragedy to the Roman stage. Others soon followed with closer or looser forms of translation and adaptation: Gnaeus Naevius with plays on the Trojan War; Ennius, Pacuvius and Accius with tragedy; Caecilius Statius with comedy. Translation, that is, had the effect of directly inaugurating Roman epic and drama at a time when these genres were barely emergent in their own right.

As a cultural phenomenon in antiquity, the history of translation is every bit as diverse as it will later become in the anglophone world. Horace's famous claim about rendering Greek lyrics into Latin (*Odes* 3.30.13) covers what is in almost every respect a different kind of thing from the exotic Latin framing by 'Lucius Septimus' of the Greek *Diaries of the Trojan War* by 'Dictys'.[4] The Roman experience is likewise an emphatic but not unique instance of the centrality of translation. In the European Renaissance the medieval literary tradition was invigorated and the literary idiom much enriched by fresh contact with classical sources through translation and imitation, sometimes of a directly experimental kind. It can be said without qualification that in every phase of English literature, and for that matter many phases of other western literatures too, much of the innovative impulse comes directly or indirectly through translation from ancient Greek and Roman texts, and in some eras their impact is fundamental. The effect is often one that is hidden or hard to discern, partly because of the frequent difficulty of determining whether originals or translations were being used in a given instance – did Shakespeare know Ovid's Latin epic, Arthur Golding's English *Metamorphoses*, or

3. Simpson (2002); Ousby (1993).
4. 'Lucius Septimus' is the name attached to the fourth-century CE Latin rendering of an earlier Greek prose narrative purporting to be an eye-witness account of the Trojan War by Dictys of Crete, supposedly the companion at Troy of the Cretan hero Idomeneus. For an English translation, see Frazer (1966).

both? (The answer here happens to be 'both'.) What is certain is that translations from the classics have been enormously widely read in the West, and that their readers and their creators have over the centuries included the most influential of figures (not only artistic figures). Today more than ever, the number of individuals who will read a classical text in one of the readily available series of modern English translations (Penguin Classics, Oxford World's Classics, Everyman's Library, and so on) is many times the number that will read it in Greek or Latin, whether as part of an educational programme or not.

It's a good question what continuity might be said to exist in terms of individual translation practice between, say, Livius Andronicus' Latin rendering of the *Odyssey* and a popular twentieth-century English version of the Homeric poem.[5] In respect at least of how translation has been theorized in the West, continuity over the centuries has been ensured by the influential, though hardly extensive remarks on the subject by Cicero in *De oratore* and *De optimo genere oratorum*, Horace in the *Ars poetica*, Pliny the Younger in the letter *To Fuscus*, Quintilian in the *Institutio oratoria* and Aulus Gellius in the *Noctes Atticae*.[6] Much Renaissance thinking on translation was done around Horace's and Cicero's brief statements especially; their drift is against over-scrupulous, word-for-word translation.[7] But Christianity has successfully intervened in this tradition, with St Jerome and St Augustine, in particular, battling over the translatability of the Word in a fourth-century controversy. Many of the subsequent striations of western theory derive from Augustine's promotion of the idea of a single, true translation.[8]

Because of its sheer scale, the growth and development over time of the corpus of classical texts translated into vernaculars is still imperfectly documented. By as early as the seventeenth century, publishing activity in this area had become so voluminous that a comprehensive bibliographical record even of translations of classical texts into English has not yet been assembled.[9] But perhaps a few statistics will be suggestive. The latest bibliographies of English classical translations for the 250-year period 1550–1800, a period which might be held to constitute the golden age of the tradition, run to some 1,500 items for about 100 ancient authors.[10] These are not comprehensive listings of every individual translation, but

---

5. For Livius' *Odusia*, see Conte (1994), 40–1; Mariotti (1952). For the acclaimed twentieth-century version of the *Odyssey* by Robert Fitzgerald, see Chapter 11, below.
6. These texts are conveniently assembled in English translations in Weissbort and Eysteinsson (2006), 20–33.
7. For continental Renaissance translation theory as derived from classical sources, see Rener (1989), esp. 261–326.
8. For the 'striations', see Robinson (1992).
9. There are, however, currently research programmes undertaking the cataloguing of translations, as for instance for early modern translations into English at the Centre for the Study of the Renaissance at the University of Warwick. Earlier bibliographies covering classical translation in the more manageable period to the first half of the seventeenth century are Palmer 1911 and Lathrop (1933); Bolgar (1954) is supplemented for English by Nørgaard (1958).
10. Cummings and Gillespie (2009); Gillespie (2009).

records of the more substantial and significant for these years. They may represent the complete works of an ancient writer, a selection, or a single text; the single texts may range from an epic poem to a satire, but are usually substantial enough to have been printed as a book, whether long or short, in themselves. Virgil, for instance, collects 103 entries, 95 of which are in verse. The most substantial of these are half-a-dozen complete *Works* and the same number of separate *Aeneid*s, followed by nine or ten complete translations apiece of the *Georgics* and *Eclogues*. Most of the remainder are selections of one kind or another, frequently one or more Books of the *Aeneid*, with a few 'translations' into burlesque or parodic form thrown in. Naturally enough, because the originals are of a more manageable average length, Horace attracts more translations: some 160 are listed, with interest taking off after 1650, and with satires as popular as odes during the eighteenth century. Ovid's total is about 100 translations for the same period. But a checklist for Ovid continuing on to the present finds a similar total again for the years 1800 to 2004, even with the more routine prose translations and school texts excluded for the nineteenth and twentieth centuries. It also records a further 37 English translators who were responsible for short excerpts or individual items such as elegies.[11] That's almost 250 Ovid translations all told, many of them by very recognizable English literary figures, and including 28 complete *Metamorphoses*. All these totals are confined to printed works, whereas I will be suggesting later that texts remaining in manuscript often made up a significant part of translating activity too. There is absolutely no shortage of material to address here.

But there is no difficulty in sketching out a general history of classical translation in post-classical times, thanks not least to the pioneering work of the *Oxford History of Literary Translation in English* (soon to be joined by the *Oxford History of Classical Reception in English*). Such a narrative might begin with a prequel to the accounts such sources make available for the vernacular, which is to say with the continuing tradition of translation from Greek into Latin. The lead was given by Boethius (480–524/5 CE), who prepared literal Latin versions of the Greek philosophers which he intended would create an archive for civilization, together with Jerome (*c.* 341–420), whose methods of biblical translation prioritized accuracy. The Greek East and Latinate West had to communicate, and there was a Greek presence along the northern coast of the Mediterranean for much of the early Middle Ages. The Roman senator Cassiodorus (*c.* 480–*c.* 550) founded a monastery where monks were to translate works of philosophy and theology from Greek into Latin. By the eighth century it was the Muslim world that was making the running with Greek material: in Toledo and Baghdad, in Sicily and Seville, could be found Muslims active in turning classical Greek works of philosophy and physical science into Arabic. When Aristotle and other Greek philosophers were introduced into European universities in the twelfth and thirteenth centuries, it

11. Gillespie and Cummings (2004).

was through Latin versions of these Arabic translations, one result being that Aristotle was condemned by some authorities as a pagan influence.

Nevertheless, the relative marginality of translation to the 'universalizing' Latin culture becomes clear when this picture is contrasted with the role translation will come to play as a vehicle of cultural exchange within vernaculars. For much of the Latinate Middle Ages, down to the late fourteenth century, translation was not actually necessary, as Stephen Medcalf has recently spelled out. 'As long as to be literate normally involved belonging to the clergy, whose language was Latin,' Medcalf writes, 'the Latin classics were a literary heritage to be retold, continued or imitated, like the *Aeneid* in Geoffrey of Monmouth's *Historia Regum Brittaniae*, but there was no great point in translating them. Nor indeed did the *Aeneid* or the works of Ovid, Lucan, or Statius have the status accorded them in the Renaissance, of works whose meaning and style needed to be recovered.'[12] Greek texts, too, were still much more often turned into Latin than other languages – the natural impulse following the recovery of ancient Greek was to resume the work of Boethius and late antiquity and translate into Latin. As Greek scholars from the Byzantine Empire reached fourteenth-century Italy, the humanist translating tradition began to take shape. Both Galen and Hippocrates were Latinized by an early figure, Niccolo da Reggio (1280–1350). The first humanist rendering of Aristotle, again into Latin, was Leonardo Bruni's of 1423. Bruni, more than any other, made the treasures of the Hellenic world available to the Latin reader through his literal translations of Greek authors, among them Plato, Plutarch, Demosthenes and Aeschines. Marsilio Ficino, Georgio Valla, Theodore Gaza and Angelo Poliziano followed in Bruni's footsteps. Translations of Plato, a considerable challenge, extended to the full corpus by the first half of the fifteenth century; Ficino then consolidated the work of numerous hands by preparing a humanistic *Opera omnia* in 1463–9. Direct translation from Greek into vernaculars had been occasional since the twelfth century through the agency of such figures as James of Venice (*fl.* 1125–50). In England the Anglo-Norman Robert Grosseteste, Bishop of Lincoln, had placed several works at the disposal of a learned European audience in this way in the 1240s, among them Aristotle's *Nicomachean Ethics* and *De caelo*.[13] But it was not until the arrival of Greek instruction at Oxford during the second half of the fifteenth century, along with the contemporaneous development of printing, that English translations of Greek texts appeared in significant numbers.

Meanwhile the English language had been emerging as a literary medium. While it is evident that some classics were rendered into Old English, the limitations on our knowledge of the results are severe. A tantalizing indication of the non-survival of such texts is an early eleventh-century manuscript fragment of the Greek romance *Apollonius of Tyre*, translated into Old English. Woefully incomplete as it is, it forms the first known vernacular translation of the story and 'arguably the

---

12. Medcalf (2008), 364.
13. For a recent overview of Grosseteste's work, see Rosemann (2008).

first English romance'.[14] Or again, after the Norman Conquest Marie de France claimed in the late twelfth century to have translated a collection of Aesop's *Fables* from an English rendering by King Alfred, but if anything along these lines was available to her, neither it nor other mentions of it survive. The arrival of printing naturally had the effect of ensuring a much higher survival rate for translations as for other kinds of texts.

Chaucer (*c.* 1343–1400) has his Man of Law say that the poet 'hath told of loveris up and down | Mo than Ovide made of mencioun'. In fact, most of Chaucer's 'loveris' are derived from Ovid's *Metamorphoses* and *Heroides*. In some cases (Ceyx and Alcyone, Thisbe, Philomela) Chaucer shares Ovidian material with Gower. But Chaucer, in particular, acquired much more from Ovid than narrative material, whereas he acquired nothing from his Anglo-Saxon predecessors.[15] His principal formal translation from Latin is, however, his *Boece* – one of four medieval versions of the *Consolation of Philosophy*.[16] The impact of Boethius is apparent in the language and thought of several works central to the Chaucerian corpus: *The Book of the Duchess, The Knight's Tale, Troilus and Criseyde*.

On a pan-European view from the beginning of printing in the mid-fifteenth century to 1600, and speaking quantitatively, classical translation moved fastest in Italy and France, with German, Spanish and English following some distance behind.[17] The material translated was broad in range, including medical, military and technical texts. In this era there are as many printed vernacular translations from Greek authors as from Latin ones overall: Plutarch is felt to stand more in need of translation than Ovid, Lucian more than Martial. But they are not often translations from the Greek language: 'secondary' (or 'indirect') translation from intermediate versions in other languages is common, especially so in England from French texts of Greek classics. Plutarch's *Lives* were expressly translated by Sir Thomas North in 1579 from Jacques Amyot's French of 1559, and not from the Greek (the relationships are explored further in Chapter 4, below). Similarly Aristotle's *Politics*, englished in 1598 by I.D. (John Dee?) from Louis Le Roi's French of 1568. Equally, the Latin versions of Greek works produced by many European translators alongside translations into the vernaculars were very often the source of English versions. Among the first direct translations from Greek texts, though, are Thomas Elyot's version of Lucian's *Necromantia* (bilingually in English with Thomas More's Latin, 1530) and Gentian Hervet's *Oeconomicus* of Xenophon (1532).

14. So Archibald (1991), 184; for a summary account of the manuscript and related scholarship, see 183–4.
15. For Chaucer and Ovid, see Calabrese (1985).
16. *Boece* draws on Jean de Meun's French prose translation, collating and supplementing it with the Latin original. For a major study of medieval receptions of Boethius, see Minnis (1993).
17. Bolgar (1954), Appendix 2, presents comparative tables for first translations of individual works into the respective European vernaculars. The French picture for the sixteenth century is well described by Hutton (1980).

Why was the acquisition of classical works a slower process for English than for Italian or French? There was clearly a ready audience: a verse translation of the *Aeneid* (by Phaer and Twine) went through six editions between 1573 and 1620. But the effort was unofficial and uncoordinated, largely a matter of individual initiative. This included the initiatives of patrons, but translation did not enjoy the kind of royal patronage provided for it in France. Nor was there in England a scholarly publishing house comparable to those of Aldus and Paulus Manutius in Venice, the Estiennes in Paris, or Plantin in Antwerp. But the tide washed in new literary translations continuously, as well as all manner of practical, technical, political, polemical and in particular doctrinal translated material, to contribute to what was by 1600 an extensive translating culture. In one bibliography of 'literary' English translations, broadly defined, for the period 1550 to 1660, Latin originals (classical and contemporary, along with some medieval religious texts) are estimated to account for 40 per cent of the material.[18]

In addition to the literary arrivals already mentioned, sixteenth-century England embarked on the vernacularization of Ovid, extending to most of the corpus in published verse translations by 1572; of Horace's *Satires* and *Ars poetica*; of Martial and Ausonius; of Seneca's tragedies; of Homer; of Longus, Heliodorus and Apuleius. Other new arrivals in part or whole included Euripides and Sophocles, Moschus and Musaeus, Theocritus and Achilles Tatius. The exemplary and informative works of classical historians gained them much attention: Sallust (*c*.1520), Caesar (1530, 1565), Livy (1544, 1570), Thucydides (1550), Herodian (1556), Polybius (1568), Appian (1578) and Tacitus (1591, 1598). For the sixteenth century, 'letters' could also include such texts as Proclus (1550), Euclid (1570) and Vegetius (1572), as well, of course, as moralists such as Epictetus (1567) and orators and rhetoricians such as Isocrates (1534, 1576, 1580) and Demosthenes (1570).[19]

At the most familiar level of classical learning, school texts often comprised translations of selections from suitable authors such as Aesop or Terence. These are easy to overlook. The translations are prosaic and, what (in aesthetic terms) is worse, they are often 'grammatical' – that is, with the English syntax following the Latin for pedagogical purposes. In terms of readership and of publishing history, however, the scale involved was large. One famous compilation is by a schoolmaster, Nicholas Udall, whose *Flours for Latine Spekynge selected and gathered oute of Terence, and the same translated into Englysshe*, first appeared in 1533. Another is *The Distichs of Cato*, used in England with the annotations of Erasmus, presented as an aid to Latin language learning in 1540 by Richard Taverner in a bilingual text reprinted in 1553, 1555 and 1562, then supplanted in 1577 by an anonymous version 'newly englished to the comforte of all young schollers', itself reprinted in 1584. 'Cato', as it was called, has been singled out as '*par excellence*

---

18. Braden, Cummings and Gillespie (2010), 9.
19. For a complete chronological listing of printed English translations of this era by classical author, see Cummings and Gillespie (2009).

the first of schoolbooks, and the elementary moral treatise of the Middle Ages'. It was edited, augmented, selected, and in time translated into a dozen European vernaculars, 'first as a means to assist in the understanding of the original, or in verse, emulating the Latin in a modern language'.[20] Such compilations – texts sometimes printed together with *Cato* include the proverbs of Publilius Syrus and the *Dicta Sapientum* – were in use on a scale out of all proportion to their barely perceptible profile today. Their users, we might bear in mind, will have included almost every historically identifiable male of Renaissance England. Much of Shakespeare's experience of Latin writing, like that of all other sixteenth-century grammar school boys, thus came in the first instance not in the form of complete works of verse or prose but from such collections of *sententiae*, 'dicta', and the like, in which the Latin was often accompanied by more or less literal English translations – the traces of which can sometimes be found in his own works.[21]

By the mid-sixteenth century, English vernacular writing begins consciously to seek to remodel itself according to Latin standards, whether of linguistic purity or literary quality. Translation, in fact, is often felt to reveal the poverty of the vernacular. Humanist teachers were concerned with the quality of the vernacular and not only with language learning, so that their instruction in Latin and Greek rhetoric laid the foundations of literary English from the Tudor era on. Nor was the translator's role necessarily servile, at least once training was complete. At the highest level the instinct of classical translators and imitators is competitive. Edmund Spenser's ambition is to 'overgo' his sources; Ben Jonson, translator of Horace, imitator of Martial, Virgil, Tacitus, invokes the classics as 'guides, not commanders'.[22] And, as is revealed by some of the metaphors its exponents use, translation was seen not just as a method of fertilization, but, in other moods and contexts, as a form of invasion, colonization or conquest.[23]

If we are to believe Thomas Warton, the 'first English classical poet' had already come and gone by 1550 in the shape of Henry Howard, Earl of Surrey (1517–47).[24] Surrey translated Books 2 and 4 of Virgil's *Aeneid*, drawing on the compelling, but isolated and posthumously published, early sixteenth-century version in Scots by Gavin Douglas.[25] Surrey's best original poems, with their close attention

---

20. Lathrop (1933), 16.

21. For Shakespeare's use of Publilius Syrus, see Smith (1963); of Aesop, Gillespie (2001), 9–13; of Taverner's Cato, Baldwin (1944), 603–6. A list of school translations in use in the period appears in Tuck (1950).

22. *Timber, or Discoveries*, Jonson (1975), 379. For Jonson's attitudes to classical authority, see further pp. 44–5. below.

23. See Chapter 3 for some of these tropes. For attitudes to the practice of translation in the Tudor period, see Morini (2006).

24. Warton (1774–81), III, 2: 'Surrey the first English classic poet' (section heading); Warton's discussion of his work is at III, 10–25.

25. Sources on this material include Jones (1964) for Surrey and Cummings (1995) for Douglas's *Aeneid*. Douglas's translation was completed in 1513 and published in 1553.

to individual words and phrases, are those of one who has appreciated Martial, Virgil and Horace. Thus Surrey's work reflects the effort to discover new possibilities for English writing as an impetus to translation of the classics. But translation could have many different purposes (and, as we have begun to see, different readerships). A few years after Surrey's death, Thomas Hoby suggested others in the dedication to his English rendering of Castiglione (1561):

> the translation of Latin or Greeke authours, doeth not onely not hinder learning, but furthereth it, yea it is learning itselfe, and a great stay to youth … and a vertuous exercise for the unlatined to come by learning, and to fill their mind with the morall vertues, and their bodies with civill condicions, that they may bothe talke freely in all companie, live uprightly, though there were no lawes, and be in a readinesse against all kinde of worldlye chaunces that happen, whiche is the profit that commeth of Philosophie.[26]

Such sentiments will echo through translators' prefaces over many decades to come. Though their conventionality is apparent, their rehearsal reveals that justification for englishing the classics was felt necessary. There have perhaps been opponents of vernacularization for as long as it has gone on.

By 1600 there was still in English no full translation of Latin authors as considerable as Lucretius, Persius or Quintilian, to say nothing of some even larger Greek lacunae. But developments towards the end of the sixteenth century had been rapid. Older favourites such as Cicero were being freshly translated, but there was also a taste for later, sometimes post-classical, texts – William Aldington's Apuleius of 1566 would be one example. Some Renaissance English translators produced work which has remained squarely within the English literary canon, and indeed the translators were often well-known writers independently of their translating work: for example, the poets and playwrights Christopher Marlowe (who translated Ovid and Lucan), George Chapman (Homer, Hesiod, Juvenal and Musaeus) and Ben Jonson (Horace's *Ars poetica* line for line; Martial, Ovid, Catullus, Horatian satire and other texts more freely). In England translators usually worked outside the academic world as their contemporaries abroad did not. They were courtiers, students at the Inns of Court, gentleman-soldiers and many other things. Far from operating on scholarly principles, they are regularly found using a French or Italian intermediate text where access to a Latin or Greek original must have been feasible – and indeed sometimes seeing this as a virtue. But many of their productions have proved more durable than more scholarly undertakings.

'After the age of Jonson,' Thomas Greene writes, 'ancient culture acquired in England that straddling status it already possessed on the Continent: it was foreign but at the same time it *belonged*. It had undergone its process of reception, and

---

26. Hoby (1588), ¶3[r].

now it was progressively a native possession.'[27] For 'reception' we could read 'translation', which for most readers – as contemporary discussion shows – was easily the most significant aspect of the 'process'. That is, a classical text, author or even genre is felt to have been definitively acquired for the anglophone world once successful translations have become available. So Jonson welcomes Chapman's Hesiod (the first in English, in 1618, following Chapman's 1611 *Iliad*):

> Whose worke could this be, Chapman, to refine
> Olde Hesiods Ore, and give it us; but thine,
> Who hadst before wrought in rich Homers Mine?
>
> What treasure hast thou brought us! and what store
> Still, still, dost thou arrive with, at our shore,
> To make thy honour, and our wealth the more![28]

More metaphors than one are at work here, but the idea of 'acquisition' (and indeed 'possession', to use Greene's word) is central. In spite of this example, however, with this period Greene's generalization works better for Latin than Greek: Plato might have been translated into Latin by Jonson's time, but a full-scale English version took until 1701, and even then it came by way of a French text. In the Latin-based culture of Christendom, a poem like the *Iliad* was in so many ways an 'alien text',[29] not readily accommodated to the Renaissance epic norms of moral teaching, allegory and romance. It had probably been experienced by relatively few English readers by the time Chapman began publishing his translations in 1598. But increasingly through the seventeenth century, classical texts are no longer there to be 'discovered' by the translator. One of the purposes of fresh translations is to broaden the range of what translators themselves wish to write about. This means, as Richard Stoneman puts it, that 'even those works which to us read like a translation ... in fact often diverge in directions the author himself wished to expand'.[30] Translators speak in the person of their authors. Sometimes it is the pressures of contemporary politics that make themselves felt, as in Thomas May's version of Lucan's *Pharsalia* (1627), which idealizes Pompey as a republican leader and regrets Rome's drift into empire. May's dedications to the individual Books situate his work among a politically independent and hawkish nobility tending towards parliamentary opposition to royal policies.[31] May's Latin and English verse are symbiotically related: he also composed in English couplets a continuation of Lucan's epic down to the death of Caesar which, when later

---

27. Greene (1982), 293.
28. Jonson, 'To my worthy and honour'd Friend, Mr George Chapman', in Chapman (1618), A4ᵛ.
29. Sowerby (1994), 9. See 1–29 for his account of Homer's Renaissance standing, with particular reference to Chapman.
30. Stoneman (1982), 10.
31. Norbrook (1999), 57–66.

recast by him into hexameters, found its way into editions of the *Pharsalia*. On the other side of the political divide, during the Civil War period many Royalists turn to classical translation, whether as exiles of one kind or another, like Sir John Denham, or in postwar retirement at home, like Abraham Cowley, who worked Horace, Claudian, Seneca, Martial and Virgil into his reflections on the good life in his *Essays in Prose and Verse*, 1668. Thomas Stanley, another Royalist, after retiring to his estate from an inhospitable London following the execution of Charles I in 1649, combined his lyric bent with his considerable Greek scholarship in translations of 'Anacreon', Bion and Moschus. By this time it was becoming common, as in Stanley's case, for an English poet's translations of individual short poems, selected according to his tastes and affinities, to appear within a miscellaneous collection of his original and translated verse, an arrangement foreshadowed in the innovative Jonson *Works* of 1616.

New markets emerge among readers after the 1660 Restoration: women, and the non-classically educated middle classes, are targeted by publishers specializing in literary translation such as Jacob Tonson (1656?–1736).[32] However, at least some classical translation had already been aimed at a wide audience: the Elizabethan Seneca, for example, in the *Tenne Tragedies* gathered together in 1581, seems to have spoken to all those who enjoyed the contemporary stage. These and other early translations of the Renaissance now start to look comprehensively dated, so that new versions are felt necessary – not only of Seneca (by Sir Edward Sherburne in 1679 and 1701, and others), but Plutarch (by several hands, 1683–5), Virgil (Dryden, 1697), Josephus (Roger L'Estrange, 1702), Ovid (Samuel Garth and others, 1717) or Homer (Alexander Pope, 1715–26). But translators are often deeply aware of their predecessors, and may seek deliberately to use and embody within their work the best parts of the tradition in which they can now see for the first time they stand. Whereas his predecessors had stressed novelty and innovation, Dryden's *Works of Virgil* draws on previous English Virgils repeatedly, attempting to fashion a kind of summation of English versions. The most recent editor of Dryden's Virgil, William Frost, remarks the way 'the neo-classical translators read, studied, and reacted to each other's versions, borrowing lines or phrases from each other ... and generally operating under the stimulus of an enterprise felt to be cumulative and mutual'.[33]

Notable over the eighteenth century is the popularity and longevity of the leading classical translations. Dryden's Virgil (1697) goes through ten editions by 1790, while Pope's 1715–20 *Iliad* and 1725–6 *Odyssey*, with some 50 editions

---

32. And by his star translator, Dryden, who is explicit about this in 1693, writing of his target audience as consisting of 'Gentlemen and Ladies, who tho they are not Scholars are not Ignorant: Persons of Understanding and good Sense ... not ... conversant in the Original'. *Discourse of Satire*, Dryden (1956–2000), IV, 87.

33. Frost (1988), 93, with documentation from eighteenth-century Persius translations. For recent discussion of Dryden's Virgil in this regard, see Frost's edition of Dryden's *Æneis* in Dryden (1956–2000), VI, 862–70.

separately or together, can fairly be said to make Homer a classic for the Enlightenment English reader.[34] But different kinds of translation had differing purposes. Utilitarian cribs met pedagogical needs. At the opposite extreme, for readers with good Latin or Greek, a translation could become a kind of commentary on its original, generating at the highest artistic pitch a complex intertextual play, as with Pope's satirical *Imitations of Horace* (1733–8), which appeared with the Latin texts of the relevant epistles *en face*. Pope's choices of English equivalents for characters and their actions (and sometimes his silence, as when blank space corresponds to Horatian approbation of a public figure) are in themselves telling.[35] Such effects are only likely with the most familiar of classics. Much misunderstanding is today caused by ignorance of a translator's ambitions: Pope's Horace is simply not meant as a guide to verbal meaning. Once again, a divide opens up between current expectations and the very different assumptions of previous eras; the prime objective in the eighteenth century was usually understood to be semantic accuracy only when it came to school texts. Otherwise, the priority might very often be the reproduction of 'classic' aesthetic qualities by any available means. Hence the centrality of the medium of translation to the movement later known as English Augustanism, which took as the guiding lights for its poetics Virgil, Ovid and Horace. Translations, that is, were meant as stylistic experiments, or as models for modes of English verse writing – in short, as making available for emulation and development some of the qualities of a classical text not yet assimilated to contemporary poetic possibility. Translators and theorists are perfectly explicit about this.[36]

The period from Dryden's first translations in the 1680s to Samuel Johnson's death in 1784 has a good claim to be regarded, no less than the Renaissance, as a golden age of English classical translation – it is, in fact, at the core of the present book. Its two most eminent poet-translators concentrated on the classics, and were both versatile enough to work across a number of genres. Dryden's Virgil and Pope's Homer in an important sense *became* Virgil and Homer for the eighteenth century.[37] Beyond this, Dryden and Pope translated (or imitated) between them the whole of Persius and substantial parts of Homer, Ovid and Juvenal (Dryden), Horace and Statius (Pope), together with sometimes highly influential versions of poems or segments from Lucretius, Horace and Theocritus (Dryden), Boethius, Martial, Ovid and Tibullus (Pope). The work of these and other higher-profile figures is naturally underpinned by a great deal of activity from less illustrious names – for translation, like other art forms, cannot nurture its stars without an extensive supporting cast. Pope's *Odyssey* was itself a collaboration, a practice Pope inherited primarily from Dryden, the editor of a number of 'several hands' transla-

---

34. For the Pope statistics, see Young (2003), 412.
35. A sample is quoted in Chapter 8. The fullest account of these aspects of the *Imitations* is Stack (1985).
36. For eighteenth-century translation as a stimulus to innovation in English writing, see recently the overview in Gillespie and Sowerby (2005).
37. See p. 32, below.

tions. Examples of specialist eighteenth-century translators, prominent in their time but well below the horizon today, are Gilbert West (Euripides, Lucian, Pindar, Apollonius Rhodius), William Melmoth (Pliny the Younger, Cicero) and Thomas Gordon (Tacitus, Sallust).[38] To give an indication of the proliferation of activity: some 120 book-length translations and imitations of Horace, mostly selections but including about a dozen collected versions, were published in the eighteenth century. Some 40 of these appeared in the 1730s alone[39] – an average of four per annum, or one per quarter.

Plainly, the eighteenth-century literary world is a translating culture, with the greatest prestige attaching to classical translation. Once this fact comes into focus, the absence of this dimension from the received literary-historical account becomes equally obvious. Pope and Dryden always emerged from the orthodox narratives until the late twentieth century primarily as (original) satirists. Indeed, they were original satirists, but this is certainly not the part of their *œuvres* for which they were most celebrated in their own lifetimes, nor is it the principal emphasis, by the 1770s, of Johnson's authoritative accounts of their life and work. This culture is one in which works of translation have full continuity with other literary output, so that it becomes common for writers to publish volumes of their 'Poems and Translations', while perhaps also contributing to joint translations, whether of short works like Horace's *Odes* (where variety of hands leads to pleasurably various English verse) or within large undertakings such as the *Plutarch's Lives* translated by some 42 contributors under the editorship of Dryden (1683–6). Widely read collections, such as poetry miscellanies, integrate translations in quantity into the material they print.[40] It's a culture in which some writers come to translation late, like Dryden in his fifties, while others found their careers on it, like John Oldham (1653–83), translator of Horace, Ovid and Juvenal, imitator of Moschus.[41] It is a culture in which classical translation is not confined to authors of high social rank (Rochester, Roscommon) or even in which contributors need to be of professional standing (Oldham, Samuel Garth, Philip Francis); translation can be published by women, as with an Ovidian epistle Aphra Behn contributed to a Dryden collection, or the learned Elizabeth Carter's Epictetus of 1758.[42] It is one in which writers so far below the notice of literary history as to be virtually unheard of today could make handsome livings by translating (or even, on occasion, by merely promising

---

38. For the work of these figures and brief biographical notices, see Gillespie and Hopkins (2005).
39. Gillespie (2009), 196–202. 'Book-length': publications sold as individual items or volume-sets; appearing as separate published entities in the *English Short Title Catalogue*, a database of publishing activity 1473–1800.
40. Such is conspicuously the case with classical translation in the highly successful verse miscellanies published by Jacob Tonson, 1684–1709. For a full account of the place of translation in them, see the introduction to Gillespie and Hopkins (2008).
41. Significantly, the first book-length study of Oldham's work did not appear until Hammond (1983).
42. Behn, 'Oenone to Paris', in *Ovid's Epistles*, 1680. Carter's *Enchiridion* was still in use as late as the twentieth century, as the basis of the Everyman's Library text.

to do so: Thomas Cooke followed up his heroic couplet Hesiod of 1728 by collecting 700 subscriptions for a verse translation of Plautus; he published only one play, in 1746).

Naturally, the mix of translated classics evolved as the eighteenth century went on. Before 1800 the works selected were often, on a broad definition, philosophical. After that date genres we would today label 'literary' tended to take precedence, among which the previously seldom translated texts of Greek drama should perhaps receive special mention. In spite of the discouragement Romantic theories of original genius appear to give translation, and in spite of the promotion of alternative models (modern or sometimes native models such as, for epic, Ossian), poets of the Romantic era were engaged in translating and otherwise reworking classical texts all the way across Europe. The most prominent English example is Shelley (1792–1822), who made direct versions of Euripides' *Cyclops*, the *Homeric Hymns*, Theocritus and the *Symposium*, and modelled other works on Aeschylus and Bion.[43] As will be explored in Chapter 9, literary history has played down the importance of classical knowledge, as well as of translation, to this generation. Such memorable but superficial comments as Byron's on his schoolroom experience of Horace ('Then farewell Horace! whom I hated so') have often been allowed to discourage further probing. The Hellenisms of (say) Keats, Landor and the novelist Thomas Love Peacock are different things, and manifest themselves in different ways, but we can be certain that plenty of their reading of Greek literature was in the form of English translations, sometimes historical ones. Appreciation of Chapman's Homer, for instance, undergoes a revival at this time, and Keats's well-known poem 'On First Looking into Chapman's Homer' is not the only recorded reaction to it.[44]

Further into the nineteenth century, Homer, by now generally preferred over Virgil, was at the centre of the debate over translation conducted publicly between Matthew Arnold and his opponent F. W. Newman, a Classics professor at University College London, in the 1860s. German scholars had pressed for the principle of 'facsimile' translation, which would reproduce not only meaning but also idiom and metrical form. In translating Homer, then, should a translator register the archaic and alien, disrupting contemporary English-language norms (as Newman argued), or should Homer be made to sound simple, natural, unquaint (as Arnold contended)? Subsequent English versions of Homer – and there was no shortage – could go in either direction.[45] Newman's Homer wrote in ballad metre, whereas Arnold argued for hexameters; Victorian writers as diverse as Tennyson, Clough, the scientist William Whewell and the politician Gladstone would later try their hands at reproducing classical metres in English. The prestige of classical Greek

---

43. The first general modern account of Shelley's translations was Webb (1976).

44. For Keats's, Shelley's and Coleridge's responses, see Webb (2004) and pp. 33–4, below.

45. For the issues at stake in the controversy, with reference to subsequent translations, see Ricks (2006). For a sampling of these translations, see Steiner (1996).

and the emphasis on school training in it were two factors behind the many English treatments of previously little-translated Greek poets. Poems and fragments of Sappho were translated by Byron, George Eliot, Landor and D. G. Rossetti. Theocritus attracted Matthew Arnold, Elizabeth Barrett Browning, Charles Calverley, Leigh Hunt, Andrew Lang and John Addington Symonds. Nonnus appealed to Thomas Love Peacock and Elizabeth Barrett Browning.

Plenty of distance still obtained between different types of translation, both in the product and the intended audience. Shelley did not write for the benefit of those who wanted uncoloured translations, but others did. From the early nineteenth century many works of translation, hitherto normally marketed as separate, individual publications, were issued within series intended for readers who would not have possessed copies of the originals. Henry Bohn (1796–1884) became the best known of the series publishers, with the 100 volumes of 'Bohn's Classical Library' (mainly issued 1848–63) a core part of his list, and sometimes embracing historical translations as a supplement to freshly commissioned items. For example, Bohn's 1850 *Satires of Juvenal, Persius, Sulpicia, and Lucilius, literally translated into English Prose by the Rev. Lewis Evans, M.A.*, also carries William Gifford's metrical version of Juvenal and Persius, first published in 1802.[46] Similarly, the Bohn Horace of 1850, translated by Theodore Alois Buckley, also prints Christopher Smart's literal prose rendering dating back to 1756. It has been imagined that this type of series publishing was aimed at radically challenging the expected audience norms: 'to find new markets for classics and to break the upper-class monopoly on classical learning'.[47] But the reality is more complex; as noted above, publishers had targeted the middle-class market for classical translation as early as Dryden's time.

For all this activity, it is with some justice that the nineteenth century has been found wanting for its achievements in the arena of classical translation. That it is also a period in which the prestige of the classics reached a very high pitch is only superficially paradoxical: the 'inhibiting force of excessive respect', the 'accepted inequity in the relation' between past and present, is said to explain a certain counterproductive humility with which translators seem to approach Greek and Latin texts.[48] An archaizing technique is one tangible outcome of a felt distance between classics and moderns, and the resulting vocabulary is apt to look stilted when, for example, instead of 'hungry' Calverley in his translation of 1869 makes Theocritus say 'not on an o'erfull stomach'. This language was, of course, already remote from contemporary norms in Calverley's own day. Calverley's ear was not insensitive, so perhaps this type of phrasing is meant as evoking Theocritus' Doric. An explicit statement is made by J. M. Edmonds, the early twentieth-century translator of Loeb's *Greek Bucolic Poets*:

46. For Gifford's Juvenal, see further Chapter 9 below.
47. Kenneth Haynes in France and Haynes (2006), 165.
48. Poole and Maule (1985), xlv.

> In the prose parts of my translation of the pastorals I have adopted the archaic style because the shepherd in modern literature does not talk the only modern dialect I know, that of the upper middle-class, and partly in an endeavour to create in them an atmosphere similar to that of the songs. I have extended archaism to … mimes for kindred reasons, to the Love-Poems because they are so Elizabethan in spirit, to the Epic poems because the Epic is necessarily, under modern conditions, archaic, and to the rest because it is the fashion of the day.[49]

'The Epic is necessarily, under modern conditions, archaic': there could hardly be a plainer statement of felt distance between ancient and modern.

Calverley died in 1884. Edmonds lived only a few years beyond the first appearance of *The Greek Bucolic Poets* in 1912. The next generation took a fresh approach. The early Modernists, say the editors of *The Oxford Book of Classical Verse in English Translation*, 'will not have anything to do with [the] cripplingly reverential position' of the Victorians.[50] Certainly, the central figure where translation was concerned, Ezra Pound, made a point of irreverence. His *Homage to Sextus Propertius*, 1919 – of which more in Chapter 2 – outraged the establishment with its apparently cavalier attitude to interpretation and by implicitly claiming that intuition can be more important than scholarship in understanding a classical text. Pound's epic *Cantos* had set out in 1915 with a version of part of Andreas Divus' Renaissance Latin version of *Odyssey* 11.[51] Euripides (*Elektra*) and Sophocles (*Trachiniae*) were much later targets for Pound, in quirkily idiomatic, not universally acclaimed versions of the 1950s.[52] His often less direct responses to Sappho, Catullus, Ovid and Pindar have been explicated. The nature of the poetic he promoted meant that Pound's followers often had Greek tastes – Richard Aldington and his wife Hilda Doolittle ('H.D.'), for example, producing versions of Euripides and Sappho (again see Chapter 2).

There is no doubt that Pound and his school sought to overturn Victorian and Georgian poetic convention. But why does engagement with the classics through translation represent a means of doing so? For translation, as is well recognized, constituted (in the words of Stephen Yao) 'an integral part of the Modernist program of cultural renewal, a crucially important mode of writing'.[53] Daniel Hooley has suggested that what these writers were registering was the passing away of the classics from school curricula and from common knowledge; and that the spectacle of 'translator-poets demonstrating in the manner of their engagement with old poems some terribly acute awareness of their position in time and culture

---

49. Edmonds (1928), xxvi.
50. Poole and Maule (1985), xlv.
51. Why Divus? See Kenner (1990), 17, who writes: 'No one in 400 years has owed him so much.'
52. *Electra*, unpublished until 1989, was a collaboration with Rudd Fleming. For objections to the colloquial styles of *The Women of Trachis*, see Kenner (1972), 526; but for a strikingly positive assessment of this work, see Mason (1969).
53. Yao (2002), 6.

and art, of their being simultaneously at an end of things and a beginning' is what 'one refers to in describing Pound and his circle as seminal moderns'.[54] Pound's experimental translations can be seen as breaking down the foreign text and reconstituting it so as to 'make it new', as his motto ran. Pound can, as Donald Carne-Ross suggests, resuscitate elements of diction and syntax 'unfamiliar enough to sound startlingly new' and confront us with 'ancient texts that we know could only have been written in [the twentieth] century'.[55] But it is possible to discern more continuity between the Victorians and the early Modernists than might have made the latter comfortable. *Canto I* closes with some lines on Aphrodite: 'with golden | Girdle and breast bands, thou with dark eyelids | Bearing the golden bough of Argicidia'. It is perhaps less the pronoun than the clothing terminology that strikes us as redolent of the archaisms of Calverley or Edmonds; Pope's word 'zone' for the Homeric κεστός in his *Iliad* has worn better.[56] To be fair, however, Pound's archaisms sound less affected as the *Cantos* proceed.

More will be said of Pound's influence on translators in Chapter 2, but this was not ubiquitous. Twentieth-century diversity can be suggested by a sample list of translators whose lives overlapped with Pound's but whose priorities did not: Hardy (Sappho and Catullus), Housman (Horace), Allan Tate (*Pervigilium Veneris*), J. V. Cunningham (Martial and Catullus), W. S. Merwin (Persius), Peter Porter (Martial) and, for a prose example – a one-off in every way – Stephen McKenna (Plotinus). The last was eventually accommodated within the twentieth century's best-known classics in translation series: Penguin Classics, established by Allen Lane in 1946 under the editorship of E. V. Rieu, previously a distinguished but obscure classicist and publisher who had whiled away his wartime service perfecting his prose version of the *Odyssey*. Rieu promoted prose translations written in 'plain English' and without extensive annotations. Over time, with emphases shifting in schools and universities in the UK and USA, more use was made of translations in classrooms (on Great Books and on Classics in Translation courses, for example) and a more scholarly flavour was sought. This was developed by Rieu's assistant and eventual successor Betty Radice, herself a translator of Roman comedy, Pliny and Erasmus.[57] Today in the Penguin Classics list there can be found a second or third successive translation of several major classical texts (three *Aeneids* to date) – a sign of success, or of a fast track to obsolescence?[58]

---

54. Hooley (1988), 20.

55. Carne-Ross (1990), 137.

56. See especially (for Venus' *cestus*, with Pope's discursive notes) Pope's 14.210, 245; Pope (1939–69), VIII, 170–3.

57. For further history of the Penguin Classics, see Radice and Reynolds (1978).

58. While it is usually assumed that translations age more quickly than original works, and while this may be true of contemporary works for the textbook market, I have set out statistical evidence of the historical unreliability of this assumption from the book trade in the long eighteenth century. See Gillespie (2005), 143–4.

Greek tragedy deserves mention as a contemporary translation phenomenon. Pound and Eliot looked to Aeschylus, but more diffuse interests have absorbed drama translators in recent decades.[59] Seamus Heaney's *The Cure at Troy* (after *Philoctetes*, 1990), for the Field Day Theatre Company, holds on to the Greek scenario, but the verse has the flavour of Irish speech. Heaney's *Antigone* followed in 2005 under the title *The Burial at Thebes*. Just as common have been adaptations which explicitly parallel settings and situations with modern equivalents. Contemporary concerns are clearly reflected in the popularity for theatre purposes of a play like Euripides' *Medea*.[60] But perhaps the unexpected development of the late twentieth and early twenty-first centuries is simply the widespread revival, in Britain especially, of the Renaissance poet's habit of undertaking classical translation at intervals in a writing career. A few passages or poems from (say) Ovid or Horace is routine, but a more regular commitment is often apparent. Greek theatre is in this context frequently to the fore: Tony Harrison has translated the *Oresteia*, Euripides' *Hecuba* and Aristophanes' *Lysistrata* (twice). Between translating a chunk of the *Odyssey* in 1960 and Euripides' *Alcestis* in 1993–8, Ted Hughes, at whom Chapter 11 will look more closely, undertook Seneca's *Oedipus* and selections at volume length from Ovid's *Metamorphoses*.[61]

But there are, as ever, many further layers of activity beyond this highest-profile level. The career-long classical translator is still with us – C. H. Sisson is one twentieth-century example, with Catullus, Horace, Lucretius and Virgil to his credit. Over 40 book-length translations and imitations of Ovid in English appeared between 1950 and 2004.[62] Daniel Hooley is right to note that 'for the sheer number and stylistic variety of its classical translations, the first half of [the twentieth] century ranks with the Renaissance and the age of Pope'.[63] It should give pause for thought that a much larger number of English translations from the classics were published in that century than any previous one.

◆   ◆   ◆

If classical literature has been formative of western literary traditions, translations of it have probably been no less so. This is partly a practical matter: a writer cannot make use of a work she cannot read. But it is also a more subtle question of how the most ambitious translations make a text 'available' to the native tradition. Perhaps more than that: through translation, and only through translation, it can be argued, can a classic fully take its place within the vernacular culture, becoming

---

59. For an overview, see Hall, Macintosh and Wrigley (2004).
60. For performance history, see Hall, Macintosh and Taplin (2000).
61. The developments outlined in this paragraph are explored further in Hardwick (2000). Three essays on Hughes's *Tales from Ovid* and one on his Seneca appear in Rees (2009).
62. Gillespie and Cummings (2004), 216–18.
63. Hooley (1998), 18.

an adoptive child, an immediate member of the family, rather than a distant (or dead) cousin – however deeply respected a distant cousin. In the aggregate, translations are crucial to the process of 'making the classics belong'. Understanding how this occurs, which includes attending to the individual acts of translation which are fundamental to it, is one of the things this book is about.

2

Creative Translation

Over the centuries, debates about translation have sometimes focused on biblical texts or on translation from modern languages and literatures. But issues of cultural value clustering around the classics, as well as the extensive history of English versions, have always tended to lend classical translation a special status. In order to understand the Arnold/Newman controversy of the 1860s (briefly summarized in Chapter 1), for instance, it is necessary to appreciate Homer's role as the most prestigious poet of the most prestigious foreign culture in the Victorian era. At other times what is relevant is the shock value of new departures within such an apparently stable, settled arena as classical literature – which ceased being written centuries ago and which was, for nearly all of the more recent centuries during which English has been a literary language, an unavoidable part of the schooling of most of those who wrote works in English. The Elizabethan take on Ovidian erotic verse (see Chapter 3) is but one example.

I referred in Chapter 1 to the predilection of early modern translators for imposing their own time, place and personality on classical texts. This period tendency has been expressively described by James Ruoff:

> The English translators brought their own cultural values with them and did not hesitate to impose them on the foreigners they aspired to conquer. Thomas North's Greeks and Romans wear Elizabethan doublets and hose and speak in the idiom and cadences of Elizabethan gentlemen; Arthur Golding's Ovid is converted from joyful pagan to profoundly allegorical Calvinist, and Richard Stanyhurst's Dido is not so much a love-crazed Carthaginian queen as a jilted English girl expressing her indignation in colloquial Elizabethan ... They consistently changed their original authors

English Translation and Classical Reception: Towards a New Literary History, First Edition. Stuart Gillespie.

into mirrors of themselves, bringing the art of translation to the very boundaries of ingenious plagiarism.[1]

There are several ways we can look at this. We might ask how we know that our own constructions of Ovid ('joyful pagan') or Virgil's Dido ('love-crazed') are more appropriate than Golding's or Stanyhurst's. We could steer towards the terms of contemporary discussion of translating modes, 'foreignizing' versus 'domesticating'.[2] But perhaps the most interesting thing we can do is to ask what are the conditions for creative engagement with a classical text. This could be seen as a question about how linguistic and cultural alterity may be processed; hegemony and acculturation play out in many different ways. Colonizing another culture imperialistically is one. Others include competing with another culture or with other versions of another culture. One might allow a foreign text to suggest new ways of inhabiting one's own culture or use it to explore the fault-lines within one's own identity. Appeal can be made to a work's cultural authority; cultural authority can be faked by distortion or outright fabrication of sources. All of these things can be found in the history of English engagements with classical texts in translation, and perhaps none is confined to one era.

It's striking that although Ruoff is characterizing Elizabethan translation at large, not one of his illustrations here is drawn from the many modern poems, plays and stories enthusiastically englished from French, Italian, Spanish and other languages in the Elizabethan period. Neither is any of them drawn from the translation work which in many ways occupied centre-stage in the sixteenth century – on the English Bible. If Elizabethan attitudes were so uniform, the same thing could easily be illustrated there; but a moment's reflection will indicate that it does not, in fact, happen there, at least in the obvious ('doublets and hose') way.[3] We appear to be looking at a phenomenon specifically related to classical texts. Unlike the special case of the Bible, such texts are, in the sense outlined in Chapter 1, available for adoption and assimilation; yet unlike most modern European texts, they can only be 'made English' through a process of cultural negotiation, for their world is much more remote. This, of course, takes us back to what I just called 'the conditions for creative engagement' with such texts. With Ruoff's 'They consistently changed their original authors into mirrors of themselves, bringing the art of translation to the very boundaries of ingenious plagiarism' we could compare Dryden on Jonson: 'He invades Authours like a Monarch, and what would be theft in other Poets, is onely victory in him.'[4] Between 'plagiarism' and 'victory', we might say, lies the creativity of translation. Is invasiveness a necessary part of that creativity?

1. Ruoff (1975), 429.
2. Venuti (1995) has underwritten much subsequent treatment of this topic.
3. Elizabethan Bible translations sometimes even sought to mimic Latin and Hebraic idiom and syntax, producing strange, on occasion unintelligible, English. See recently Taylor (2010).
4. *Of Dramatic Poesy*, Dryden (1956–2000), XVII, 57.

◆ ◆ ◆

The possibilities of imitation – for the Renaissance an ambition, for the Romantics an evil – allow us to start answering that question. Imitation arises partly as an alternative to the constraints of the discipline of translation. In ancient Rome, translation was seen as a technically demanding version of the much wider practice of imitation of Greek models. However, as Glenn Most has pointed out, 'what counted as translation ... often allowed considerable leeway for adaptation and variation'; hence 'the precise point at which translation stops and imitation begins is often very hard indeed to discern'.[5] The choices open to any translator 'on the ground' are perhaps reducible to two: either accommodating the translation's texture to the source's features, or accommodating the source to a smooth and 'invisible' translation.[6] Robert Browning's *Agamemnon of Aeschylus* (1877) was written, he noted, 'in as Greek a fashion as English will bear', whereas Alexander Tytler maintained in his *Essay on the Principles of Translation* (1795) that a translation 'should have all the ease of original composition'. Dryden tried to break away from the binary in proposing a tripartite scheme in the 'Preface to *Ovid's Epistles*' (1680): 'metaphrase' is literal, 'paraphrase' involves 'latitude' and 'imitation' is looser still. Dryden's own translations usually mix these approaches promiscuously enough to suggest severe limitations on the usefulness of the categories. To confuse matters further, the term 'imitation' has been used to mean different things in different eras.[7]

Dryden defines imitation in the same preface: it is writing what the 'ancient' might have written had he lived in the England of Dryden's own day, using the original merely as a 'pattern'. This is by no means indefensible, but the principle can sanction a very broad range of approaches. Christopher Logue's is at one contemporary extreme: his 'accounts' or 'rewritings' (as he variously calls them) of the *Iliad*, appearing piecemeal since 1962, can take a page to deal with a couple of Homeric lines. Better this than slavishness: 'What we do not want,' Logue has underlined, 'is bad writing hiding behind efficiency in ancient languages.'[8] But what is indispensable to authenticity, and just what qualities are to be imitated, or prioritized? Form, metre, sense, sound and many other elements have their claims. The experiments of the Americans Celia and Louis Zukofsky led to a complete 'homophonic' Catullus in 1969, in which sound is paramount. A random example: in Catullus 55 the line 'Oramus, si forte non molestum est' is translated 'A rum asks me – see, fortune won't molest you.' The reproduction of phonetic values is what directs this version, though there is a concomitant attachment to rhythm and

5. Most (2003), 388.
6. For the ubiquity of binaries in theories of translation down the centuries, see Pym (1995). These choices are further illustrated in Chapter 11, below.
7. Two well-known studies are Pigman (1980), for the Renaissance, and Brooks (1949), covering the succeeding period down to Pope.
8. For the background of Logue's Homer, see Chapter 11.

word order (sort of). But it is experimental rather than readable. On the other hand, when another member of the School of Pound, H.D., singles out the dramatic picture as the element to concentrate on, dispensing with syntax and even (largely) with the 'sense' of Greek lyrics, the result is, as Donald Carne-Ross enthuses, 'a sequence of images as fresh and unexpected as though they had just been disinterred from the sands of Egypt'.[9] These are the first lines of H.D.'s remarkably spare version of the first chorus of Euripides' *Iphigenia in Aulis*:

> I crossed sand-hills
> I stand among the sea-drift before Aulis.
> I crossed Euripos' strait –
> Foam hissed after my boat.
>
> I left Chalkis,
> My city and the rock-ledges.
> Arethusa twists among the boulders,
> Increases – cuts into the surf.[10]

There may indeed be times when only radical strategies will work, when it is enough that a few aspects of the original, or a small stretch of it, can be made to come over. H.D.'s own complete *Ion* fails to extend the Imagistic discipline convincingly over a whole play. Translations can make us feel freshly connected with works we thought had slipped below the horizon, but their reappearance may be as tentative as the movements of the ancient gods Pound once imagined making their way back to Earth:

> See, they return; ah, see the tentative
>   Movements, and the slow feet,
>   The trouble in the pace and the uncertain
>   Wavering![11]

The father-figure of Ezra Pound lies behind both the Zukofsky Catullus and H.D.'s Euripides. Few can have disagreed with George Steiner when, in 1966, he observed that Pound's translations had 'altered the definition and ideals of verse translation in the twentieth century as surely as Pound's poetry has renewed or subverted English and American poetics'.[12] One could go further and say that in terms of his practice Pound brought translation and original writing together in such a way as to allow translation almost to be identified with the process of literary invention as such. The message was not lost on Eliot. John Hollander points

---

9. Carne-Ross (1961), 7.
10. H.D. (1986), 71. See for a fuller analysis Gregory (1997), 143–5.
11. 'The Return', lines 1–4, in Pound (1975), 39.
12. Steiner (1966), 33.

out that 'the job of the poet' in Eliot's seminal essay 'Tradition and the Individual Talent' is 'strangely like that of an Ideal Translator'.[13]

One of the main reasons for his influence is that Pound's translations push at the limits of what translation is or can be. Anxiety over terminology is not a reason for raising the issues here, but there is no denying that the terminology – 'definition', as Steiner put it – has been a bone of contention, and not only among translation theorists or academic commentators.[14] Pound himself originally styled his *Homage to Sextus Propertius* (1919) a translation, but quickly abandoned the term when classical scholars began to challenge his credentials. The work was not printed in his *Collected Translations*. But Eliot also excluded it from his edition of Pound's *Selected Poems*, on the grounds that he

> felt that the poem ... would give difficulty to many readers because it is not enough a 'translation' and because it is, on the other hand, too much a 'translation' to be intelligible to any but the accomplished student of Pound's poetry.[15]

Eliot went one step further in 1950, writing:

> I am aware of the censure of those who have treated it as a translation; and if it is treated as a translation, they are of course right.[16]

Eliot produced an alternative term for the *Homage* in his introduction to the *Selected Poems*: 'It is not a translation,' he wrote; 'it is a paraphrase, or still more truly (for the instructed) a *persona*.'[17] What Eliot meant was that by filtering and emphasizing what he chose, Pound had made Propertius into a vehicle, a spokesman, for himself – by no means a new departure for a translator, as we have already seen. The characterization, typically of Eliot, gives much pause for thought, even if the term 'persona' has had its gloss dulled during its passage through a great many critical hands since he used it.

The other side of the coin of Pound's adoption of Propertius is the side that has seemed to matter most for classicists: does Pound's Propertius distort (misread, misrepresent, change) Propertius? As always with reception issues, it seems, it is easy to construct an original which meets the requirements of an interpretation.

---

13. Hollander (1959), 209. Eliot's pronouncements on translation as such were limited, but in more subterranean ways the growing prominence of translation within the Modernist movement is partly attributable to him. His role requires more attention elsewhere, but see below for his 1920 comments on translating Euripides.
14. The best recent discussion of the general problem is Reynolds (forthcoming), who identifies at the root of it the difficulty that 'the word "translation" has been used to name more activities than can be reduced to [one] model'.
15. Eliot (1928), 19.
16. Russell (1950), 33.
17. Eliot (1928), 19.

One of Pound's mid-twentieth-century supporters, G. S. Fraser, suggested one of the poem's virtues was that it found (or was it 'made'?) a new Latin poet. The *Homage*, Fraser wrote, 'will send you ... to Propertius, looking for a wry humour, which is perhaps only Pound's, or which anyway no one would have seen in Propertius until Pound had read it into him'.[18] But this is doubtful: Propertius was routinely presented in Pound's own day as possessing these very qualities of modernity and humour. 'In his employment of sentiment,' J. P. Postgate had suggested in his school edition of 1881, 'Propertius is modern and even romantic' and 'has a vein of humour which we should not have expected.'[19] More explicitness about the premises of this type of critique, and more sharpness about the issues, are achieved in a later essay by Gordon Messing, at the time a senior member of Columbia University's Classics Department. After a convincing demonstration of the philological shortcomings of the *Homage qua* translation, Messing writes:

> Something more fundamental, a violation of the spirit of Propertius, is at stake. Pound has forced the tone; he has created a Propertius in his own image. He has exaggerated, for example, an ancient *topos*, dear to all the elegiacs or even to all writers of love poetry, that the poet who serenades his mistress is unfitted to attempt martial poetry ... [or] has compelled his Propertius to inveigh against Virgil in the savage way he himself lashed out at British imperialism ('Upon the Actian marshes Virgil is Phoebus' chief of police'). Above all, he has erratically imparted to many formal and traditional compositions a levity, an easygoing modern formality, that would be appropriate only occasionally.[20]

This has the virtue of laying bare the assumptions: looked at in this way, Pound's task is to convey without interference 'the spirit of Propertius'. But where is this spirit to be found? Are classical scholars able to call it up, and if so, by what magic?

Many years after the *Homage* Pound himself set out his own position in two lucid paragraphs at the end of his book *Cavalcanti* (1934):

> In the long run the translator is in all probability impotent to do *all* the work for the linguistically lazy reader. He can show where the treasure lies, he can guide the reader in the choice of what tongue is to be studied, and he can very materially assist the hurried student who has a smattering of a language and the energy to read the original text alongside the metrical gloze.
>
> This refers to 'interpretive translation.' The 'other sort,' I mean in cases where the 'translator' is definitely making a new poem, falls simply in the domain of original

18. From Fraser's essay 'Pound: Masks, Myth, Man', in Russell (1950), 172.
19. Postgate (1881), lxxv–lxxvii.
20. Messing (1975), 129–30.

writing, or if it does not it must be censured according to equal standards, and praised with some sort of just deduction, assessable only in the particular case.[21]

We have known for some time that all readings are responses. 'Making a new poem', as Pound describes it, is also a response. It does not, presumably, represent a claim that this new poem is an equivalent for, let alone a substitute for, the previous one. But it may, if successful, strike us as an exciting way of looking at it. Such lines in the *Homage* as these will not be wholly satisfactory translations to a Latinist, but they are lines which give us some idea about how Propertius relates to the poetry of our own language and time, something no Latin edition or textbook can do:

> 'quo tu matutinus', ait, 'speculator amicae'
> (Propertius)

> You are a very early inspector of mistresses
> (Pound)

> 'What!' said she, 'do you come spying at
> dawn on your sweetheart?'
> (Loeb)

or:

> incomptis vidisti flere capiliis
> (Propertius)

> She wept into uncombed hair,
> And you saw it
> (Pound)

> You saw your mistress weeping and with
> hair awry, a flood of tears streaming from
> her eyes
> (Loeb)[22]

'Relating to the poetry of our own language' does not just mean in this case 'replicating the features of early Modernist verse'. There is a strangeness, an unaccommodated surfeit of the foreign, extending particularly to the rhythms of Pound's long lines, which tend towards the syllabic rather than accentual, but do

---

21. Pound (1954), 200. For one exposition see Hollander (1959), 213–14. Happily, after entertaining the hypothesis that *Homage* should be judged as a translation, Messing arrives *a priori*, and without reference to this essay of Pound's, at a conclusion identical to Pound's: 'The only even partially satisfactory solution is to take *Homage* as an English poem' (132).
22. Sullivan (1965), 156–7, 128–9; Goold (1990), 221 (2.29B), 271 (3.7).

not seem readily identifiable as Propertian rhythms. In *Homage*, if Carne-Ross is right, 'we hear English moving to a music not heard elsewhere in our poetry':[23]

> Flame burns, rain sinks into the cracks
> And they all go to rack ruin beneath the thud of the years.
> Stands genius a deathless adornment,
>   a name not to be worn out with the years.

or:

> Nor at my funeral either will there be any long trail,
>   bearing ancestral lares and images;
> No trumpets filled with my emptiness,
> Nor shall it be on an Attalic bed;
>   The perfumed cloths shall be absent.
> A small plebeian procession.
>   Enough, enough and in plenty
> There will be three books at my obsequies
> Which I take, my not unworthy gift, to Persephone.[24]

Looked at in one way, no doubt Pound has 'invaded' Propertius to find a voice, a mask, a persona. *Personae* was the title of a collection of his verse in 1909 and the concept occupies a central position in his poetic process. But looked at in another, it is Propertius who generates new effects, thus imposing himself, we might say, on Pound. 'To construe the classics now,' writes Daniel Hooley, 'is to construe them as one writes modern poetry, according to the demands, the authority, of the age.' That might be a description of almost all successful literary translation, but it is an apt rider for the twentieth century to add, as Hooley does, that 'the requirements of an age and the nature of a classic text are too often at fundamental odds ... and their translational synthesis an enormous difficulty'.[25] It would be claiming too much to say that Pound overcame that difficulty more than occasionally. Yet by such means as we see here – the suggestions of quantitative verse on the one hand, the avoidance of embellishments such as metaphor and simile, alliteration and assonance on the other – he escaped the tired cadences of nineteenth-century verse and freed himself to use the wider poetic vocabulary of the *Cantos*.[26]

23. Carne-Ross (1990), 136, who goes on to suggest that this is because the verse has a quantitative as opposed to stress dimension – 'it is because quantity is one (*one* – I am claiming no more) of the elements that have gone to their making' (*ibid.*).
24. Quotations from Sullivan (1965), 119, 139.
25. Hooley (1988), 14.
26. Longer quotations would be needed to bring out other devices which Pound develops from *Homage* to the *Cantos* such as non sequitur and lacuna/aporia.

Pound's Propertius also changed the possibilities for twentieth-century poetry and translation more widely (as Steiner rightly claimed).[27] H.D. has already been named as one of those he caused to think about these possibilities. In 1920, a year after *Homage* was published, Eliot reviewed the *Medea* translation of Gilbert Murray, at the time Regius Professor of Greek at Oxford, and it was H.D.'s Euripides that Eliot invoked as a foil to Murray's work. Murray's efforts to produce an acting version of the play (the show was being staged at the Holborn Empire), Eliot lamented, created 'a barrier more impenetrable than the Greek language' by replacing sharp-edged Greek with the fuzzy poetic idiom of the previous genera-tion – with couplets of William Morris's cast and 'the fluid haze of Swinburne'.[28] Eliot condemns Murray for 'leaving Euripides quite dead' and asks how Euripides may be made to live:

> Greek poetry will never have the slightest vitalizing effect upon English poetry if it can only appear masquerading as a vulgar debasement of the eminently personal idiom of Swinburne … It is to be hoped that we may be grateful to Professor Murray and his friends for what they have done, while we endeavour to neutralize Professor Murray's influence upon Greek literature and English language in his translations by making better translations.

Eliot went on to indicate how he thought this might happen:

> The choruses from Euripides by H.D. are, allowing for errors and even occasional omissions of difficult passages, much nearer to both Greek and English than Mr. Murray's … We need an eye which can see the past in its place with its definite dif-ferences from the present, and yet so lively that it shall be as present to us as the present. This is the creative eye; and it is because Professor Murray has no creative instinct that he leaves Euripides quite dead.[29]

Here we have, at least by implication, a definition of creative translation. The 'creative eye' which can make Euripides live will make the past seem present, seem as contemporary as the present.[30] It will not merely adopt the idiom of the present, since that would be to ignore the past's 'differences'. It will, rather, release into the present the possibilities of past ways of thinking, feeling, expressing. This I understand to be what Carne-Ross means when he writes that 'every age has to work out its own relations to the creative achievements of the past, and the task of the translator, like that of the critic, is to define those works of other times and places which are most living and reveal those aspects of them which we most need

27. For a study of Pound's impact on subsequent translators, see Apter (1984).
28. Eliot (1967), 74–5.
29. Eliot (1967), 72, 77.
30. For H.D.'s explicit presentation of Euripides as a modern, see Jenkins (2007).

today'.[31] It follows that creative translation is translation which (in Eliot's word) 'vitalizes' contemporary poetry.

In commenting on Pound I have emphasized his cultural role beyond translation and imitation, or rather the way those activities became integral with his wider role. From the fragment to the epic, Greek and Latin verse were at the centre of what he 'revealed' about what was 'needed'. Translation has had its impact in every era. Writers as well as readers can be shown to engage with a given classic far more intensively once a translation accords it a vigorous vernacular existence. Others respond to Propertius after Pound has opened up the poems: Lowell's 'The Ghost (after Sextus Propertius)' would have been 'impossible without the example of the *Homage*', in J. P. Sullivan's view; a generation later Michael Longley achieved a 'break-through' by evolving a ten-line stanza from Propertius' death-poem on Cornelia.[32] In seventeenth-century Italy, Lucretius was a model for neo-Latin poets but, in the absence of an Italian translation (largely because of Church discouragement and suppression), much less so for vernacular Italian-language writers.[33] While in Britain Latin editions had been freely available for many years, readerly interest in Lucretius is exponentially greater after the capable complete translation of Thomas Creech (1683) and the poetically impressive selection by Dryden (1685). But what is more, succeeding generations of poets too – poets of the stature of Pope and Gray – can be shown to draw on these translations, particularly Dryden's.[34] That seems a workable definition of a creative translation: a translation which creates new possibilities or begets new works. What else would a translation create, other than itself?

And this is why, for me, the impact translations have on the literature of the receiving language is an integral part of any study of them. The impact of classical translation on English writing has taken many forms. Let us sample them, for they are only now coming to be appreciated.[35] Whatever may have become of Eliot's aspirations with Greek tragedy in the twentieth century, poetic diction has at times been strongly affected by translations – very much including translations which we might today label 'domesticating' ones. Pope's Homer was felt to have made available a highly influential new poetic idiom, Johnson writing in his 'Life of Pope', a couple of generations after its first publication, that 'Pope's version may be said to have tuned the English tongue, for since its appearance no

---

31. Carne-Ross (1961), 6.

32. Sullivan (1965), 183; Longley (2009), 106.

33. Prosperi (2007).

34. For Pope's use of Dryden, see Fabian 1979; for Wordsworth's and Arnold's, see Chapter 9; for Gray's, see Lonsdale (1969), 121. More widely on English poets' Lucretianism 1650–1800, see Hopkins (2008).

35. Scattered scholarly treatments of the topic are overdue for synthesis and development, pending which the structure of *The Oxford History of Literary Translation in English* provides for the impact of translation (from all literatures) to be expressly addressed in a chapter of each period-volume, as well as more diffusely.

writer, however deficient in other powers, has wanted melody'.[36] Translation has led to the discovery and development of metrical forms. English blank verse derives from Surrey's invention of the line in his *Aeneid* excerpts of *c.* 1540, thence migrating to the original verse of Marlowe and eventually Milton.[37] The influence of translations on the theory and practice of vernacular poetry is particularly strongly felt in the debate surrounding Elizabethan attempts to introduce the Greco-Roman metrical system into English verse, otherwise termed the Elizabethan quantitative verse movement.[38] And Dryden's enormously influential contribution to the development of the couplet owes much to what he learned from translating Virgil.[39]

Poetic forms have been imported via translation and imitation. Cowley's *Pindarique Odes*, 1656, at whatever angle we may feel they stand to Pindar, are behind the vogue for English odes over the ensuing century and more, and the highly popular enthusiastic style they offered eighteenth-century poets.[40] 'During some 150 years of experiment,' Howard Weinbrot writes, 'poets invent, vary, refine, exhaust, and redefine the form that becomes so British that even Greek relics take the native hue.'[41] But a fuller description of what happened would be given if at the beginning of that sequence the verb 'invent' were replaced by 'imitate' or 'appropriate'. Interestingly, the earlier, much more disciplined, regular, and therefore arguably more authentic 'Pindaric' odes of Jonson had not had a comparable effect.[42] History shows that many kinds and degrees of 'mistranslation' can be productive, as can faked translations and invented classics. A whole classical Greek poet, Anacreon, claimed a prominent place in English and continental verse through an extensive tradition of translation dating from the time of Ronsard, then in England via Thomas Stanley and (once again) Cowley, even though not one of his genuine works was available.[43]

George Puttenham lists in his *Arte of English Poesie* (1589) the forms 'such as time and usurpation by custome have allowed us out of the primitive Greeke & Latine, as Comedie, Tragedie, Ode, Epitaphe, Elegie, Epigramme' and others.[44] By 'primitive' Puttenham means 'original'. But as far as Shakespeare's 'Comedie'

---

36. Johnson (1905), III, 228. For the pivotal role of Pope's Homer in perceptions of English poetic idiom, see further Gillespie and Sowerby (2005), 28.

37. For Surrey's *Aeneid* and the development of blank verse, see Cummings (2010), 42–3.

38. For a comprehensive treatment of this movement, see Attridge (1974); for a recent account of the translation context, see Schmidt (2010).

39. For Dryden's Virgilian couplet verse, see Gillespie and Sowerby (2005), 26–7.

40. For one conspicuous example of the formal odes which followed from Cowley's lead, see Chapter 5, below.

41. Weinbrot (1993), 334.

42. For the Pindaric basis of the showpiece Cary-Morison Ode, see Revard (1982).

43. The original Anacreon of Teos, if he existed, was widely imitated by Hellenistic and Byzantine Greek writers. The collection of some 60 post-classical lyrics known as the *Anacreontea* was first printed by Henri Estienne in 1554. For a checklist of English translations, see Gillespie (2002).

44. Puttenham (1589), 47. For Jonson's Pindarics, see Moul (2007).

and 'Tragedie' are concerned, while the dramatist may have delved into Latin texts of Seneca or Plautus, there is not much doubt that the 'primitive Greeke' mostly came to him via translation, often at several removes.[45] And a sudden rash of Senecan inspiration and Senecan motifs in English drama around 1590 corresponds decidedly well to the publication of Thomas Newton's *Seneca his Tenne Tragedies, translated into Englysh* in 1581.[46] In a word, at this date it was largely through translation that English writers took possession of the classical inheritance Puttenham is (aspirationally) outlining.

More than this: rather than simply incorporating foreign literary models in order to complement the native tradition, early modern translations were often a site for literary experiment, provoking controversy and stimulating reflection on vernacular practice. Classical works and their vernacular descendants forced a reassessment of the literary system, in terms of genre and beyond. Chapter 3 will outline how early modern translations of the classics even had the effect of forging a new past for English poetry. And, through the process of cultural negotiation often deliberately initiated by translators, the received tradition might be as much transformed as the receiving one.

Classical translation has been decisive in the formation of vernacular literary canons. In English, the key works of translation were by 1800 established as integral parts of the English literary canon itself, as we shall see in Chapter 7. Their proud inclusion in the several large-scale editions of 'the English poets' from the late eighteenth century onwards bespeaks a situation partly resembling that of Roman culture, in which translation helps create a national literature of universal aspirations. Johnson takes occasion in his *Lives of the English Poets* (1779–81) to comment on the rare examples of English poets who are *not* translators.[47] Classical translations could even be said to act sometimes to suppress native writing: it is often remarked how Dryden and Pope failed to write epics of their 'own' while producing highly successful versions of Virgil and Homer. But to make so stark and simple a distinction between translated and original works, and to use the word 'failed' in this connection, is to accept post-Romantic priorities. We should remember that Dryden's Virgil was in his own age felt to be a greater achievement than any of his original works. Pope called it 'the most noble and spirited Translation I know in any Language',[48] while himself becoming the

---

45. See Chapter 4, and Gillespie (2001) *s.v.* 'Euripides', 'Sophocles', 'Aeschylus', 'Plautus'.

46. Newton compiled a number of considerably earlier play translations and added to them; his volume contained the only printed translations of Seneca available to the Elizabethans. Playwrights using Senecan materials around 1590 include Kyd, Marlowe, Chapman, Jonson, Marston and Webster. Two different accounts of Seneca's role within English Renaissance drama are Braden (1985) and Helms (1997).

47. Of Matthew Prior he writes: 'Scarcely any one of our poets has written so much and translated so little.' Johnson (1905), II, 204–5.

48. Translation, that is, of any work – not only of the *Aeneid*. Preface to *The Iliad of Homer*, Pope (1939–69), VII, 22.

equivalent of a multi-millionaire through his Homer. We should also keep in mind – to sum up one of my themes in this chapter – the remarkable way in which Pope's Homer and Dryden's Virgil, so to say, *gave* Homer and Virgil to eighteenth-century English poetry, and in so doing established its foundations. In Douglas Knight's words: 'The stability and range, not only of Pope's poetic world but of the Augustan world around it, are established in part by their "possession" of the great heroic poets – an achievement impossible without the living knowledge, the living poetry of Dryden's *Aeneid* or Pope's *Iliad* and *Odyssey*.'[49]

♦   ♦   ♦

In a recent book dealing in depth with writers' and critics' ways of conceptualizing translation, Matthew Reynolds has drawn attention to Elizabeth Barrett Browning's description of her work in the preface introducing her first attempt at an English version of *Prometheus Bound*. She presents it as something which 'takes its place in a relay of inspiration, a visionary chain-reaction'. Translation, Reynolds observes, is 'visualized as continuing the inspiration that had given rise to the original'.[50] This is to view translation not merely as reviving a past work, but as passing on life, or conferring new life ('inspiration', in the bodily sense, is a condition of all human life). We have seen Eliot, too, speaking of the 'vitalizing effect' that Greek poetry might have upon English poetry. 'Inspire', 'animate', 'vitalize': these words do not point merely to the 're-creation' of the past. They imply the creative power which those translations properly said to belong to the English literary tradition have proved to possess by virtue of their effects on English writing of the future.

49. Knight (1959), 204.
50. Reynolds (forthcoming).

3

English Renaissance Poets and the Translating Tradition

According to F. O. Matthiessen, 'a study of Elizabethan translations is a study of the means by which the Renaissance came to England'.[1] Nor is their importance confined to that era: early modern English translations have been a reference point for later eras too. The Victorians saw the early translations they congratulated themselves on rediscovering as adventurous, pioneering works. They are presented, for example, in the 44-volume series 'Tudor Translations', overseen by W. E. Henley in 1892–1903, as reflecting early progress towards the supremacy of English as the medium of world literature. A decade or two later, some of the same Tudor translations figured in the responses to Latin and Greek literature of those highly influential poet-critics glanced at in Chapter 2, Eliot and Pound, as they took up Catullus and Homer, Seneca and Sappho.[2] But the early twentieth-century Modernists, themselves heavily invested in creative translation, were the last generation fully to appreciate the importance of early modern translation. In the last 50 years, discussion of it has been far from central within scholarly study of English Renaissance writing.

Yet this account, while true as far as it goes, is superficial. Within the course of English poetry a much steadier reception process has been at work than the discontinuous affair of oblivion followed by sudden recovery just implied. In Chapter 1, the way Keats and some of his contemporaries embraced Chapman's Homer

---

1. Matthiessen (1931), 3. He is referring to translations of classical rather than continental Renaissance authors.
2. Eliot's review of the 'Tudor Translations' series can be found in his essay collection *The Sacred Wood*. Eliot was himself involved in a second series published 1924–7; his well-known essay 'Seneca in Elizabethan Translation' was originally composed to introduce its reprint of *Seneca his Tenne Tragedies*, 1581.

English Translation and Classical Reception: Towards a New Literary History, First Edition.
Stuart Gillespie.
© 2011 Stuart Gillespie. Published 2011 by John Wiley & Sons, Ltd.

afresh was mentioned. The episode can be seen as the turning-point in the fortunes of Pope's Homer, which by Keats's time had reached an apparently unassailable eminence.[3] But this is precisely why the later eighteenth century is atypical where Chapman's Homer is concerned: tastes formed on Pope's *Iliad* and *Odyssey* are tastes formed through reaction against Chapman's version. In fact, Chapman's Homer translations, though they make sufficiently taxing reading to be unlikely ever to reach a very wide audience, were reprinted several times in the earlier seventeenth century and were perfectly familiar to succeeding English poets and translators.[4] Because Chapman, unlike Marlowe, Jonson and the next generation of Virgil translators, Denham and Waller, did not aspire to emulation of the Roman Augustans, it is not surprising that Dryden recoiled from his 'harsh Numbers, improper English, and a monstrous length of Verse' (Chapman had adopted the fourteener in his *Iliad*). Yet in spite of all these shortcomings, Chapman's translation could not be ignored. Dryden wrote that his fellow poets Mulgrave and Waller, 'two of the best judges of our age', had assured him 'they cou'd never Read over the Translation of Chapman, without incredible Pleasure, and extreme Transport'.[5] The very terms of this description are reminiscent of Keats's reported first reaction to Chapman's *Iliad*, a 'delighted stare' (see p. 168, below). As for Pope himself, while accusing Chapman of 'negligence' in the Preface to his own version, he warms to the 'daring fiery Spirit that animates his Translation', making apparent his meaning by singling out 'above all things' in anyone who seeks to translate Homer the ability 'to keep alive that Spirit and Fire which makes his chief Character'.[6] In his 'Life of Pope' Samuel Johnson suggests, in fact, that Pope 'had very frequent consultations' of Chapman, 'and perhaps never translated any passage till he had read his version, which indeed he has been sometimes suspected of using instead of the original'.[7] Pope's Preface and the first instalment of his *Iliad* translation were first published in 1715. It was not until Pope's translation had had its effect that Chapman's Homer, as Johnson also reports, became 'totally neglected'. This neglect, then, was confined to a relatively brief interlude. As well as by Keats, Chapman's translation was endorsed by Coleridge, Godwin, Lamb and Shelley – Coleridge, for example, finding Chapman's work to give a 'far truer' idea of Homer than Pope's 'epigrams' (i.e., couplets).[8] A new edition of Chapman's *Odyssey* appeared in 1818. His *Iliads* were issued with

3. For the Romantic rejection of Pope's Homer, see Webb (2004), 305–7.
4. After the first collected edition of the Homer in 1611 there were reprints of the *Odyssey c.* 1614–15, then of the complete Homer *c.* 1616 and *c.* 1634.
5. Dryden (1956–2000), IV, 374.
6. Pope (1939–69), VII, 21–2. I owe this and the preceding reference to Robin Sowerby, whose account of Chapman's reputation from Dryden to Pope is found at the end of his own recuperative study of Chapman's Homer: Sowerby (1992), 48–9.
7. Johnson (1905), III, 115.
8. Letter to Sara Hutchinson, April 1808; Coleridge (1955), 503. For Lamb's comments on Pope and Chapman see pp. 175–6, below.

Flaxman's late eighteenth-century illustrations in 1843; edited by Richard Hooper in 1857 (two further printings following); and again by Richard Shepherd in 1875. An appreciative essay on Chapman's Homer by James Russell Lowell appeared in *Harper's Magazine* in 1892.

This outline implies an unexpected continuity in the appreciation of earlier English classical translations, particularly among English poets. Poets of one generation react against their immediate predecessors to strike out anew. But that effect is temporary, and in no way prevents their participation in the longer-term community of English followers of Homer or Ovid or Virgil. Indeed, they have no choice, for, as I will suggest later, the most powerful English readings and realizations of classical texts, such as (in Chapter 4) North's and Shakespeare's of Plutarch's *Lives*, or (in Chapter 10) Dryden's Lucretius and Virgil, have a tendency both to create and to delimit future possibilities for readers and writers at large. This 'participation' also means feeling free to emulate and borrow from previous translations, whether locally for a handy rhyme or strategically for one's whole approach.[9] All of this makes it possible, in spite of the ever-shifting priorities in English writers' receptions of ancient Greek and Latin texts, to speak of a tradition in English classical translation – a tradition which for most purposes gets under way in the sixteenth century. Towards the end of this chapter we shall see this in miniature in examples stemming from the work of Sir Thomas Wyatt and others.

♦　　♦　　♦

This chapter describes some of the ways in which English Renaissance writers approached the translation of ancient literary texts, and in which these translations mingled with their original writings and meshed with their other priorities. Generically, the English predecessor-term for literature, 'letters', embraced much more than its successor normally covers today, but in the educational sense, to study 'letters' quite literally meant following a curriculum of Latin learning (Latin, and in the higher forms Greek, being the only languages normally taught in schools in sixteenth- and seventeenth-century Britain). As for translation, those who had followed such a curriculum at grammar school had already perforce become translators of sorts, since this activity was part of their training. It is easily possible to believe, as Jonathan Bate claims, that 'Shakespeare's first lessons in poetry were lessons in the imitation of Ovid'.[10] Translation inculcated language skills, introduced literature and taught the craft of translation itself. The humanists attached weight to this, Roger Ascham calling translation the 'most common, and most commendable of all other exercises for youth'.[11] To see how it might be done, pupils could compare their efforts, or might find their teachers comparing

---

9. For an extensive example of the second, see pp. 112–14, below.
10. Bate (1993), 22.
11. Ascham (1570), L1ᵛ.

them, with published versions of classical works. Nicholas Grimald commends his English Cicero to schoolmasters as a model with which to teach their charges 'as well in the english, as the latine, to weygh well properties of wordes, fashions of phrases, and the ornaments of bothe'.[12] A hundred years later, Charles Hoole's *New Discovery of the Old Art of Teaching School* (1661) recommends that the school library stock translations for both classroom and recreational reading, specifying the best English versions of Mantuan, Virgil, Persius and Ovid. Chapman's Homer played a similar role for Greek.[13]

In contrast to Italy or France, where the topic of translation was addressed in treatises and other formal contexts by writers like Bruni, Du Bellay, Dolet and Peletier,[14] pre-Restoration Britain can lay claim at most to only one treatise on the theory and practice of translation: the *Interpretatio Linguarum* (1569) of the Oxford divine Laurence Humphrey. This, however, was written in Latin, published in Basle during Humphrey's exile under the Marian regime, and neither widely read nor reprinted. Until Dryden's well-known formulation of 1680 which we glanced at in Chapter 2, defining the three categories of 'paraphrase', 'metaphrase' and 'imitation', the formal definitions for types of translation and imitation were the humanistic Latin ones used in schools – *translatio, paraphrasis, imitatio, allusio*. Thomas Greene suggests that such distinctions are rather too sharp to describe how most actual translations operate; that the boundaries they denote are somewhat arbitrary.[15] Perhaps a more promising way of discovering how English translators envisaged what they were doing is to ask how they thought of the activity when they came to find metaphors for it.[16]

All eras have their metaphors for translation. For example, our own discussions in the twenty-first century exhibit severe moral reservations about cultural appropriation, reservations which underlie the use of such terms as 'foreignization' and 'domestication'. Those labels would have caused puzzlement in the Renaissance, but more so the assumptions they reflect. For early modern translators, not only is the appropriative nature of the translations which they carry out a good thing, appropriation is one of the primary *ends* of translation. Philemon Holland, the 'translator general' of the age (as Thomas Fuller called him), thinks of the translation of Latin works as a kind of subjugation of Roman culture – or perhaps worse still, as a payback for the Roman conquest of Britain. Those who would rather

12. Grimald (1556), ❪❪vii^r.

13. For translation within English Renaissance education, see further Kelly (2010), on which the preceding paragraph draws, and for further specifics of the curriculum, Baldwin (1944).

14. For an overview, see Morini (2006), 13–24.

15. See on the terminology generally Greene (1982), 51–2, who, as well as noting doubts about the humanist categories, suggests that Dryden feels his own distinctions are 'too rigid to be of value' (51).

16. A complementary recent discussion is found in Morini (2006), 35–61, on 'The Use of Figurative Language in the Discourse about Translation'. The most recent account of English Renaissance translation theory and procedure is Braden (2010).

Latin works remained untranslated, Holland notoriously pronounces in the preface to his Pliny, must be supposed to

> thinke not so honourably of their native countrey and mother tongue as they ought: who if they were so well affected that way as they should be, would wish rather and endeavour by all meanes to triumph now over the Romans in subduing their literature under the dent of the English pen, in requitall of the conquest sometime over this Island, atchieved by the edge of their sword.[17]

Such formulations are largely predicated on the degree to which the source text and its language are successfully assimilated into the translation. George Turberville is frank in the address to the reader in his 1567 English *Heroides*: 'It is,' he asserts, 'a work of prayse to cause | A Romaine borne to speake with English jawes.'[18]

But usually this is expressed in a more abstract discourse of strangeness and familiarity. Terms which seem happily assimilated into English are 'natural', 'native', 'plain', 'proper', 'pure', 'apt and mete'.[19] This means that questions about the procedures and purposes of translation are wrapped up with debates about linguistic assimilation. Two central issues structure these debates: the adequacy of English as a language of culture and knowledge, and the specific character of the English into which foreign (especially Latin) texts are translated. English was often seen at this time (and far beyond) as an inadequate language, lacking both authority and copiousness, and translation was one way of putting right these shortcomings: the unprecedented expansion of English vocabulary in the hundred years from 1550 was largely the result of the effort to translate texts into English (literary texts, but also practical, religious and other kinds). And this drive was, as Charles Barber makes clear in describing the expansion of English vocabulary in this period, 'highly conscious'.[20] Or, as Richard Foster Jones spells it out further, 'the key to an understanding of the dominant attitude toward the vernacular … is found in the unhappy comparison with Latin and Greek and in the strong desire and earnest effort to educate the unlearned by translations and by original works written in English'.[21]

Early modern translators often apologize that their work falls short of Latinate copiousness, eloquence or diction – which is to say that these qualities tend to be thought significant, but not crucial. Arthur Golding suggests that one of his translations 'in his playne and homely English cote' might be as acceptable to the reader as the original 'when it were richly clad in Romayn vesture'.[22] But the other side of this coin is the way translation is viewed as the means by which the necessary

17. Holland (1601), π2ᵛ.
18. Turberville (1567), X2ᵛ.
19. These adjectives are all taken from Wilson (1553), 82ᵛ–83ʳ.
20. Barber (1997), 53. The recognized precedent of Latin borrowings from Greek was significant.
21. Jones (1953), 168.
22. Golding (1564), viᵛ.

enrichment of English can be achieved. The importance attached by translators to the status of the vernacular (to which, after all, they have a built-in commitment) is entirely compatible with the view that the stock of English words needs to be augmented and the language's expressive power improved via the process of translation itself. Disparagement of the English language is found alongside earnest efforts to improve it.

It is no coincidence, then, that a period in which the vocabulary of English expands so rapidly is also one in which translation is such an influential literary mode. Although we might be tempted to suppose that vocabulary growth would have proceeded from the need to find new terms of a functional or practical kind to correspond with foreign ones, in actuality it seems more often to have been driven by stylistic and literary motives. A simple piece of evidence would appear to point this way: the central role of literary translation is implied by the heavy preponderance of new lexical items having Latin origins (as often shown by spelling), rather than deriving from modern languages. When language historians count the new words they identify for this period, they find borrowings from Latin heavily outnumbering those from modern languages.[23]

As is well understood, the outlines of ancient literature looked different to early modern readers and scholars. Just as 'letters' was a broader category than 'literature' is today, a more inclusive sense of the available range of ancient writings obtained too, so that Virgil, for example, was accepted as the author of the pseudo-Virgilian text, a mock-heroic trifle, known as *Virgil's Gnat* (it was translated by Spenser); or, as was mentioned in Chapter 2, so that Hellenistic poems written in imitation of much older ones attributed to Anacreon of Teos were accepted as genuinely ancient works. This is one of the reasons why, although they did not put it in these terms, writers and translators could also choose from among several 'classicisms' – on occasion, it may be, doing so with as much self-consciousness as when we think about these matters today. The Greek and Latin authors Marlowe translated and imitated included Lucan, Musaeus and Ovid, all of whom were known as subversive or dissident writers in his era as well as in their own. Ovid was also known to be pornographic, and Marlowe's spirited, clandestinely printed translations from the *Amores* (under the title *Ovid's Elegies*) were scandalous enough to be burned by the official censor in London in 1599.[24] Ovid was perhaps the most imitated and influential classical author for the English Renaissance; as the perceived shape of the Ovidian corpus shifted, and ways of reading him moved away from the medieval practices of moralizing and Christianizing towards delight in luxuriance and eroticism, his cultural capital evidently remained secure. If some

23. The ratio of Latinate to French words is estimated at more than 3:1. For the arrival of Latin and Greek loan-words from 1500, with lists of examples and some discussion of the issues in distinguishing Latin from French, see Serjeantson (1935), 259–70. For translation and the changing English language in the Renaissance, see further Clarke (2010), on which the preceding two paragraphs draw.
24. On Marlowe's elective Ovidianism, see Cheney (1997).

translations acquired notoriety, others, such as George Sandys's, make it evident from the way they are printed, with the full paraphernalia of prefaces, notes and illustrations, that they are designed to become cultural monuments. The multifaceted experience of Renaissance Ovidianism is worth pausing over here.

Because of his wide appeal Ovid is revisited and replayed in many different ways by English writers, his works having a place in theatre and prose contexts as well as a more substantial one in poetic responses.[25] He is mediated through Marlowe as well as others: enough copies of Marlowe's *Elegies* survived the bonfire for his contemporaries to echo his Ovidian translations in their own productions, and it seems to have been Marlowe's book itself that prompted several of them to publish collections of love poems titled 'elegies' in the mid-1590s. He is the only classical author named by Shakespeare and perhaps the only one to whom Shakespeare was compared by a contemporary.[26] Ovid's concerns are in the air of the age: metamorphosis, metempsychosis, poetic immortality, the impermanence of the past, the multiple forms of sexual desire – and writing itself. Shakespeare's Sonnet 60, 'Like as the waves make towards the pebbled shore', is closely modelled on *Metamorphoses* 15.178–85, and, as Colin Burrow has written, 'ends in an uneasy balance between loss and recuperation which is typical of responses to Ovid in this period: Ovid is revived and imitated, but with a lasting impression that texts may be weak opponents to Time's destructive energy'.[27] However, we are entitled here to place the emphasis on the recuperation, for English Ovidianism is in one of its aspects a tradition, enduring over many years, of cross-fertilization between his translators, imitators and other 'respondents'. For example, by the time Shakespeare used a couplet from the *Amores* (1.15.35–6) as the epigraph to *Venus and Adonis*, it is more than likely he had read Marlowe's version of that collection. Or there is Shakespeare's much-discussed relation to Golding's and other English Ovids in the playlet of *Midsummer Night's Dream*.[28] Golding's Ovid is 'undoubtedly a monument', Raphael Lyne writes, a work which, because he makes Ovid think in terms of English scenes and details as well as giving him a full-flavoured English idiom, sits well with 'the ambitions on behalf of their native tongue shared by many renaissance writers'.[29] Sandys's succeeding translation of 1621–32, mostly carried out in Virginia while Sandys was working as Treasurer of the struggling Jamestown colony, could be presented as both a national triumph and a triumph for the English language, as by Michael Drayton in his commendatory verses. Drayton imagines the two languages concerned walking together, 'the neatness

25. No single study covers all this ground, but some attractive recent general accounts of English Renaissance Ovidianism are Pearcy (1984); Barkan (1986); Lyne (2001).
26. 'Ovidius Naso was the man', says Holofernes (*Love's Labours Lost*, IV.2.119). 'The sweet wittie soul of Ovid lives in mellifluous and hony-tongued Shakespeare', writes Francis Meres in *Palladis Tamia*.
27. Burrow (2002), 303.
28. See Brooks (1979), lxxxvi–lxxxvii; Taylor (1989). For Ovid and Shakespeare more widely, see Bate (1993); Brown (1994).
29. Lyne (2002), 254.

of the *English* pace' comparing favourably with the 'jetting' (strutting, boastful) Latin that 'came | But slowly after, as though stiffe and lame'.[30]

Here we return, then, to national pride and self-assertion. But there could be no serious English claim to have dominated or overtaken the ancients; quite the contrary, in that as the classics were 'made English' they proffered a new ancestry for English poetry, supplanting the native one and making English junior in the relationship. In Chapter 1, I wrote that 'classical works and their vernacular descendants forced a reassessment of the literary system' and undertook to outline how translations had the effect of forging a new past for English verse. Robert Cummings has most recently described this process. Translation gave English writers a sense of the contingency of style and led to their rejecting the home-grown: 'Isocrates, Cicero, or Seneca did not determine what English prose should look like, nor Virgil, Horace, or Ariosto how English verse should move, but they supplied a perspective on the stylistic landscape. They offered a new way of think-ing about the map of English writing.' Thus English writing began to be conceived in relation to other writing and not in relation to medieval English, now largely 'irrecuperable in the required terms and hence written out of the record'. So it is that while Jonson advises poets to beware of tasting Gower or Chaucer, English writers begin to look for other masters and 'the translators from classical literatures supply an alternative past for English poetry'.[31] As well as at the level of shifting elective affinities like those instanced here, this effect can be illustrated from con-temporary thinking about the art of poetry. We see how the controversy about quantitative verse, 'instead of simply confirming the natural prevalence of accus-tomed native verse forms over "newfangled", artificial imitation … forced vernacu-lar writers to reconsider some of the very laws that were traditionally thought to govern English poetry'. Gabriela Schmidt shows how translators attempting to imitate quantitative metres thus turn out to have been taking 'an important step on the road towards a more consciously regularized English vernacular poetics, which, consequently, became capable of entering into a more confident and dis-criminating dialogue with the classical tradition'.[32] In answering the question of how to establish an English literary identity while drawing from other traditions, translations were the focus of a great deal of interest.

But this chapter did not set out from foreign or classical traditions, rather with the early development of the English translating tradition. The renegotiation of the past, the influence of ancient poetics, or the arrival of sequences of translations of the same texts over time, might be parts of such a project, might even be necessary conditions for its realization, but a tradition is not necessarily constituted from them – they are not, that is, sufficient conditions. This book as a whole aims to suggest what the requisite conditions might be, but some idea of what such a

30. Drayton, 'To Sir Henry Reynolds', 160–2; Drayton (1931–41), III, 230.
31. Cummings (2010), 32.
32. Schmidt (2010), 304.

tradition looks like can be supplied, for the moment, from one small group of early modern translations and imitations.

The seventeenth-century development of a nexus of themes and ideas around Horace's Second Epode has been studied in some depth. *Beatus ille*, the Happy Husbandman, country/city, retirement/solitude, *via media*: these linked ideas, in the words of the most comprehensive twentieth-century expositor of this episode in English poetry, Maren-Sofie Røstvig, 'form the core of the neo-classical philosophy of retirement as it is expressed in English poetry from Phineas Fletcher and Ben Jonson to Pope and Gray'.[33] Røstvig identified John Ashmore's 1621 translations, *Certain Selected Odes of Horace*, as one of the early watersheds; translations of Horace are more frequent after this date. But Horace was not the only classical writer to elaborate these themes, and the role translators played in developing them lies more in the way they turn to a range of individual poems and passages for celebration of the retired life. As well as Horace (the Second Epode often englished in curtailed form, without the usurer's closing words), translators repeatedly quarry Martial (10.47), Seneca (the second Chorus from *Thyestes*) and Claudian (*De sene Veronesi*), other texts such as Virgil's Second Georgic more occasionally.

What can be discerned in this activity is not merely a fashion for retirement poetry to which classical texts are laid under contribution, or a sudden access of enthusiasm for certain Latin poems, or merely a series of translations reflecting the popularity of those poems. We might say rather that a collective enterprise gets under way, a shared effort to make English, and to make contemporary, the concerns of these Latin poems. The contemporary angles are implied in the lives and times of the translators, from Sir Thomas Wyatt, precariously placed at the Henrician Court in the mid-sixteenth century, to Cowley and others who lived through the Civil War in the seventeenth. One way of demonstrating the collective nature of the enterprise is by showing that English poets develop from each other over time a vocabulary for englishing these poems and passages. For instance, Seneca's Chorus beginning 'Stet quicumque volet potens | aulae culmine lubrico' was imitated early by Wyatt, who used the word 'slippery' (in the older adjectival form 'slipper') for the Latin *lubrico*:

> Stond who so list upon the Slipper toppe
>   Of courtes estates, and lett me heare rejoyce;
> And use me quyet without lett or stoppe,
>   Unknowen in courte, that hath suche brackishe joyes[34]

Jasper Heywood's near-contemporary version shows there was nothing inevitable about Wyatt's adjective: Heywood speaks of standing on a 'tickle' (insecure,

33. Røstvig (1954–8), I, 73.
34. Ed. Muir (1950), no. 176.

precarious) 'top'. But Wyatt's poem, 'doubtless written', Thomas Greene notes, 'after the execution of Wyatt's patron Cromwell',[35] became extremely well known through its inclusion in the most popular English verse anthology of its day, Tottel's Miscellany (1557).[36] Down through the seventeenth century his word 'slippery' begins to leak into original English verse in similar contexts (involving kings and courts):

> Of fickle Fortunes false and slippery Court
> (Francis Quarles, 1633)

> Praising a Cottage, bove a slippery Court
> (Robert Baron, 1650)

> Pow'r and Greatness are such slippery things,
> Who'd pity Cottages, or envy Kings?
> (Katherine Philips, 1664)

> the slippery state of Kings
> (Sir John Denham, 1668)

It was this adjective which was then accepted and adopted in later translations of the Senecan chorus, as by Cowley in 1656 –

> Upon the slippery tops of humane State,
> The guilded Pinnacles of Fate,
> Let others proudly stand ...[37]

– until Marvell, responsible for perhaps the best-known English version, wrote:

> Climb at court for me that will
> Giddy favour's slippery hill;
> All I seek is to lie still.[38]

It might be added that despite its being in some sense the culmination of a tradition, as well as a powerful and accessible poem, Marvell's contribution regularly

---

35. Greene (1982), 245. See 245–6 for analysis of Wyatt's highly charged ten-line poem, constituting for Greene an early example of 'mature English imitation', and of its relation to the Latin.
36. This printing of Wyatt's poem gives 'slipper wheel' in the first line. This no longer accepted variant, a reference to the medieval Wheel of Fortune, was common in printed texts up to the twentieth century, but the point does little to affect the present discussion of the adjective.
37. Cowley (1905), I, 399–400.
38. This text, from Donno 1972, is based in part on a manuscript which belonged to Marvell's nephew William Popple, whom we will meet in Chapter 8. The second line exists in more than one version; for discussion of the alternative readings, see Daalder (1989).

goes unprinted in modern selections of his work, one reason being that it is a translation.[39]

Finally, and briefly, a further example will link to the major Dryden translation which will be the subject of Chapter 5. The climactic stanza of Dryden's version of Horace's Ode 3.29 begins with the phrase 'Happy the man' and includes the line 'To morrow do thy worst, for I have liv'd to day'. These two pieces of phraseology may be said to reflect Horace's Latin (in which the words corresponding to those to which I wish to call attention are simply *felix qui* and *vixi*), but they are rooted in the expressions English poets had previously found to summon up the happy life within translations and original poems in the *Beatus ille* tradition. So we may pick up the first signs of the word 'live' being used emphatically, to mean something active as opposed to mere existence, in Ralph Freeman's *Lucius Annaeus Seneca the Philosopher: His Book on the Shortnes of Life. Translated into an English Poem* (1663):

> That man hath certainly too late begun
> To live, who onely lives when life is done …[40]

And we might look to Cowley's Claudian, in his *Essays* of 1668, for Dryden's opening phrase:

> Happy the Man, who his whole time doth bound
> Within th'enclosure of his little ground.
> Happy the Man, whom the same humble place,
> (Th' hereditary Cottage of his Race)
> From his first rising infancy has known …

Cowley was one of Dryden's favourite authors, and Dryden would have known this translation intimately. But we would then find Cowley had been anticipated by Thomas Randolph in translating Claudian in 1638:

> Happy the man that all his days hath spent
> Within his grounds, and no further went

and was succeeded by Bulstrode Whitlock in translating Horace's Second Epode in 1692:

39. For example, Wilcher (1986). The poem is not part of the Marvell selection in the major teaching anthologies of English poetry/literature either. For a collection of sixteenth- and seventeenth-century versions of the Senecan chorus, see Costa (1974), 197–201; for comparisons between them, see Mason (1959), 181–6.

40. Jonson had used the same Senecan epistle (Ep. 83) in the rather different context of the Cary-Morrison ode, without quite arriving at the emphatic verb: 'For, what is life, if measured by the space, | Not by the act?' (21–2; Jonson (1975), 212).

Happy the Man from toilsome cares set free,
Who does regain Man's ancient Liberty,
Ploughing his Ground with Oxen of his own,
By Parents left;'s free from Usurious Loan

again by Elijah Fenton when translating Claudian in 1720:

Happy the Man who all his days doth pass
In the paternal cottage of his race.[41]

and by Pope, in one of his earliest poems, one not announced as a translation:

Happy the man whose wish and care
A few paternal acres bound,
Content to breathe his native air,
In his own ground.[42]

It is nothing new to say that the words and phrases used by their predecessors are one of the fundamental forms in which a tradition can present itself to poets, and in which they may embrace it. What we have just seen shows, more specifically, that the English translation of classical verse sponsored its own traditions. Here we make contact with another distinctive feature of classical translation, for whereas successive vernacular translators tend to turn to new sources, especially contemporary foreign writings, each generation of English poets retranslates the classics in the light of changing circumstances. What we have just seen also suggests something more unexpected: that in this context the borders between individual classical texts, and again between translations and original English verse, are of little account.

◆ ◆ ◆

In Chapter 1, I quoted Jonson on the use of the classics as 'guides, not commanders'. In Chapter 2, I argued that the idea of creative translation still bears examination. For the early modern period these things need stressing because of the negative light in which it is so easy to see its doctrine of imitation. That negative light is by no means always inappropriate: even Jonson can have trouble making imitations and translations seem creative, as much of his line-for-line version of Horace's *Ars poetica* illustrates. As it happens, though, one point at which it breaks further away from literalism than usual is when Horace is discussing imitation:

41. A collection of English versions of *De sene Veronesi* is assembled in Claudian (1993), from which all these quotations are taken.
42. 'Ode on Solitude' (*c.* 1700), 1–4; Pope (1939–69), VI, 3.

> Publica materies priuati iuris erit, si
> non circa uilem patulumque moraberis orbem,
> nec uerbo uerbum curabis reddere fidus
> interpres nec desilies imitator in artum,
> unde pedem proferre pudor uetet aut operis lex.

Horace thus sanctions the use of the common stock of cultural material, *publica materies*, and warns against the type of *fidus interpres* who will allow himself to be constrained by *pudor* or *lex operis* – by a sense of modesty or by the laws of genre. Jonson seems to appreciate the creative freedom this formulation allows: his version is at this point itself an expansion, and handled more freely than he permits himself elsewhere. He also introduces the word 'translate' to accompany Horace's 'imitate':

> Yet common matter thou thine own mayst make,
> If thou the vile broad-trodden ring forsake.
> For, being a poet, thou mayst feign, create,
> Not care, as thou wouldst faithfully translate,
> To render word-for-word: nor with thy sleight
> Of imitation, leap into a strait
> From whence thy modesty, or poem's law,
> Forbids thee forth again thy foot to draw.[43]

'Making common matter thine own' is what Wyatt could be said to do in the Senecan imitation we glanced at as standing at the head of a line of English responses to the *Thyestes* chorus. Here Wyatt composes a drama of his own time and place in language that marks him as an Anglo-Saxon countryman. His idiom ('brackishe joyes', 'lett or stoppe') is, in fact, radically anti-Latinate, and, as Greene writes, 'calls attention to his own parochial rusticity' in order implicitly to criticize the facility, the elegant Latinism, of the Senecan subtext.[44] Here is Wyatt's poem as a whole:

> Stond who so list upon the Slipper toppe
>   Of courtes estates, and lett me heare rejoyce;
> And use me quyet without lett or stoppe,
>   Unknowen in courte, that hath suche brackishe joyes
>   In hidden place, so lett my dayes forthe passe,
>   That when my yeares be done, withouten noyse,
>   I may die aged after the common trace.
> For hym death greep'the right hard by the croppe

43. Lines 187–94; Jonson (1975), 358–9.
44. Greene (1982), 246.

> That is moche knowen of other; and of him self alas,
> Doth dye unknowen, dazed with dreadfull face.[45]

Wyatt's early modern successors often found it all too easy to create reproduction antiques, something which could appear to be permitted, if not encouraged, by the Renaissance doctrine of imitation. But their best impulses were towards innovation. Like Wyatt here, they were, as Robin Sowerby has expressed it, 'concerned with the ways in which the classics might be used to aid fresh creative endeavour in the present' and 'desired through their commerce with the ancients both to extend their own poetic range and to raise the standards of contemporary achievement'.[46] All I would add is that that a fundamental part of that commerce took place in translation, over the full range of its forms.

45. Ed. Muir (1950), no. 176.
46. Sowerby (1994), 375. See this work *passim* for Jonson's attitudes to classical authority.

4

Two-Way Reception: Shakespeare's Influence on Plutarch

Critical discussions, not unlike what are sometimes called 'works of the imagination', all have their starting points, and one of this chapter's is a recent essay by Michael Silk titled 'Shakespeare and Greek Tragedy: Strange Relationship'.[1] This leads the reader from the issue of Greek tragedy's apparently very limited influence on Shakespeare to that of 'Shakespearean "influence" on Greek tragedy'. Accepting that Seneca is 'no doubt "the closest Shakespeare ever got to Greek tragedy"',[2] Silk intriguingly suggests that one effect of the 'profound affinity' between Shakespearean and Greek tragedy, of their 'common inner logic', has been that the English dramatist 'has exerted a multifarious interpretive pull' over the ancient Greek plays – 'a kind of reverse, Eliotian influence'.[3] Shakespeare, that is, has been 'read back' onto the Greeks, helping to stimulate modern critical awareness of the thematic function of Aeschylus' imagery or of features in Euripides that might be regarded as comic or tragicomic. Most fundamentally, Silk suggests, Shakespeare has sponsored our 'expectation of the unitary–heroic matrix', the supposition in place since the seventeenth century that Greek tragedies are structured around a single hero. One result of this, he speculates, is the current assignment of the role of normative Greek tragedian to Sophocles (though efforts have had to be made to bring *Antigone* into line), whereas it is Euripides who was more highly esteemed in Shakespeare's time.

Such speculation has a heady attraction. We might pause to reflect, though, that Sophocles was also the normative Greek tragedian for Aristotle. Or we might want to ask whether Shakespeare would actually have recognized some of the

1. Silk (2004).
2. Silk (2004), 241, quoting Charles and Michelle Martindale.
3. Silk (2004), 246.

English Translation and Classical Reception: Towards a New Literary History, First Edition. Stuart Gillespie.

features said to link his plays profoundly to the Athenian ones. Don't such entities as 'thematically functioning imagery' belong rather specifically to twentieth-century critical thinking? (And are they perhaps reaching their sell-by date?) Later, I will suggest that more may remain to be uncovered about the impact Greek tragedy had on Shakespeare, as well as his impact on it. But to start at the beginning: how did Shakespeare come to place his own writing within this 'matrix' – to acquire his idea of how a tragic play could or should be constructed? This seems to have happened under the influence neither of classical Greek theatre nor of the later tragedies Shakespeare knew which derived from it, namely Senecan drama as mediated by English translators and by the sixteenth-century Italian plays of Cinthio and others. Rather, where this question leads us was suggested 50 years ago when J. A. K. Thomson wrote: 'I believe it was from Plutarch that Shakespeare learned how to make a tragedy of the kind exemplified in *Hamlet* and *Othello*, *Macbeth* and *Lear*. It was … in the course of writing *Julius Caesar* that he learned it.'[4] This proposition has since won general acceptance, and even those to whom it is still unfamiliar should not be unduly surprised by it. Shakespeare is believed to have written *Julius Caesar* before any of the other plays named, under Elizabeth in 1599, and his source was Plutarch. *Julius Caesar* may not in itself have a straightforwardly tragic structure, but it leads to Shakespearean tragedy because in it Shakespeare, in the words of a more recent commentator, Cynthia Marshall, 'crosses his own Rubicon', moving from 'largely plot-driven plays' to 'deeply characteriological drama'. Marshall suggests further that 'what happens … in Shakespeare's conversion of [Plutarchan] narrative into drama, is the establishment of our culture's prevailing model of character as one that is at once intensely performative and putatively interiorized'.[5] As I hope will become clear, what I think this formulation obscures is that Shakespeare's 'model of character' is itself one that looks backwards to the classics, as much as forwards to ourselves.

◆   ◆   ◆

Lest I be thought to stray from my path, translation is decisively involved here, for, knowing nothing of the Greek Plutarch, Shakespeare was the beneficiary of the work of two of the most accomplished prose translators of the sixteenth century. They were the Englishman Sir Thomas North and behind him the admired Jacques Amyot, of whose 1559 French rendering, rather than the original Greek, North's *Lives* (1579) was expressly a translation. Everyone knows that Shakespeare used Plutarch's narrative material; he was also attracted to North's way with words. Verbal parallels, at some points so extensive as to give the impression that Shakespeare is merely versifying North's prose, occur throughout the Roman plays. Enobarbus' speech 'The barge she sat in', his description of Cleopatra

4. Thomson (1952), 242.
5. Marshall (2000), 80, 73.

in *Antony and Cleopatra* II.2, is the most often cited example, but there are many others, including one case in which North's text actually allows us to reconstruct and restore a lost line from *Coriolanus*.[6] That's how closely Shakespeare sometimes follows North. Unless Shakespeare owned a copy of North's translation (a very expensive folio production), it would appear he must have been able regularly to consult one for his work over the years. There was Southampton's library, perhaps, or for the 1595 edition the London print shop of his fellow Warwickshireman, Richard Field.[7]

Shakespeare used North, but did not use Amyot. We know this because Shakespeare's texts reflect North's adjustments of Amyot (inadvertent as well as deliberate), and indeed the very mistakes of North's printers. An example of Shakespeare capitalizing on a touch which must have been consciously introduced by North comes when Coriolanus' mother Volumnia tells him that he'll be the death of her if he persists in his campaign.[8] The words Plutarch gives her about him 'treading underfoot the dead body of the woman who bore you' were closely followed by Amyot. North, though, brings the subtext to the fore, introducing the word 'womb', and has Volumnia explicitly say 'thy foote shall treade upon thy mothers wombe, that brought thee first into this world'[9]. Shakespeare sees he can use this, and his Volumnia complains:

> thou shalt no sooner
> March to assault thy Country, then to treade
> ... on thy Mothers wombe
> That brought thee to this world.
>
> (V.3.123–6)

Such appropriations of North's changes are significant in that those who feel Shakespeare has an intuitive ability to reach back beyond the translators and imitators whose versions of Greek texts he used so as to grasp the authentic Homer, or the authentic Greek tragedians, have so far been unable to explain how it is that he is simultaneously so happy to use (and indeed conspicuously felicitous in his use of) such inauthentic accretions.

This example may be trivial enough as far as the overall conduct of *Coriolanus* is concerned, but the point about Shakespeare's 'intuitive ability' is worth pausing on, not least because the claim is made by some of the most distinguished recent commentators on his response to the classics. A. D. Nuttall, writing about an accepted debt to Ovid in a passage on the amours of the gods in *The Winter's*

---

6. Braden (2004), 188.
7. It is not known which of the available editions of North (1597, 1595, 1603) Shakespeare used; their textual differences are small. Citations below are from the first. For Field's Shakespeare connections, see Duncan-Jones (2001), 114–15.
8. For fuller discussion of this moment, see Braden (2004), 190–1.
9. North (1579), 257.

Tale, a debt which he thinks can explain the material but not its flavour, explains that Ovid transmits the Greek gods in a 'consciously delinquent' way. What Shakespeare does is to 'ignore' this flavour and instead 'pass ... through the ... Roman medium to the Greek material on the far side'. Nuttall then generalizes: 'I am suggesting that Shakespeare had a facility for driving through the available un-Greek transmitting text to whatever lay on the other side.'[10] In this case it happens to be a matter of flavour, but Nuttall and others are also given to claiming that Shakespeare has a capacity to 'reimagine', that is to reconstruct, original Greek material of narrative and other kinds too.[11] The ultimate motive to such claims, I would suggest, is the allure of being able to show that first-division Greek literature (especially Homeric epic and Athenian tragedy) provides models for Shakespeare directly, not only via such routes as English translations of Seneca or the *Gesta Romanorum*.[12] Such thinking is of specific concern here because it has been hypothesized that Shakespeare has the facility to divine what Plutarch wrote independently of how North and Amyot, through local error or more diffusely through their own emphases, distorted the *Lives*. Distort them they did: Amyot was a humanist Catholic clergyman and North a Puritan English gentleman, and their ideological distance from Plutarch is only too evident in many of their local decisions as translators. To take a simple example from the *Life of Brutus*: later on in the narrative, Brutus, typically of Plutarchan political men, expresses the glory of dedicating his life to his country – this, he says, is what the Ides of March meant to him, and (I paraphrase the Greek) 'since then, for my country's sake, I have lived another life of liberty and glory'. But Amyot, followed by North, instead makes Brutus conclude his speech with a vision of the afterlife:

> For, I gave up my life for my contry in the Ides of Marche, for the which I shall live in another more glorious worlde.[13]

This Brutus sounds oddly like a Christian who has wandered into republican Rome.

The hypothesis that Shakespeare could 'see through' these distortions has been propounded most recently in the outstanding work of Christopher Pelling, whose edition of the *Life of Antony* (Pelling 1998) has much to offer Shakespeare scholars and whose more recent essay on *Julius Caesar* (Pelling 2009) lays out in detail the signs that in this play 'Shakespeare can sense the real Plutarch ... even when his translators stray.'[14] Pelling, to be sure, does not commit himself as fully as

10. Nuttall (2004), 214.
11. For example, Pelling (2009), 270, of elements in *Julius Caesar* (see further below) 'extending to imagery and theme as well as particular adaptation'.
12. Kragelund (2009), 281–2, sets out the same point in relation to Greek tragedy and Renaissance drama at large.
13. North (1579), 1074.
14. Pelling (2009), 268.

Nuttall, offering this proposition as one way of describing an impression the text creates rather than simply as 'what must have happened', but his language resembles Nuttall's when he remarks on the 'uncannily similar paths' Shakespeare's and Plutarch's sensibilities took them along. Pelling concedes that on occasion, while Shakespeare abandons a misreading in North, he also fails to arrive at 'what Plutarch's original said'. But he then presses the claim that what Shakespeare does is often 'truer to the genuine Plutarch … than … to the translators'.[15] Now this, as it stands, can be happily accepted without its implying anything 'uncanny'. Amyot and North are both very good translators, but their task is enormous, neither is perfect, each has his own mental habits and assumptions, and there is a double possibility of transmission error. Shakespeare may simply feel that a passage Amyot and/or North has messed with doesn't sound right – isn't true to life, doesn't make the narrative compelling or simply doesn't make sense – and what seems more plausible to him may well be how Plutarch originally presented things. In fact, there is an example at the point in *Julius Caesar* where he would have found the anomalous reference to the afterlife. Shakespeare, as it were, silently corrects North, and his Brutus says nothing of survival after death:[16]

> this same day
> Must end that work the ides of March begun.
> And whether we shall meet again I know not;
> Therefore our everlasting farewell take.
>
> (V.1.112–15)

At other times, Shakespeare's departures from Amyot and North may be occasioned by dramatic purposes and priorities which can overlap with Plutarch's. But there is no doubt that Shakespeare is sometimes taken many leagues away from Plutarch by a 'false reading' in Amyot or North. Most anecdotally, the creation of the two scenes on Enobarbus' desertion in *Antony and Cleopatra* seems to be made possible by Amyot's misreading of an aorist as a present tense.[17]

Attention focuses, therefore, on the few concrete instances Pelling proposes of Shakespeare's moving in the opposite direction, back towards Plutarch, and the robustness of the evidence available for 'uncanny similarity'. His leading example in *Julius Caesar* is the 'picturing of the murder as sacrifice' in Brutus' words 'Let us be sacrificers, but not butchers' (II.1.165; Pelling 2009: 270). This Pelling associates with Plutarch's depiction of the assassination, in which the word *katarkhesthai* (often used of ritual slaughter – it refers to a particular kind of blow) is used to describe how the conspirators ensure communal responsibility when Caesar is run through. Plutarch says that 'each had to take part in the sacrificial

---

15. Pelling (2009), 270–2.
16. For a more detailed account of this moment in Shakespeare, see Braden (2004) 191–2; Cantor (1997), 71–2.
17. Pelling (1998), 274, *ad* 18.4.

blow' (*Caesar* 66.11). One must agree the word 'sacrifice' is not there in Amyot's or North's account of the murder.[18] But it isn't actually there in Shakespeare's account of the murder either, only in Brutus' words ahead of it – an entire Act ahead, so that it isn't a question of the dramatist 'restoring' something which has dropped out of North's narrative. Instead, we are required to suppose Shakespeare first intuited one feature of the way Plutarch presents the assassination at the point when it is carried out, then applied it to the way a *character* presents it in a scene of conspiratorial discussion – a scene of his own invention, which did not actually exist in Plutarch – which came many hundreds of lines earlier in his play.

Surely it is much more likely that the logic of Brutus' character itself suggested to Shakespeare the idea that he would wish to view the assassination in the light of a sacrifice and not a slaughter? In any event, it is simply not the case that 'it could not have been North that suggested the figure of sacrifice',[19] for the word does, in fact, appear in North's *Life of Antonius*. After telling of how the Triumvirate come together to divide up the world between themselves, North adds that Antony, 'to gratefie Cæsar, was contented to be chosen Julius Cæsars priest and sacrificer'.[20] Antony will not, of course, be one of those involved in 'sacrificing' the Dictator, so there is no particular irony here; but North's use of the word in connection with Caesar must weaken the contention that Shakespeare arrived at it in Brutus' speech by intuiting what Plutarch's Greek text said or implied.

♦   ♦   ♦

Two strands of this discussion now need to be further attended to. Earlier I quoted Cynthia Marshall to the effect that that Shakespeare's use of Plutarch can be seen as establishing our culture's 'prevailing model of character'. And I quoted Michael Silk to the effect that the pull of Shakespeare's works has altered perceptions of classical Greek texts. Drawing these two matters together leads us to ask for some close definitions of how Plutarch envisages (and hence presents) character, how Shakespeare does so, and how we are accustomed to do so.

But no sooner do we start to look at Plutarch than the Plutarchan foundations of so much historical western writing seem to rise up in front of us. This was the experience of Reuben Brower, whose book *Hero and Saint: Shakespeare and the Graeco-Roman Heroic Tradition* contains an instructive attempt to describe and define Plutarchan history. Brower takes the *Life of Alexander* (in North's translation particularly) as his example, and finds in it much that looks familiar. There are such heroic features in Plutarch's portraits as 'the Renaissance–Virgilian exem-

18. Pelling (1998), 270 n. 22, following Brower (1971), 214, points out that North at another point Christianizes the pagan idea of sacrifice in Plutarch, when, translating a passage using the same term, he has the conspirators agree that the presence of Brutus would make the deed 'holie, and just'.
19. Pelling (2009), 269–70.
20. North (1579), 985. Plutarch (*Antonius* 5.2) here uses, and explains for his Greek audience, the word 'augur'.

plar' of the hero; reminiscences of 'many of the great men whose tales are told in the *Mirror* and *The Falls of Princes*'; and an episode proving Alexander's chastity that 'sounds like something from Chrétien de Troyes'.[21] These remarks of Brower's, it is true, are stabs at describing, 'placing' Plutarch for the benefit of readers who are not familiar with the *Lives*. Such descriptions nevertheless imply that later writers, having learned from Plutarch, have tended to lay down parameters (even preconditions?) for subsequent readings of him. In fact, this becomes clear when Brower expands on the point about 'the Renaissance–Virgilian exemplar' of heroic self-restraint, writing: 'The comment that it was "more princely for a kinge ... to conquer him selfe, then to overcome his enemies", though so "Renaissance" in flavour, is Plutarch's own.'[22] We see what's meant, and Brower is not unaware of the complexities, but in a slightly different sense we could ask how far it can remain 'Plutarch's own' when it has acquired 'so Renaissance' a flavour.[23]

Next as to character. If we ask what is Shakespearean about Plutarch (or vice versa) and what is modern about either, what is ultimately at issue is not individual characters or character types, but the conception of character itself. One complicating factor for us is that Shakespeare has become prominent in connection with attitudes to 'character' which feed on post-Shakespearean conceptions. This phenomenon goes back to the eighteenth century, when his work was enthusiastically incorporated into such emergent modern ideas as 'personality', 'identity' and 'self'. Maurice Morgann's essay on Falstaff of 1777, or the planned Shakespeare Jubilee celebrations in Stratford of 1769, in which a procession of characters from the plays was to parade through the streets, are two manifestations. Shakespeare, according to this way of seeing the plays, creates characters who are 'fully rounded', who 'leap off the page', who are each and every one of them individual personalities, who stay with you for life. And there is a natural tendency to suppose these attitudes reflect more sophisticated understandings of character than those found in earlier eras.

If, as I am arguing, Shakespeare does not conceive of character in the modern way, how does he think of it? At the start of *Twelfth Night* Viola decides she is willing to trust her sea captain rescuer, telling him (I.2.50–1):

> I will believe thou hast a mind that suits
> With this thy fair and outward character.

More often in Shakespeare the word 'character' means 'written character', but he uses it here in a way that hints at the wider classical sense of 'readable signs'. Character in this sense, the developed visual and verbal language that allows us to

---

21. Brower (1971), 206–8.
22. Brower (1971), 209. The quotation is from North's *Alexander*, North (1579), 733.
23. Compare Emrys Jones (1977), 60: 'Plutarch's *Life of Martius Coriolanus* at several points throws out strange echoes of the Gospel narratives – or rather, to a prospective dramatist who obscurely associated Christ's Passion with the writing of tragedy, that is what they might seem.'

recognize and formulate the identities of others, has been even more fundamental to western culture than the 'performative' and 'interiorized' post-Renaissance model. But today the word 'character' has ceased to mean 'signs to decipher' and instead acquired connotations from other discourses (those, for instance, which have brought us 'personality' and 'self'). However, the more difficult word here is *mind*: it means something close to what 'character' ordinarily means today; as the *Oxford English Dictionary* defines it, *mind* in this historical sense means 'Inclination, tendency, or way of thinking and feeling, in regard to moral and social qualities; moral disposition; a spirit or temper of a specified character'.[24] Indeed; but in Viola's circumstances, which happen to bear a close resemblance to those of the audience members at a play, this inner 'character' can only be guessed at through outward 'character', through reading of signs, which have a complex and suspect relationship to the qualities they seem to 'suit'. This complexity, and this discourse of character, is important not just in these lines but over *Twelfth Night* as a whole.

It's here that Shakespeare helps us to recover the classical and Plutarchan conception. Yes, Shakespeare's drama moves away over time from plot and towards character as its motivating force – and this he learned in large part from Plutarch. And no, Shakespeare's tragic figures do not possess the 'roundedness' of novelistic characters. It's not only the twentieth-century debates about apparent inconsistencies in their presentation ('How many children had Lady Macbeth?') that tell us he could not have 'stood a stiff cross-examination' on them, as Henry James reported feeling himself capable of undergoing on Mrs Brook in *The Awkward Age*. We can recognize and 'read' Macbeth's character, and it is plainly what drives the play from first to last; but it is based on only a few traits rather than constituting a full-blown Jamesian self complete with developmental history. As we have said, it's agreed that Shakespeare learned from Plutarch how character as opposed to plot could become the structural principle of a play. My further suggestion is that alongside this, in fact facilitating it, was the way Shakespeare and Plutarch entertained a similar conception of character itself. I'd like to suggest how this works in *Antony and Cleopatra*, which, together with *Coriolanus*, is one of the Shakespearean tragedies that makes the most of the notion of character I am pointing towards.

Plutarch offers his *Life of Marcus Antonius* as an example of κακία, ethical badness, which seems a crude enough starting point. The lives of Antony and his Greek precedent, Demetrius Poliorcetes, 'confirm', we're told, 'the saying of Plato, that from great minds, both great vertues & great vices do procede'.[25] But while his starting point may look reductively programmatic, readers of Plutarch's *Antony* do not think of this biography as a sordid tale of lofty ambition ruined by lust, because, having served it up, Plutarch goes on in the course of the life to deepen

24. *OED*, 'Mind', *sb.*1, 15.
25. *Life of Demetrius*, I, 7; North (1579), 942.

and refine on his initial statement, working in a tradition accustomed to progressive development from a basic opening proposition.[26] And although his Antony is more harshly portrayed than Shakespeare's, the depiction is by no means purely negative: in both we find 'the same expansiveness, nobility, generosity, and largeness of spirit'.[27] Plutarch shows an awareness of the interrelation, almost identity, of Antony's strengths and failings. In North too, 'liberalitie' (North's principal term) can be read as licentiousness or as generosity, prodigality or charitableness.

It's a favourite technique of Plutarch's to pass comment on his subject by reconstructing how observers would have responded at the time. He often delivers his own judgements provisionally, because he is himself interpreting the far from uniform evidence he has available about a long-gone historical figure. Perhaps Shakespeare caught something of this in his well-recognized technique in this play of offering mutually incompatible views of Antony (soldiers, Romans, Eros, Octavian, and so on) without attempting to resolve them. At all events, Shakespeare and Plutarch both tend to offer Antony's character as a variously interpretable set of data. Inconsistencies which surface in the presentation do not mean that the character itself is contradictory or 'conflicted'. Plutarch carefully distinguishes the impulses of licentiousness/generosity, prodigality/charitableness in Antony, whereas Shakespeare tends to concentrate on his magnanimity. Shakespeare's word is 'bounty', and the plenary example, placed at the most decisive juncture, is his treatment of the 'master-leaver' Enobarbus.

The term is first used in a purely material sense by the soldier who reports Antony's generosity to the fugitive Enobarbus, telling him:

> Antony
> Hath after thee sent all thy treasure, with
> His bounty overplus.[28]

The word is taken up a few lines later by Enobarbus:

> O Antony,
> Thou mine of bounty, how wouldst thou have paid
> My better service, when my turpitude
> Thou dost so crown with gold!
> (IV.6.32–5)

And before long it is positioned centrally in Cleopatra's extraordinary dream-vision of the dead Antony as emperor:

---

26. Here I am more than happy to join Pelling (1998), 12–13, whose comparison of Shakespeare's and Plutarch's Antony I draw on in what follows.
27. Pelling (1988), 42.
28. Ed. Wilders (1995), IV.7.21–3; subsequent quotations from *Antony and Cleopatra* are taken from this edition cited by line number in-text.

> For his bounty,
> There was no winter in't; an autumn it was
> That grew the more by reaping.
>
> (V.2.85–7)

Both Shakespeare and Plutarch are clear that this generosity is a given. In fact, it appears to be viewed by Plutarch as an inherited characteristic – in the very first sentences of the life we read that Antonius' father was, as North has it, 'specially very liberall in giving'.[29] The trait is compatible with both positive and negative views of Antony because both positive and negative possibilities flow from it. He is loved and reverenced for his 'magnificence' but his treasury is plundered because he is too trusting towards the officials; he is more effective 'in geving, then in punishing'.[30] And this is why Shakespeare would have been able to discern in Plutarch a very strong causal sequence that lent itself to tragic form: the same qualities raise Antony to greatness and then destroy him.[31] While Shakespeare doesn't place these emphases exactly where Plutarch places them – he doesn't, for example, make Antony's extravagant gifts of whole principalities to Cleopatra count against him with the Romans as Plutarch does – it's plain that a broadly similar mechanism governs the career of his Antony. In Shakespeare, his trust in his captains inspires them, while his devotion to Cleopatra loses him Actium; these behaviours spring from the same character trait, which we may call 'loyalty'. And ultimately, of course, this presentation of the hero's *agon* is expressed in the most famous of lines: Antony is 'a Roman by a Roman | Valiantly vanquished'. North's Plutarch had come close to this, but missed the tragic twist: in North, Antony lays his death at Caesar's door, describing himself as 'overcome, not cowardly, but valiantly, a ROMANE by an other ROMANE'.[32] That 'an other' makes all the difference. On the other hand, nothing could be more fundamental to Greek characterization than the propensity of heroes to destroy themselves, and Plutarch reflects it in his lives of Alcibiades, Alexander, Caesar, Coriolanus, Pompey – and, of course, of Antony too.

This seems to bring us full circle, back to Greek tragedy, and my observations seem to suggest a little-discussed way in which Shakespeare may at one remove have learned something crucial from it. For Plutarch himself was closely conversant with the classical Greek stage – 'thoroughly imbued with Sophocles and the tragic tradition both directly from the plays and from all those other genres that they

---

29. North (1579), 970.
30. North (1579), 981.
31. Shakespeare's ability to see this in Plutarch helps us, too, to see that the *Lives* are not (or at least not always) the collections of detail and anecdote that Plutarch himself sometimes implies. In particular one should be wary of the view that *Antonius* is 'rambling, episodic, full of circumstantial detail, but lacking in clearly visualisable shape' (Jones (1971), 225).
32. North (1579), 1007.

had already influenced'.[33] A range of effects which Plutarch might have mediated from Greek tragedy to Shakespeare can readily be enumerated. For *Julius Caesar* recent discussion has proposed mirroring scenes, the struggle against the continuing past and the ambivalent relevance of a distant figure.[34] But is there something still more fundamental than these features? Can it be that the 'doubleness' of character traits, the idea that human beings undo themselves not through their bad qualities but their good ones, the tragic sense of the destructiveness inherent in greatness, was one of the Greek tragic motifs that shaped Plutarch's *Antony*, and thereby made its way into Shakespeare's field of vision? While I have gone no further than to suggest this idea in relation to *Antony and Cleopatra*, it could be explored in Shakespeare's output from *Julius Caesar* onwards – from the point, that is, when he first experienced Plutarch's *Lives*.[35] This tragic self-destructiveness may, for example, be discerned in Shakespeare's *Coriolanus*, whose alienation we can readily see would have attracted the writer of *Richard III*, but who as a tragic figure in Plutarch harks back to Sophocles' Ajax and Homer's Achilles. And so I find myself, after all, joining in the pastime of asking how Greek contributed to Shakespearean tragedy and also asking whether, after all, we must accept (with Michael Silk) that Seneca was 'the closest he ever got' to it. Certainly we may say that Antony's own despair at his inability to tell whether his actions will lead to good or ill not only implies precisely such a double-edgedness to everything he is and does; it also sounds, as he expresses it, reminiscent of Sophoclean self-discovery:[36]

> when we in our viciousness grow hard –
> O misery on't! – the wise gods seel our eyes,
> In our own filth drop our clear judgements, make us
> Adore our errors, laugh at's while we strut
> To our confusion.
>
> (III.13.116–20)

In the distinctively Greek stress on the selfsame traits operating to create as well as destroy a hero (as clear if not clearer in Shakespeare's Coriolanus as in his Antony), we may be touching not only on what Shakespeare learned from Plutarch, but on what Greek tragedy gave to English.

33. Pelling (2009), 288.
34. Pelling (2009), 287, noting also (288) that Seneca must also be a mediating route for 'the tragic manner' more widely than in *Julius Caesar* alone.
35. Honigmann (1959) produces evidence that Shakespeare's reading in the *Lives* went well beyond the parts immediately relevant to his plots for the Roman plays, and suggests (29) that even as early as *Julius Caesar* he may have looked at several lives presenting figures relevant to the play in addition to the three usually cited as sources.
36. 'Sounds' is perhaps the operative word: as Emily Wilson points out to me, in 'laugh at's' Shakespeare is probably thinking mainly of the goddess Fortune, while aiming to suggest something more like the Greek divinities (who however do not laugh at men) in his plural 'gods'.

But reception runs both forward and backward in time from Shakespeare, and I choose to conclude in a different way by moving, in equally speculative mode, to the post-Shakespearean side. I began by referring to the 'single hero' model of tragedy which has been drawn from Sophocles and Shakespeare and Aristotle to create, as Brower puts it, 'the concept usually implied when we speak of "tragedy" in western literature'.[37] Undoubtedly so; but *Antony and Cleopatra* is not such a tragedy, whereas Plutarch's *Life of Marcus Antonius* is. Shakespeare completely omits the first third of Plutarch's story, which relates to Antony and Antony alone: quite simply, Shakespeare's theme was a couple and not an individual. Cleopatra's presence is felt from line one of the play. True, Shakespeare might have arrived at his dual theme partly for pragmatic reasons. For one thing, the first third of Plutarch's *Antony*, covering the period before his removal to Egypt, was, as it happened, also the least suitable for dramatic transposition.[38] But I don't think it's been adequately remarked how radically Shakespeare's decision, in combination with subsequent developments, has affected the cultural history of Mark Antony. By the year 2011, Cleopatra is to most people a figure readily separable from her consort, a figure of independent fascination and symbolism (whether an image of eastern voluptuousness, independent female power, or whatever else), but the converse is hardly the case at all: Marcus Antonius, that is, scarcely exists for most of us outside the collocation 'Antony and Cleopatra'.

That figure of Cleopatra seems to have acquired much of its definition, prominence, and independence of Antony in the course of the nineteenth century. One might think, for example, of the long scene in Charlotte Brontë's *Villette* where Lucy Snowe discusses a portrait of Cleopatra in a Belgian picture gallery she is visiting.[39] It's of great interest to note that this timeline suggests the stage history of Shakespeare's play might provide some explanation for the rise of Cleopatra and the decline of Antony's cultural collateral. The play has historically been viewed as deeply problematic for the theatre, owing to considerations ranging from the resources needed to stage naval battles to the expressive range Cleopatra's role requires. Such considerations help explain why the play went unstaged for most of the eighteenth century.[40] Only one production is recorded in the entire century, with Antony played by the leading actor of the day, David Garrick, in 1759. By this time things had moved on considerably from the Shakespearean era both in textual and in theatrical terms. Shakespeare's frequent reliance on messengers in this play suggests he was himself often content to depict events in narrative, rather than full-blown dramatic, mode. But early Shakespeare editors, in particular

37. Brower (1971), 80.

38. Pelling (1998), 33.

39. See Ewbank (1986), 64–8, who identifies the portrait behind the scene as De Biefve's *Une Almé* of 1842.

40. Also relevant are the continuing popularity on the stage of Dryden's version of the story, *All for Love* (first performed 1677), and pronounced critical disapproval of the play on neoclassical grounds – its failure to confirm to the unities of time and place, etc.

Nicholas Rowe, had divided up the free-flowing Folio text into Acts and scenes, breaking its continuity and formally allotting a geographical location to each scene. In a separate development, movable scenery had come into use in London theatres, both 'flats', which could be rolled on and off the stage in grooves, and 'drops' lowered from the flies.[41] The effects of all this on the Garrick production, and beyond that on other productions of the play throughout the nineteenth century, are explained by one of its recent editors:

> Some adaptation of the text had ... to be made in order to reduce the number of scenes and to avoid frequent scene changes, a process which went on up to the end of the nineteenth century. Hence some of the Roman scenes were omitted and the many short battle scenes conflated. Since the role of Cleopatra remained substantially intact, however (the last act was performed in its entirety), the emphasis of the play was significantly altered. It became essentially a tragedy of love played out within a sketchy political context.[42]

Garrick's production was not a success, but it did set the direction, and nineteenth-century productions grew increasingly elaborate, so further cuts were needed, manoeuvring the distribution of weight still further away from what editors today believe Shakespeare implies.[43] This unusual stage history would help explain how, over two millennia or so, we have moved from Plutarch's life of Antony, to Shakespeare's tragedy of Antony and Cleopatra, to the post-eighteenth-century downgrading of Antony in tandem with the rise of Cleopatra's cultural stock.[44] Or, to put it another way, from an exemplary story about an individual man, to an ambivalent play about a couple, to an image of glamorous if morally question-able femininity.

◆   ◆   ◆

My account has tried to do justice to both sides of the equation that reception always implies. Reading Plutarch helps us read Shakespeare and may even help us put our finger on where Shakespeare is coming from (with character, with tragedy). But from the other side, even if Shakespeare stands between us and Plutarch, giving us a Plutarch already comprehensively reprocessed, it is nevertheless the case that thinking about Shakespeare is a way of thinking about Greek literature, not only the *Parallel Lives* but Athenian tragedy too, and about our response to it.

41. Southern (1952), 32–4.
42. Wilders (1995), 16.
43. See Lamb (1980), 54–105.
44. For documentation of the rapidly growing prominence of Cleopatra in nineteenth-century Shakespearean criticism, see Steppat (1980), 161–81.

5

Transformative Translation: Dryden's Horatian Ode

In this chapter the focus narrows to a single short text in translation – a translation that has regularly been viewed as one of the finest ever to appear in English verse. This enables us to see something of the detail of how translators can respond to classical texts; wider issues will also be at stake. In assessing translations, questions commonly arise as to whether it is their 'fidelity' by which they should be judged (however we define this), or whether they should be approached as though they were independent English works. Dryden's version of Horace's Ode 3.29 has plenty of intrinsic appeal; Dryden can also lay claim to quite sufficient linguistic and scholarly knowledge to produce a nuanced account of a Horatian poem. Again, some commentators stress the 'dialogue' between translator and source-author – a dialogue in this case continued in the Preface to the Dryden collection (*Sylvae*) in which this translation appeared in 1685, where Dryden offers a lively critical discussion of Horace's character as a poet.[1] In a reception context prominence will tend to be given to a third figure, the reader, and my further questions are about how that figure's relation to a classical poem can be affected by such a translation as this. I propose Dryden's version can change our sense of the Latin work; that is, I want to suggest how a translation of a classical poem can transform it for us. Dryden's work helps to bring this out because it is a translation of a particular kind: it operates at so marked a distance from its source, freely expanding 64 lines into 104, that some would prefer to call it an imitation. In this respect Dryden's approach contrasts with that of Ted Hughes to the *Odyssey*, as we shall see in Chapter 11; Hughes actually condenses Homer's lines into fewer English ones. But this is not the primary sense in which I use the word 'transform' here.

1. See Hopkins (2010) for a recent presentation of the dialogic aspect of translation, with substantial reference to Dryden.

English Translation and Classical Reception: Towards a New Literary History, First Edition.
Stuart Gillespie.
© 2011 Stuart Gillespie. Published 2011 by John Wiley & Sons, Ltd.

Any powerful translation is transformative because it is inescapably a construction of the text it sets out from, a way of enacting or envisaging it.

In this case, Dryden's poem is neither identical with, nor necessarily even an equivalent for, Horace's ode. But Ode 3.29 is affected – has already been affected – by it. Dryden's translation, Dryden's representation of this poem, can be presumed already to have flowed into perceptions of Horace in the English-speaking world. Not only was it well known to Dryden's wide readership for the entire duration of his eighteenth-century fame (as well as, no doubt, to all or nearly all subsequent English translators of Horace); it is nowadays becoming familiar again, anthologized in compilations such as *The New Penguin Book of English Verse*.[2] Hence the translation is part of what 'Horace' now means. All the same, it will have much more effect on the way some readers think of Horace than others. As will be seen, I am particularly concerned to ask how far it can mesh with the responses of those Horatian readers upon whose bookshelves it is perhaps least likely to have a place: Latin scholars of the present and the recent past.

A complete text of Dryden's translation appears as an Appendix to this chapter.

◆   ◆   ◆

It is much more difficult to discover English poets of the later seventeenth century who were not imitators of Horace than to name ones that were. Between 1660 and 1700, new translations and adaptations of poems from the *Odes* alone were published by at least 50 different hands.[3] If the frequency with which gentleman-authors turned out their versions of Horatian odes did not quite match the rate achieved a generation or two later, in Pope's heyday, the uniformity of their productions and, one may thus infer, of their response to the *Odes* was perhaps even greater. Dryden himself is conventional enough in classifying the *Odes* in the Preface to *Sylvae* into 'panegyrical', 'moral' and 'jovial' types, and in his apparent preference for the latter.[4] And the 'jovial' Horace – the *bon viveur*, the voluptuary, the lover – is a figure so frequently encountered in later seventeenth-century translators' work that we must suspect the period's usual sense of the poet to be extremely selective, if not positively eccentric. At least, as seen with the benefit of several centuries of hindsight, most Restoration efforts to present this favourite Horace in English translation very clearly reflect the translators' own tastes and conspicuously lack qualities found in the *Odes* by readers of other periods. Horace tends to be made a spokesman for the Restoration gentleman's 'libertine'

---

2. Keegan (2000). Or there are the impressions of Emrys Jones: Dryden's 'versions of Lucretius and Juvenal and his paraphrase of Horace's ode … are now recognized as being among his finest poems, and no selection of his poetry is likely to leave them out'. Jones (2004), 123.

3. Gillespie (1992). For further discussion of seventeenth-century translation of the *Odes*, see Edden (1973); Røstvig (1954–8); Scodel (2010), 213–20.

4. Dryden (1956–2000), III, 16. All quotations from Dryden's Horace translation are taken from this edition, III, 81–4, with its line numbering adopted.

attitudinizing; what other eras have seen as his characteristic poise becomes unbalanced in the process, as moments of moral seriousness disappear and the wit is blunted and coarsened. Dryden's own work on Horace might on the face of it seem to fit this pattern only too well. Like many contemporary translators he englished only the handful of short Horatian poems which took his fancy, and the one he confesses to having spent most pains on, Ode 3.29, is a poem standing firmly in the *carpe diem* tradition.[5] Yet this translation has been recognized in each century after Dryden's death as a conspicuous success – as one of the most attractive and convincing renderings of classical verse in his wide and varied work.[6]

Those who have tested out the scholarly discussion available on Horace's Ode 3.29 have sometimes found conviction lacking there. At worst it may seem, as to one recent writer, that 'although all [commentators] praise it, nobody has given a convincing reason for the praise'; that the available accounts tend to be so external that discussions of 'arithmetical correspondences of line lengths, of consonant and vowel interplay, are offered as constituting what makes this the most impressive of the odes', and that there is 'the maximum possible amount of difference of opinion' about how the poem can be said to cohere.[7] Undeniably, I think, interpreters of the ode, both scholars and translators, have generally tended to make it seem either too slight to satisfy or more weighty than its apparently slender frame can sustain. Perhaps the following bald summary (from an introductory edition) is enough to suggest how both possibilities arise:

> A warm welcome awaits you, Maecenas, at my house: come then at once. Cease merely to gaze longingly on the country, and leave Rome for a while and all its magnificence and cares. Rich men sometimes find the change to a humble household a relief. The dog-days moreover are coming on, and yet you linger in town and worry about political contingencies. What is the good? Providence has sealed the future and mocks our efforts to read it. Calmly to deal with the present is wisdom; for life is like a river and moves along uncontrolled by us sometimes peacefully, sometimes like a raging torrent. He lives best who enjoys today; tomorrow Jupiter may send trouble but he cannot undo the past. Fortune is ever fickle: I accept her favour and put up with her frowns. In stormy weather I am not like a merchant fearful lest his rich cargo he lost: it is enough for me if I weather the tempest myself.

5. Preface to *Sylvae*, Dryden (1956–2000), III, 16–17. Dryden writes: 'I have taken some pains to make it my Master-Piece in English.' At least three translators other than the several who composed complete versions of the *Odes* attempted 3.29 in the period 1660–1700: for details see Gillespie (1992), 57–9.
6. Modern commentators who have regarded Dryden's Ode 3.29 as an especially impressive performance include Mason (1981), Ramsay (1975), 23–4, Steiner (1975), 426–9 and Wasserman (1964), 134–5. But Dryden's work was perhaps regarded even more highly by readers of previous centuries: see, for example, Samuel Rogers' comment to the effect that Dryden's Horatian translations surpass the originals in Dyce (1887), 89–90.
7. Mason (1981), 102–3.

On the one hand, there have been those over the centuries who have seen the ode as very largely the invitation to the pleasures of friendship and wine which its starting point and general structure seem to imply it is, and Horace's wider reflections as a mere extension of this (however elaborate a transformation of the traditional format might thus be produced). On this interpretation, Horace's references to change and loss are there to enhance the attractions good company offers, much as snow outside is supposed to enhance the attractions of a log fire. Yet the ode seems to bear readings of an altogether more rarefied kind too. Fraenkel went so far as to speak of the 'almost religious fervour that breathes in this ode', while the nineteenth-century scholar William Sellar spoke of the 'ethical grandeur' to which he felt it to rise.[8] How does a poem proposing the pleasures of a country weekend come to bear this freight of 'philosophy'? Again, it requires little experience of Latin and Greek literature to see that nine-tenths of the 'precepts' Horace offers in the second half of his ode must be thought of as conventional if not hackneyed: should we take these parts of the poem seriously, or is Horace, after all, committed only to the enjoyment of hedonistic pleasure?

If we plunge in at the centre, to the consequences the poet draws from the realization that the future is unknowable, the weightier and more difficult side of the ode will come to the fore. But where is the weight placed? Although Fraenkel was convinced that the poem had extensive hidden depths of thought and feeling, he seems to have felt that it touches only lightly on the world outside. For him, that world is presented in self-contained *tableaux* of which Horace's description of the Tiber is one – the 'finest ornament' of a poem which shows Horace's supreme 'eye for the picturesque' and 'ear for the suggestive sound'.[9]

> quod adest memento
>
> componere aequus; cetera fluminis
> ritu feruntur, nunc medio alveo
>   cum pace delabentis Etruscum
>   in mare, nunc lapides adesos
>
> stirpisque raptas et pecus et domos
> volventis una non sine montium
>   clamore vicinaeque silvae,
>   cum fera diluvies quietos   40
>
> irritat amnis.

Remember to make the best of the present moment with equanimity: the rest is carried along like a river, at one time peacefully flowing down in mid-channel to the

8. Fraenkel (1957), 228; Sellar (1899), 166.
9. Fraenkel (1957), 225, 227.

Etruscan sea, at another whirling rocks it has eaten away and trees it has uprooted and cattle and houses all together, with a roaring echo from the mountains and nearby wood whenever a fierce flood excites the quiet river.[10]

What has Dryden made of this river? For him it is no 'ornament'; its importance does not seem to have lain for him merely in Horace's eloquence, but in the weight of experience the description imposes, as it were, on the utterly conventional sentiment which introduces it. Dryden translates:

> Enjoy the present smiling hour;   50
> And put it out of Fortunes pow'r:
> The tide of bus'ness, like the running stream,
> Is sometimes high, and sometimes low,
> A quiet ebb, or a tempestuous flow,
> And always in extream.
> Now with a noiseless gentle course
> It keeps within the middle Bed;
> Anon it lifts aloft the head,
> And bears down all before it, with impetuous force:
> And trunks of Trees come rowling down,   60
> Sheep and their Folds together drown:
> Both House and Homested into Seas are borne;
> And Rocks are from their old foundations torn,
> And woods made thin with winds, their scatter'd honours mourn.

Dryden begins by turning the river explicitly into an image of the implacable power of Fortune. This suggestion is only latent in the Latin through the connection between Fortune and the watery grave the merchant's goods suffer at the close, yet once it is made it becomes inevitable that the river's destruction evokes human powerlessness in the face of the unpredictability of things. Dryden makes *cetera* refer to the whole of life outside the present hour; inspired by one of Cowley's Horatian poems, it seems, he calls this the sphere of 'bus'ness' (52). Here the power of Fortune dominates.[11] And the damage Fortune wreaks is not merely physical, but also, Dryden's language of transience and desolation implies, spiritual. It is possible to see in Dryden's lines a reflection of the arbitrary, chaotic

10. The Latin text of 3.29 is quoted from Shackleton Bailey (1985), 106–9; for the editions used by Dryden, see Bottkol (1943). There is only one minor textual variant affecting passages discussed here (see below). The literal English prose translation quoted here and below is that of Williams (1969), 146–7.

11. It is Dryden who introduces Fortune here. Compare Cowley's couplet in 'Upon Liberty': 'The st[r]eam of business does begin, | And a spring-tide of clients is come in', Cowley (1905), II, 389. Dryden's 'tide of bus'ness' should be construed as a tide not only of 'official or professional duties' (*OED*, 'business', *sb.*, 12), appropriate to Maecenas, but in the light of more general senses such as *OED* 5, 'anxiety, solicitude, care; distress, uneasiness'.

changes, the abrupt discontinuities of his own life and times (a point to which I shall return); but whatever lies behind Dryden's words, the result of his recasting of the Latin at this point is to suggest unmistakably the feeling which some have discerned at various points in the Horatian text: an 'awareness of what is essentially a tragic view of man's condition'.[12] And yet there is something more. To some commentators, Horace's burden in this poem is that once the *fugiens hora* has been arrested, happiness is attainable because Man has overcome Nature's restrictions on him.[13] Dryden's rendering suggests a quite different possibility, and it is one which seems to account more fully for what all have praised as the astonishing descriptive vigour in this central stanza. The tragic note is only one element in Dryden's translation here. For all the destruction the flood unleashes, Dryden seems with one part of himself almost to relish its awesome force, and to communicate in the confident surge of his own verse a positive pleasure in contemplating the irresistible operation of Nature's process. The hero, so to speak, of Dryden's ode is not one who success-fully resists the laws of Nature (to adopt a phrase Dryden used in translating Lucretius), but one who gladly accepts them. I shall later suggest reasons for finding this a convincing construction of Horace's mood rather than a wilful dis-tortion of it.

'Mood' is a better word here than 'thought'. It is crucial in responding to Horace's ode not to imagine, as some have done, that its profundity is of the kind we might find in an exposition of philosophical principles.[14] This is particularly important with the stanza immediately following, a passage which has been taken to sum up 'Horace's philosophy of life' or to contain 'precepts' which constitute a recipe for happiness.[15] In commenting on his reasons for translating Horace in the Preface to *Sylvae*, the collection in which his handful of Horatian translations appeared, Dryden will have little to do with any of this, and concentrates instead on the special importance of his manner. He singles out Horace's 'elevated flights' and 'sudden changes of his subject with almost imperceptible connections' – 'Pindaric' features, as Dryden sees them, much in evidence in his own version of the stanzas on the river – and explains that the characteristics of Horace's style are inseparable from the animating spirit of his poetry:

12. Hornsby (1958), 136. Hornsby's stress on this aspect of the *Ode* has been generally felt to be too exclusive, however.
13. For example, Commager (1961), 315.
14. Thus far one might wish to concur with Fraenkel's comparison of 3.29 with several passages in the *Epistles:* the latter are 'not inferior to the ode in dignity ... but they demonstrate and teach, they do not sing' (Fraenkel (1957), 228). For the importance of ethics in Horace's *Odes* see the various pieces gathered in Macleod (1983).
15. This section of the ode was excerpted by several Restoration translators for separate treatment in this way: John Norris of Bemerton, for example, includes a version of lines 25–56 titled 'The Advice' in his *A Collection of Miscellanies,* 1687.

That which will distinguish his Style from all other Poets, is the Elegance of his Words, and the numerousness of his Verse; there is nothing so delicately turn'd in all the *Roman* Language. There appears in every part of his Diction, or, (to speak *English*) in all his Expressions, a kind of noble and bold Purity. His Words are chosen with as much exactness as *Virgils*; but there seems to be a greater Spirit in them. There is a secret Happiness attends his Choice, which in *Petronius* is call'd *Curiosa Felicitas,* and which I suppose he had from the *Feliciter audere* of *Horace* himself. But the most distinguishing part of all his Character, seems to me, to be his Briskness, his Jollity, and his good Humour: And those I have chiefly endeavour'd to Coppy.[16]

There can be nowhere all this is more obvious than in this passage of Ode 3.29:

> ille potens sui
> laetusque deget, cui licet in diem
>   dixisse 'vixi. cras vel atra
>   nube poluat Pater occupato
>
> vel sole puro: non tamen irritum   45
> quodcumque retro est efficiet, neque
>   diffinget infectumque reddet
>   quod fugiens semel hora vexit.'[17]

That man shall live as his own master and in happiness who can say each day 'I have LIVED': tomorrow let the Father fill the sky with a black cloud or clear sunshine, yet he shall not make null whatever belongs to the past nor shall he alter and render undone what once the fleeting hour has carried away.

Horace's ode does not *reason* that life should be lived for the present: in the coiled finalities of the Latin at this point, it dramatizes the attitude of one who is already living according to that principle. And there is no translator who has so clearly brought over this attitude, this dramatization, as Dryden. In the buoyancy of the rhythms and the vibrant simplicity of the language, and with a 'secret happiness' attending his lexical choices of just the sort he identified in Horace's, Dryden discovers in his own English the joyful energy which he felt inseparable from Horace's wisdom – and hence discovers a much more deeply and convincingly 'jovial' Horace than the one his contemporaries so readily embraced. Here in the quite independent conviction of the English verse we can discern something of what Dryden was able to bring to Horace from his own resources:

> Happy the Man, and happy he alone,
>   He, who can call to day his own:

16. Preface to *Sylvae*, Dryden (1956–2000), III, 16.
17. *Pater* is taken to be vocative by Shackleton Bailey (1985); the quotation here is adapted to accord with Dryden's and Heinsius' readings of it as nominative.

> He, who secure within, can say
> To morrow do thy worst, for I have liv'd to day.
> Be fair, or foul, or rain, or shine,
> The joys I have possest, in spight of fate are mine.   70
> Not Heav'n it self upon the past has pow'r;
> But what has been, has been, and I have had my hour.

What kind of dialogue, if that is the word, has gone on between the two poets? On the one hand, we must not imagine that Dryden was a passive vehicle through which Horace's reflections flowed as through a conduit. No one could have written this stanza who had not given thought to the few unremarkable English words on which it turns – today, yesterday, tomorrow. Yet we have no difficulty in recognizing Horace's lines (transformed into something familiar and domesticated) as Dryden's basis. Dryden's emphasis on the word 'lived', for example, is clearly inspired by the Latin, in which language the verb *vivere* is frequently used in the sense of enjoying or using life as opposed to merely existing (one need only recall Catullus, or Thomas Campion's version of him, 'Come my Celia, let us live …'). Nor is the note we hear in this stanza the one Dryden himself more usually sounded in summing up the ends of life – the one he felt appropriate for moments such as the close of his translation of Juvenal's Tenth Satire:

> Forgive the Gods the rest, and stand confin'd
> To Health of Body, and Content of Mind:
> A Soul, that can securely Death defie,
> And count it Nature's Priviledge, to Dye;
> Serene and Manly, harden'd to sustain
> The load of Life, and Exercis'd in Pain;
> Guiltless of Hate, and Proof against Desire;
> That all things weighs, and nothing can admire.[18]

In Dryden's Horace the note struck is not one of fortitude in the face of adversity, but of triumph.

Commentators have disagreed as to what note Horace's poem itself sounds at this point. Dryden's extraordinary lines force us to say whether we hear in it something like this:

> to Maecenas he recommended a stoic indifference … Immunity to each day's vicissitudes and the security of the granted present – here is the best Horace can lay before Maecenas.[19]

18. Dryden (1956–2000), IV, 239–41.
19. Commager (1961), 314–15.

Or (from another twentieth-century exposition) something more like this:

> Triumph is the atmosphere ... so the country retreat is not ... a place of refuge where
> the timid and the insignificant may hide themselves away. In stanza 12 [Horace gives]
> an impression quite opposite to defeatism; it serves to strengthen and prolong the
> tone of unshakeable confidence.[20]

It is not that Dryden's translation provides 'evidence' about the way the Horatian
poem 'should' be read. Rather, its poetic resources can open our ears to possibilities which might otherwise be only distantly detected.

Three stanzas of Horace's text remain. Here we need to be alert to a paradox
affecting the work of both the Latin and the English poet. The most obvious form
of it has already been mentioned: although Horace's poem starts and ends with,
and seems to depend for its effect upon, our sensation of involvement in the most
individual details of the poet's life, it also purports to speak for human experience
at large. The close of the ode has been described in this way by Peter Connor:

> From the predilections of Fortuna we note immediately that the giving and taking
> of honours and dignities picture a Horace who, as involved in public life as the
> stoutest Roman, can be exalted one moment and toppled the next. This is often
> interpreted as his willingness to renounce his Sabine farm if that became necessary.
> But the language contains a larger frame of reference or, at least, he is elevating his
> farm to equal significance with the most lofty gift of Fortuna granted to anyone.[21]

And the poem as a whole has been seen as working through this dual 'frame of
reference':

> Though the poet draws us all in, he makes the words for *present* and *live* more serious,
> more intense, by his own personal concern, which is, we are made by his art to feel,
> both a concern shared with all men and the concern of a poet desirous of settling
> his principles of conduct.[22]

What is true of Horace in this respect seems to have been true of his translator.
It is not necessary for us to relate Dryden's ode to the particular details of his situation in the 1680s: but it is evident that translating this poem enabled him to
confront aspects of his own lived experience (and, again paradoxically, to do so in
ways that his 'original' writing of the period did not). At this date, in the words
of his most recent editor, Paul Hammond, Dryden 'had seen enough of public
life to feel the power of Fortune, and to understand what it was like to live as
Fortune's slave'. Tracing the play of Dryden's imagination over these subjects

20. Connor (1987), 138.
21. Connor (1987), 138.
22. Mason (1981), 104.

around this date, Hammond shows how the concept of Fortune is for Dryden a symbol of a 'multifaceted problem which he is attempting to articulate and to solve', and finds a new departure in Dryden's treatment of it in his Horatian ode.[23] In this way, we may imagine, Dryden's writing involved him in the same kind of artistry some have seen as lying behind Horace's, a process of 'testing the inherited wisdom about life by bringing it to bear on his own experience',[24] at the same time confronting that experience through creative contact with his literary inheritance.

These are the penultimate passages of the two poems:

> Fortuna saevo laeta negotio et
> ludum insolentem ludere pertinax   50
>   transmutat incertos honores,
>   nunc mihi, nunc alii benigna.

> laudo manentem; si celeres quatit
> pennas, resigno quae dedit et mea
>   virtute me involvo probamque
>   pauperiem sine dote quaero.

Fortune taking pleasure in her cruel job and stubborn at playing her high-handed game changes around her unstable honours, kind now to me, now to another: I praise her while she stays with me; if she shakes her swift wings, I give up what she has awarded me and I wrap my virtue close about me and go courting honest poverty that has no dowry.

> Fortune, that with malicious joy,
>   Does Man her slave oppress,
> Proud of her Office to destroy,
>   Is seldome pleas'd to bless:
> Still various and unconstant still;
> But with an inclination to be ill;
>   Promotes, degrades, delights in strife,
>   And makes a Lottery of life.   80
>   I can enjoy her while she's kind;
>   But when she dances in the wind,
>   And shakes her wings, and will not stay,
>   I puff the Prostitute away:
> The little or the much she gave, is quietly resign'd:
>   Content with poverty, my Soul I arm;
>   And Vertue, tho' in rags, will keep me warm.

---

23. Hammond (1985), 776.
24. Mason (1981), 121.

Once again we can say that what Dryden gives us is unmistakably his own. To 'puff the Prostitute away' might be part of a line from a Restoration satire. Even the combination with Horace's prostitute of Virgil's Dido, 'varium et mutabile semper | femina' (*Aen.* 4.569), evinces a characteristically Drydenian cast of mind. And Dryden's expansiveness with respect to the Latin might suggest an almost irresponsible attitude to his duty as a translator. But in spite, or (I would argue) rather because of all these things, Dryden may in fact be said to find an English form in which Horace can live. Most translators water Horace down at this point, unwilling to make the passage turn on what seems a mere poeticism, the most hackneyed of tropes. For Dryden Fortune is not a mere allegorical figure, but a tangible female personality, a mistress, at once both alluring and dangerous. And there are further nuances to which Dryden seems to alert us. Poised though these lines are between seriousness and self-irony, some of the gravity that seems to underlie the Latin peeps through in Dryden's language. Horace's words here have often been felt to imply more than they say; and at this point commentators have been drawn to the thought that he was doing more than expressing a conventional faith in the *virtus* and *paupertas* to which he limits his expression of his resolution. Commager's reading is suggestive:

> May not *virtus* (55) have less to do with conventional morality than with something more private, something comparable to his proclaimed *fides* or *pietas*? His glad betrothal to *probam pauperiem* (55–56) recalls ... the blend of physical simplicity and the inner resources of the poet in the Hymn to Apollo ... Horace's exaggerations are deliberate, and suggest that he is trying to find a means of dramatizing the essentially undramatic quality of inner serenity.[25]

Dryden's language of religious consolation ('Content with poverty, my Soul I arm; | And Virtue, tho' in rags, will keep me warm') has a corresponding resonance, for all the self-deflating humour both Horace and Dryden seem consciously to admit here.

But too exclusive an emphasis on the graver side of the poem would distort it. Dryden's final strophe leaves the reader not with solemnity but with a delighted enjoyment of the storm from whose dangers the poet is secure:

> What is't to me,
> Who never sail in her unfaithful Sea,
>   If Storms arise, and Clouds grow black?   90
>   If the Mast split and threaten wreck,
> Then let the greedy Merchant fear
>   For his ill gotten gain;
>   And pray to Gods that will not hear,
> While the debating winds and billows bear

25. Commager (1961), 343.

His Wealth into the Main.
For me secure from Fortunes blows,
(Secure of what I cannot lose,)
In my small Pinnace I can sail,
    Contemning all the blustring roar;   100
    And running with a merry gale,
With friendly Stars my safety seek
Within some little winding Creek ;
    And see the storm a shore.

Dryden's transformations are significant. In Horace it was not the merchant but the sea that was 'greedy' (*avaro*, 61), and Horace said nothing about 'ill-gotten gain'. Dryden has not made the merchant unsympathetic on a whim, however, but through a deliberate emphasis: in the Latin there was already scorn in 'ad miseras preces | decurrere et votis pacisci' (58–9; 'take refuge in pitiable prayers and bargain with vows'). The effect is almost comic: tonally, we are at virtually the opposite extreme from Clarence's vision of the sea-bed in Shakespeare:

> Methoughts I saw a thousand fearful wrecks;
> Ten thousand men that fishes gnawed upon;
> Wedges of gold, great anchors, heaps of pearl,
> Inestimable stones, unvalued jewels,
> All scattered in the bottom of the sea.[26]

Yet the Duke's vision of the horrors to which men lay themselves open through their lust for wealth is not totally alien to Horace's lines. The merchant is relevant to the poem not only because he depends for his happiness on Fortune; he is also one whose life is spent in hopes for the future (of his cargo), rather than contentment in the present – the condition the ode has defined as spiritually sterile. Dryden is content to end, however, with Horace's humour and fancifulness, in a final image which delights by its unexpectedness and generates a close which insists on nothing.

◆   ◆   ◆

In a survey of recent work on the reception of classical literature among the English poets, Tom Mason writes, somewhat nostalgically, of the passing of earlier habits of looking to translations and imitations for insight into ancient texts:

> It has [recently] been habitual to discuss sources, influences, origins, derivations … But although the process of moving forwards to examine later treatments of a particular poem has become fashionable, the procedure is seldom taken seriously. It is

26. *Richard III*, I.6.24–8, ed. Honigmann (1968).

assumed that the later use of an earlier poem is likely to be, in one way or another, a misreading. The practice of looking before and after, common in eighteenth-century editions of English poems – which draw as much attention to 'imitations' by later poets as to the sources of the primary text – has fallen into disrespect. From a 'scholarly' point of view, the life of a poetical work is still seen as ending at the moment the manuscript was sent to the printer. It is difficult, for example, to convince a Chaucerian scholar that Pope's *January and May* could have more than a passing interest to a reader of *The Merchant's Tale*. Similarly, the reasons why a classicist might want to look at modern poems have always been less than all-commanding. It seems to be as hard for a professor of Latin to believe that a seventeenth-century English poet could possibly show him anything about a Latin poem as it was for Bentley to feel that Pope's 'pretty poem' was in any way a reflection of the *Iliad*. There are ... good reasons for such caution.[27]

The 'reasons for such caution' are well understood. What this chapter has attempted is an illustration of how rewarding it can be to ignore them.

Appendix

Dryden's Horatian Ode

Horace. Ode 29. Book 3
PARAPHRAS'D IN PINDARIC VERSE; AND INSCRIB'D TO THE
RIGHT HONOURABLE LAWRENCE EARL OF ROCHESTER.

I.

DESCENDED of an ancient Line,
  That long the *Tuscan* Scepter sway'd,
  Make haste to meet the generous wine,
  Whose piercing is for thee delay'd:
  The rosie wreath is ready made;
  And artful hands prepare
The fragrant *Syrian* Oyl, that shall perfume thy hair.

II.

When the Wine sparkles from a far,
  And the well-natur'd Friend cries, come away;
Make haste, and leave thy business and thy care,   10
  No mortal int'rest can be worth thy stay.

---

27. Mason (1996), 213. Mason's discussion plausibly proposes several other English translations and imitations with which the attempt should be made. For Bentley on Pope, see p. 99, below.

III.

Leave for a while thy costly Country Seat;
 And, to be Great indeed, forget
The nauseous pleasures of the Great:
 Make haste and come:
Come and forsake thy cloying store;
 Thy Turret that surveys, from high,
The smoke, and wealth, and noise of *Rome;*
 And all the busie pageantry
That wise men scorn, and fools adore: 20
Come, give thy Soul a loose, and taste the pleasures of the poor.

IV.

Sometimes 'tis grateful to the Rich, to try
A short vicissitude, and fit of Poverty:
 A savoury Dish, a homely Treat,
  Where all is plain, where all is neat,
  Without the stately spacious Room,
The *Persian* Carpet, or the *Tyrian* Loom,
Clear up the cloudy foreheads of the Great.

V.

The Sun is in the Lion mounted high;
  The *Syrian* star,   30
  Barks from a far,
 And with his sultry breath infects the Sky;
The ground below is parch'd, the heav'ns above us fry.
  The Shepheard drives his fainting Flock,
  Beneath the covert of a Rock;
  And seeks refreshing Rivulets nigh:
  The *Sylvans* to their shades retire,
Those very shades and streams, new shades and streams require;
And want a cooling breeze of wind to fan the rageing fire.

VI.

  Thou, what befits the new Lord May'r,   40
  And what the City Faction dare,
  And what the *Gallique* Arms will do,
  And what the Quiver bearing Foe,
  Art anxiously inquisitive to know:
 But God has, wisely, hid from humane sight
  The dark decrees of future fate;
  And sown their seeds in depth of night;
 He laughs at all the giddy turns of State;
When Mortals search too soon, and fear too late.

VII.

Enjoy the present smiling hour;   50
  And put it out of Fortunes pow'r:
The tide of bus'ness, like the running stream,
  Is sometimes high, and sometimes low,
A quiet ebb, or a tempestuous flow,
  And always in extream.
  Now with a noiseless gentle course
  It keeps within the middle Bed;
  Anon it lifts aloft the head,
And bears down all before it, with impetuous force:
  And trunks of Trees come rowling down,   60
  Sheep and their Folds together drown:
Both House and Homested into Seas are borne;
And Rocks are from their old foundations torn,
And woods made thin with winds, their scatter'd honours mourn.

VIII.

Happy the Man, and happy he alone,
  He, who can call to day his own:
  He, who secure within, can say
To morrow do thy worst, for I have liv'd to day.
  Be fair, or foul, or rain, or shine,
The joys I have possest, in spight of fate are mine.   70
  Not Heav'n it self upon the past has pow'r;
But what has been, has been, and I have had my hour.

IX.

Fortune, that with malicious joy,
  Does Man her slave oppress,
Proud of her Office to destroy,
  Is seldome pleas'd to bless:
Still various and unconstant still;
But with an inclination to be ill;
  Promotes, degrades, delights in strife,
  And makes a Lottery of life.   80
  I can enjoy her while she's kind;
  But when she dances in the wind,
  And shakes her wings, and will not stay,
  I puff the Prostitute away:
The little or the much she gave, is quietly resign'd:
  Content with poverty, my Soul I arm;
  And Vertue, tho' in rags, will keep me warm.

X.

What is't to me,
Who never sail in her unfaithful Sea,
        If Storms arise, and Clouds grow black?   90
        If the Mast split and threaten wreck,
Then let the greedy Merchant fear
        For his ill gotten gain;
And pray to Gods that will not hear,
While the debating winds and billows bear
        His Wealth into the Main.
For me secure from Fortunes blows,
(Secure of what I cannot lose,)
In my small Pinnace I can sail,
        Contemning all the blustring roar;   100
            And running with a merry gale,
With friendly Stars my safety seek
Within some little winding Creek;
            And see the storm a shore.

6

Statius and the Aesthetics of Eighteenth-Century Poetry

Dryden, on any view one of the principal English translators, has a part to play again in this chapter, though not quite as a translator. So too, and further towards stage centre, does the other prominent eighteenth-century figure of Pope. But we now move away from individual 'masterpieces' (Dryden's own term for his Horatian ode) towards the broader current of English classical translation, where, over time, the investment poets make in Statius takes on a reciprocal character. Statius is first rejected, then embraced, by and through translators; at the same time the role of the *Thebaid* (in particular) is highly significant in eighteenth-century debates on the aesthetics of English verse. Surprisingly, this narrative concludes with what I describe as 'the transformation of Statius into something like an honorary Augustan poet', for, in this forgotten passage of literary history, Statius attracted more attention than he has been accorded either before or since. In dealing with his seventeenth- and eighteenth-century translators and the priorities of their period, one is dealing with a kind of anticipatory recovery of Statius himself.

Eventually, a decline from this prominence set in for Statius, his reputation reaching its nadir when, in the mid-nineteenth century, an influential essay by a Parisian professor of Latin presented him as emblematic of the social and political decadence of the post-Augustan age: he was a fop who minced around court in a Greek cloak at Domitian's beck and call.[1] Notwithstanding that many of the details of Nisard's essay had no foundation in surviving evidence, it was influential and widely cited. For the Victorians Statius was at best 'the greatest poet of the Decline', as one of his editors saw him.[2] It may come as a surprise to those who have noted his currently ongoing rehabilitation to learn that debates on English poetics three centuries ago took him as one of their touchstones.

1. Nisard (1834).
2. Pinder (1869), 373.

English Translation and Classical Reception: Towards a New Literary History, First Edition.
Stuart Gillespie.
© 2011 Stuart Gillespie. Published 2011 by John Wiley & Sons, Ltd.

◆ ◆ ◆

Let us begin at the beginning, with the *envoi* to Chaucer's *Troilus and Criseyde*:

> Go, litel book, go, litel myn tragedye,
> Ther God thi makere yet, er that he dye,
> So sende myght to make in som comedye!
> But litel book, no makyng thow n'envie,
> But subgit be to alle poesye;
> And kis the steppes where as thow seest pace
> Virgile, Ovide, Omer, Lucan, and Stace.[3]

Chaucer is only the first prominent follower of Statius among his countrymen, yet for English literature, as D. W. T. Vessey observes, 'the afterlife of the *Thebaid* has never been fully explored'. In the Renaissance, he adds, 'there are few major writers in whom a Statian influence has not been traced', and as late a figure as Pope considers Statius 'of the old Latin poets ... next in merit to those of the Augustan age', but no general account of his significance for English writers is available.[4] In part, this is a reflection of his low critical standing over the twentieth century, a period in which 'few scholars ... attempted to redress the balance' by 'bringing to the notice of a limited audience some of the qualities that made Statius more than a second-rate or maladroit plagiarist of Virgil'.[5] On the other hand, and characteristically of Statius' reputation through many periods, some notable dissenting voices were heard. Whereas in twentieth-century Classics departments Lucan easily outranked him in the second division of epic poets, E. M. W. Tillyard held that 'however closely he imitated Virgil, [Statius] is a poet in his own right, and a better one than Lucan'. C. S. Lewis urged more serious attention to both: 'The fatal words "silver" and "rhetoric" have done harm and modern ears are deaf ... I think Lucan, Statius, and the tragedies of Seneca are to be taken as if they really had something to say.'[6] It is at any rate clear that Statius' importance in the English literary tradition is not negligible, and one of the things I aim to provide here is a portion of the general account we lack of English writers' dealings with him. Thus I consider translations of Statius, especially the *Thebaid*, made in the hundred years or so from the first published English version in 1648, their context and their implications for literary history. It may be, as the editors of the current *Oxford Book of Classical Verse in English Translation* remark, that 'English

3. *Troilus and Criseyde*, V, 1786–92; ed. Benson (1987), 584. This passage itself imitates the closing lines of the *Thebaid*.
4. D. W. T. Vessey, introduction to Melville (1992), xlii–xliii. For Pope, see Spence (1966), I, 233 (no. 552).
5. Vessey (1973), 2.
6. Tillyard (1954), 100; see his full discussion, 99–104. Lewis (1966), 95; see for further discussion Lewis (1964), 34–40; Lewis (1938), 49–56.

translations of ... Statius ... hardly answer to the pervasive influence of the *Thebaid* [or the] *Silvae*',[7] but the translations nevertheless indicate some of the reasons for that influence by showing what qualities were discerned in the works. And even though some of the translators in this period, most notably Pope and Gray, are very considerable poets, the contexts from which their translations emerge are surprisingly little understood.

Apart from one reference in Juvenal, nothing is heard of Statius from contemporary sources, and only passing mentions are known to us before the last days of the Roman Empire. But Ausonius, Claudian and Apollinaris Sidonius read him thoroughly, and Claudian's *Rape of Proserpine* is heavily indebted to the *Achilleid*. The *Thebaid* was associated with the *Aeneid* by the sixth century – Fulgentius gave both an allegorical interpretation – a connection which helped promote Statius' standing as an epic poet in the Middle Ages, and this not only among poets: manuscripts of both the *Thebaid* and the *Achilleid* are frequently copied; both are used as texts in the medieval schools from the tenth century onwards (though the *Silvae* were almost unknown until their rediscovery by Poggio in 1416 or 1417); and the *Achilleid* is one of the six elementary Latin texts included in the standard medieval schoolbook now called the *Liber Catonianus*.[8] But two of the greatest poets of the Middle Ages became perhaps Statius' best-known disciles in any period. Dante puts him in Purgatory, attributing to him a hidden Christianity and showing himself elsewhere, as C. S. Lewis has it, 'steeped in the text of the *Thebaid*'. 'Every major character in the poem of Statius finds a mention in the *Comedy*', and Dante responds especially to Statius' dark conception of man and his often sordid gods.[9] Chaucer, in a passage which probably follows Dante, places Statius first in his House of Fame:

> There saugh I stonden, out of drede,
> Upon an yren piler strong
> That peynted was al endelong
> With tigres blod in every place,
> The Tholosan that highte Stace,
> That bar of Thebes up the fame
> Upon his shuldres, and the name
> Also of cruel Achilles.[10]

Despite the last words Chaucer seems not to have known the *Achilleid*. But he does make detailed use of the *Thebaid* over a long period, with effects amply

7. Poole and Maule (1995), 460.

8. Clogan (1968) presents the text and glosses of the *Achilleid* in the form in which they appeared in the *Liber Catonianus*. See 1–3 for Statius' medieval reputation. For the *Liber Catonianus*, see Boas (1914).

9. Lewis (1966), 95, 96–9.

10. *The House of Fame*, 1456–63; Benson (1987), 365. 'Tygres blod' alludes to the story of the two tigers in *Theb.* 7. 'Tholosan': from Toulouse – generally supposed Statius' birthplace in the Middle Ages.

documented by earlier commentators on Chaucer, most significantly in the *Knight's Tale*, *Troilus and Criseyde* and *The Legend of Good Women*.[11]

Chaucer's use of Statius effects the Latin poet's entry into the English tradition, not least in that Chaucer's name is regularly invoked by the early translators in support of a high valuation of the *Thebaid*. Thomas Harte, for example, refers in the notes to his 1727 version of Book 6 to 'Chaucer, who was perhaps the greatest poet among the moderns', having translated passages from it 'almost word for word in his Knight's Tale':[12]

> as nothing particularises the fine passages in Homer more than that Virgil vouchsafed to imitate them: so scarce any thing can exalt the reputation of Statius higher, than the verbal imitations of our great countryman. I prefer this to a volume of criticism; no man would imitate what he could exceed.[13]

And the age of Chaucer is followed by new phases of interest in Statius, reflecting different priorities into the Renaissance. The story of the education and early life of Achilles in the *Achilleid* was of special interest in the humanists' view of education, while Poggio's discovery of the *codex unicus* of the *Silvae* led to new commentaries from Calderinus on.[14] The positive assessments of Statius by Politian and Scaliger are well known, and into the seventeenth century Strada places him, once again, at the top of Parnassus in his canon.[15]

Hence it is surprising that no formal translation from Statius (or at least the *Thebaid*) appears in English until the middle of the seventeenth century. Lucan was attempted by two different English translators a hundred years earlier, and the *Pharsalia* translated in full by Sir Arthur Gorges in 1614, again by Thomas May in 1627. But no French version of Statius was published before 1648 either (though Italian and Spanish can each show one).[16] Perhaps a coincidence of translator and time was simply lacking in both countries; perhaps Statius was felt to be more of a minority taste. Tillyard observes that the *Thebaid* being 'less

---

11. The first study was Wise (1911); for more recent accounts, see Clogan (1967); Haller (1966); Magoun (1955). Boccaccio's adaptation, the *Teseida*, is important as a Chaucerian point of entry into the material.

12. It is sometimes suggested, however, that Chaucer's treatment of Statian material in the *Knight's Tale* is burlesque: see Benson (1987), 841, *ad* 2925–7.

13. Chalmers (1810), XVI, 341. William Lillington Lewis plagiarizes this note of Harte's in the Preface to his complete translation of 1767: Chalmers (1810), XX, 568.

14. See Clogan (1991). For Statius' impact on two major Renaissance poets, see Newlands (1988); Ringler (1963).

15. Angelus Politianus, 'In oratione quam habuit Statii Silvas praelecturus'; J. C. Scaliger, *Poetices libri septem*, 6.6; Famiano Strada, *Prolusiones*, 2.6. Such verdicts as Strada's obviously imply a high ranking, but not an absurd one: they are intended to reflect the 'elevation' of Statius' style.

16. For early translations of Lucan, see Norbrook (1994). For early translations of Statius into French and Italian see Moss (1837), II, 618–20. Le Bossu is scathing on the *Thebaid* in his *Traité du poème épique* (translated by W.J., London, 1695, pp. 74–8), and Boileau laments Statius' choice of Polynices and Eteocles as heroes a few years before the first complete French rendering: *L'art poétique*, 3.251.

of a school-book than Virgil or Lucan … reached a smaller audience in Renaissance and neo-classic England'.[17] No doubt it was less often prescribed than Virgil, but this scarcely means it was unfamiliar to post-medieval readers. There were cheap editions of Statius such as the widely dispersed Amsterdam 1624 (and reprints), and he appears in standard compilations such as the *Corpus omnium veterum poetarum latinorum*, a copy of the second edition of which (Geneva, 1611) was owned by Ben Jonson.[18] Moreover, the first English translation of the *Thebaid* was written by a schoolmaster 'for a help to my scholars', with 'marginall explications of the Poetick story', or as we might say today 'notes for use in schools'.[19] The schoolmaster, Thomas Stephens, is an otherwise unknown figure whose *Thebaid* 1–5 seems to have attracted little attention from his contemporaries.[20] At least, no further Books were forthcoming, though Stephens' Preface undertakes that in the event the work 'prove satisfactory … to my … Friends' he will 'progresse' with it. The translation, though containing some more fluent passages, is generally in crude, halting couplets, of which a sample follows:

> Like as a Lion, when the Shepherd's fled,
> Preyes on *Massilian* sheep: But when he's fed
> And pamper'd with their blood, which clots his mane,
> He stands i'th' midst o'th' flock, which he hath slaine,
> Tir'd, yawning, surfeited; his rage does pawse,
> A while, and lashes th' mire with's empty jaws:
> Licking, with loll'd-out tongue, their gentle fleeces.
>   Now *Tydeus* full of blood, and glorious pieces
> Of spoiles, had gone to *Thebes* …[21]

However feebly this strikes us, this was the version that excited the young Pope's interest in Statius. Pope was, he told Spence, introduced when about eight years old to a 'translation of part of Statius, by some very bad hand', but had liked it 'extremely'.[22] The hand was Stephens', and though his influence on Pope's own version of Book 1 was not extensive, Pope evidently consulted him and may be said to have 'honoured the old schoolmaster posthumously by becoming his brightest pupil'.[23]

17. Tillyard (1954), 104.
18. Jonson's copy is now in the British Library, shelfmark 11352.e.8.
19. T.S. (1648), Preface.
20. Stephens is however the subject of current research by Carole Newlands, whose initial findings suggest political motivation might be discernible behind his work on Statius.
21. T. S. (1648), 2.805–13 (p. 59).
22. Spence (1966), I, 233 (no. 551). Elwin and Courthope (1871–89), I, 46, point out that at this age Pope would have had hardly any Latin, so that 'the principal advantage … to Pope of Stephens's attempt was that it enabled him to interpret the original'.
23. Aubrey Williams (editing Pope's translation) in Pope (1939–69), I, 349. Examples of Pope's use of Stephens are given at 350–1. Pope's *First Book of Statius his Thebais* is quoted from this edition, 409–46.

If we are to believe Sir Robert Howard's own words, his choice of the *Achilleid* to translate twelve years later was not connected with the existence of Stephens' *Thebaid*. According to his Preface, he 'chose it as most pleasing'; 'there wants not ingenious men who preferr'd it before his other Poems'.[24] The volume in which it appeared was reissued once, in 1696, but Howard's rendering has remained almost as obscure as Stephens', its fortunes little promoted by Sir Walter Scott's description of Howard's 1660 writings as 'productions of a most freezing mediocrity'.[25] Passages are reproduced by Howard's biographer, who is a little over-generous as to the translation's achievement, but succeeds in demonstrating that Howard conveys pathos and manages narrative well (neither quality being conspicuous in Statius' own work).[26] Howard's enormously detailed notes on the mythology of the *Achilleid*, reminiscent of those in, say, Barten Holyday's Juvenal, are full of learning of a familiar seventeenth-century antiquarian kind, drawing on authorities such as Selden and Burton. But Howard is a gifted dilettante, not a scholar, and ultimately his work on Statius looks curiously tangential to his several careers as playwright, courtier and financial wheeler-dealer.

Howard's translation is closely connected with his contemporary (and later brother-in-law) Dryden – not least in that Dryden may have contributed to it. The volume of Howard's poems in which his *Achilleid* appeared in 1660 carried a long and conventionally eulogistic prefatory poem by Dryden, 'To My Honoured Friend, Sir Robert Howard', which constitutes perhaps the sixth work the poet published (at the age of 28). Dryden and Howard may have met through the *Poems* volume's publisher, Henry Herringman, and it is conjectured that Howard's preparation of his work involved Dryden's polishing of it: he may be the 'worthy Friend' on whom Howard says he 'prevail'd ... to take so much view of my blotted Copies, as to free me from grosse Errors'.[27] Dryden's prefatory poem disparages Statius for the sake of giving extra credit to Howard; his praise makes it sound as though Howard has rather transformed than translated the *Achilleid*:

> To understand how much we owe to you,
> We must your Numbers with your Author's view;
> Then we shall see his work was lamely rough,
> Each figure stiffe as if design'd in buffe;
> His colours laid so think on every place,
> As onely shew'd the paint, but hid the face.[28]

24. Howard (1660), A5^r. Edward Phillips reports in his *Compendiosa Enumeratio Poetarum* (1669) that Howard also translated the *Thebaid*, but no publication of it is on record and this is very likely an error.
25. Dryden (1808), IX, 6.
26. Oliver (1963), 29–31.
27. Howard (1660), A5^r. The editors of the California Dryden find it 'seems likely that Dryden was the "worthy Friend"': see Dryden (1956–2000), I, 208, and for further support Winn (1987), 99.
28. Lines 71–6; Dryden (1956–2000), I, 19. 'buffe': leather.

Dryden then singles out the annotations for special praise, praise which again turns out to be slightly self-contradictory:

> Your curious Notes so search into that Age,
> When all was fable but the sacred Page,
> That since in that dark night we needs must stray,
> We are at least misled in pleasant way.
>
> (83–6)

This seems to say that the notes are misleading, but pleasantly so. Though parts of Dryden's Howard poem have sometimes been supposed ironic, however, this passage at least must be sincere, since Dryden evidently remembered nearly 40 years later the impression Howard's 'learned and judicious observations' had made on him.[29]

The mature Dryden refers often to Statius and occasionally, as we shall see, borrows from him. The references are usually hostile: Statius is associated with Chapman in extravagance, opposed to Virgil for glitter and bluster.[30] But paradoxically there is also some lavish praise from the late Dryden. Though Statius does not know, he says, as Virgil does, 'how to rise by degrees in his expressions', making his two lines on Archemorus' horse beginning to run before the race has started (*Theb.* 6.400–1) 'the true Image of their Author', yet these lines are 'wonderfully fine' and 'would cost me an hour, if I had the leisure to translate them, there is so much of Beauty in the Original'.[31] Dryden's last discussion of Statius is negative once more, however, and proposes that his appeal is to the inexperienced – on the face of it a plausible claim for this period, in which several of Statius' translators, including the two major poets among them, Pope and Gray, translate him at an early age. Statius, contends Dryden, is most likely to be admired by

> warm young Men, who are not yet arriv'd so far as to discern the difference betwixt Fustian, or ostentatious Sentences, and the true Sublime. These are above liking *Martial*, or *Owen*'s Epigrams, but they wou'd certainly set *Virgil* below *Statius*, or *Lucan* … their Poets … affect greatness in all they write, but 'tis a bladder'd greatness … Even these too desert their Authors, as their Judgment ripens.[32]

All this is understandable, for in many ways Statius is the antithesis of the Augustan poets from whom Dryden and his successors take their very names in literary histories. He is vague where the Augustans (Latin and English) are precise;

---

29. See Dryden (1956–2000), I, 210, and for ironic interpretation of the poem, Vieth (1972).
30. For the full range see Aden (1963), *s.v.* 'Statius'.
31. *De Arte Graphica* (1695); Dryden (1956–2000), XX, 74.
32. *Dedication of the Aeneis*; Dryden (1956–2000), V, 327.

he overstrains the language where they aim at 'certainty of words, and purity of phrase';[33] or as one of his twentieth-century translators puts it:

> There are phrases which it is impossible to make sense of, if taken grammatically and literally … [Statius was] perhaps … led to write in this way by an attempt to avoid the hard glitter of Latin, so suitable to the clear-cut phrase of Horace or the snap and polish of Ovid or Martial, and a longing for occasional half-tones, for lack of precision … Virgil's genius consists in being able to give a soft, mysterious effect without any sense of unnaturalness. Statius aims at a like effect, but fails to avoid unnaturalness.[34]

The point, and its implications for the period we are considering, is very clearly brought out in a comparison regularly made over a century of English literary discussion about Statius. Thomas Rymer's Preface to his translation of Rapin's *Reflections on Aristotle's Treatise of Poesie* (1674) concludes with a demonstration of the superiority of English poetry which made famous a passage in Dryden's *Indian Emperor* (1665). Rymer quotes Dryden's description of night and compares part of it with a line in the well-known sonnet-like poem often called 'To Sleep' in *Silvae* (5.4), which Rymer says Dryden is adapting:

> We have seen what the noblest Wits both ancient and modern, have done in other Languages, and observ'd that in their very Master-pieces they sometimes trip, or are however liable to Cavils. It now remains that our *English* be expos'd to the like impartial Censure.

> > All things are hush'd, as Nature's self lay dead,
> > The Mountains seem to Nod their drowsie head,
> > The little Birds in dreams their Songs repeat,
> > And sleeping flowers beneath the Night-dew sweat,
> > Even Lust and Envy sleep.

> In this description, four lines yield greater variety of matter, and more choice thoughts than twice the number of any other Language … Here are the *flights* of *Statius* and *Marino* temper'd with a more discerning judgment, and the *judgment* of *Virgil* and *Tasso* animated with a more sprightly Wit. Nothing has been said so expressive and so home in any other Language as the first Verse in this description. The second is *Statius* improv'd.

> > Et simulant fessos curvata cacumina somnos.

> Saith *Statius*, where *simulant* is a bold word in comparison of our English word *seem*, being of an active signification; and *cacumina* may as well be taken for the Tops of

---

33. *Dedication to Troilus and Cressida* (1679); Dryden (1956–2000), XIII, 222–3.
34. Mozley (1928), I, xx–xxi. Mozley's impressions are nothing new; compare, for example, the scholiast on *Theb.* 5.364, 'raptus ab omni sole dies', who exclaims 'nove dictum!'

Trees, as the tops of Mountains, which doubtful meaning does not so well content the Reader, as the certainty.[35]

Rymer's purpose here is to promote contemporary English verse rather than to characterize Statius, but, as we have seen, Rymer's view of Statius can easily be supported and indeed overlaps with Dryden's own. On the face of it, it is difficult to understand why, given all this, the 100 years traditionally called the Augustan age which follow Rymer's comments see Statius attracting some ten English translators, as well as many other readers and admirers, instead of sinking into obscurity.[36]

The subsequent history of discussion of this Dryden/Statius comparison suggests what happened. Fifty years after Rymer, Pope's notes to his *Odyssey* (1725–6) recall Rymer's observations. At least, Pope remembers that Rymer had praised Dryden at Statius' expense. Rymer's point about Statius' 'doubtful meaning' is, by oversight or design, ignored, and Pope proposes that the *Silvae* line, correctly interpreted, refers only to one thing, the trees:

It is remarkable that almost all Poets have taken an opportunity to give long descriptions of the night; *Virgil, Statius, Apollonius, Tasso,* and *Dryden,* have enlarg'd upon this Subject: *Homer* seems industriously to have avoided it: perhaps he judg'd such descriptions to be no more than excrescencies, and at best but beautiful superfluities. A modern Hypercritick thinks Mr. *Dryden* to have excell'd all the Poets in this point.

> All things are hush'd as Nature's self lay dead,
> The mountains seem to nod their drowsy head, &c.

The last verse is translated from Statius,

> Et simulant fessos curvata cacumina somnos.

which I mention only to propose it to consideration, whether *cacumina* must in this place of necessity signify the Tops of Mountains; why may it not be apply'd, as it is frequently, to the Tops of the Trees? I question whether the nodding of a Mountain, or the appearance of its nodding, be a natural Image: whereas if we understand it of the Trees, the difficulty vanishes, and the meaning will be much more easy, that the very Trees seem to nod, as in sleep.[37]

Pope, then, whose own translation of Book I of the *Thebaid* had been published in 1712, proposes to remove the ambiguity and read one of Statius' most famous

35. Rymer (1956), 15–16.
36. One of the translators, John Potenger, is responsible for a version of *Silvae* 5.4. For a modern printing, see Poole and Maule (1995), 466–7.
37. Note to *Odyssey*, XIV, 510; Pope (1939–69), X, 61.

lines in such a way that it will become 'natural' and 'easy', accommodating it and its author to Augustan canons of propriety. We may well recall Pope's overall estimate of Statius, quoted earlier: 'of the old Latin poets ... next in merit to those of the Augustan age'. But Pope had, it seems, already made up his mind on all this in 1712, for there appears to be a hitherto unrecorded debt in one of the most admired passages of his translation to these very lines of Dryden's when part of another description of the silence of night in Book 1 of the *Thebaid* (336ff.) is rendered as 'All Birds and Beasts lye hush'd' (478).[38] It is hardly surprising that Pope would not accept Rymer's contrast between Statius and Dryden.

The transformation of Statius into something like an honorary Augustan poet seems to have been more or less routine another half-century on. His 1767 translator William Lillington Lewis, for example, invokes Pope for support against Le Bossu to urge Statius' 'singular beauty and propriety'. The *Thebaid* has faults, to be sure, but it is 'the most illustrious work of Roman antiquity after the *Aeneid*', it has suffered unjust neglect, and may not some of its faults be considered 'graces ... beyond the rules of art'?[39] And in 1774, exactly 100 years after the publication of Rymer's strictures, Mr Urban of the *Gentleman's Magazine* received from his correspondent 'Q' (Richard Gough) two letters debating the merits of the various poetic 'night-pieces' Pope mentions, and others. By this time the subject had been widely canvassed by English critics; Gough refers to previous discussions by Cooper and Melmoth.[40] (A few years later, in 1779, Johnson was to use Dryden's *Indian Emperor* speech to fault Donne's unnaturalness in the 'Life of Cowley'.) Quoting the Dryden passage, Gough predictably finds Dryden to be 'nobler' than certain other poets, including Statius, from whom 'Dryden seems to have taken the hint'. Yet it is a close-run thing, for Dryden and Statius, it transpires, both stand out above the rest. We move on to a comparison between Tasso's *Gerusalemme liberata*, 2.96, and a passage in the *Achilleid* (1.619–21) –

> Scandebat roseo medii fastigia caeli
> Luna uigo, totis ubi somnus inertior alis
> Defluit in terras mutumque amplectitur orbem

– in which Statius' '*image of sleep brooding with wings expanded over the silent globe*, is, it must be confessed, highly animated, and truly poetical'. And Tasso's lines 'Era la notte all' hor, ch' alto riposo | Han l'onde, e i venti, e parea muto il mondo', 'borrowed, as it should seem, from the *mutumque amplectitur orbem* of Statius',

---

38. Stephens's corresponding line, in a passage cited by the Twickenham editors as a source for other phraseology in Pope, bears no resemblance: 'No beasts doe roare, no birds doe chatter'. Pope (1939–69), I, 350.

39. Chalmers (1810), XX, 565, 568, 571. Lewis's phrasing is itself a variation on one of Pope's much-quoted lines from the *Essay on Criticism*, 'And *snatch* a *Grace* beyond the Reach of Art' (155).

40. The letter quoted is from *The Gentleman's Magazine* for February 1774; quotations are from the reprint in Walker (1914), II, 188–92.

fall 'much below his original, both in the prosaic turn of the expression (*parea*), and in the application of the image itself; which being a *general, uncharacteristic* one, thrust in amidst a group of *particular, appropriated* images … loses in Tasso's hands all the graces it had in the hands of Statius'.

At any rate, Pope's *Thebaid* clearly assimilates Statius to an English Augustan poetic,[41] decisively so for later translators, many of whom are Pope followers or protégés. Though according to Pope's 'advertisement' it was made almost in his boyhood, his translation was in fact carefully revised when the poet was in his twenties, and is not simply a product of the 'immature Judgment' Dryden attributed to Statius' admirers.[42] Pope's practice here is, in fact, very much of a piece with his work as a translator of Homer. Just as he omits from his *Iliad* 'low' ideas and images, so in his Statius he is not prepared to include a translation of lines 408–81 of *Thebaid* 1, which he calls 'an odd account of an unmannerly battle at fisticuffs between the two Princes on a very slight occasion', or the lines containing one of the major ironies of the conflict (150–1), in which Statius stresses the worthlessness of the prize (*paupere regno*) the brothers are fighting for – 'he gives us', Pope complains, 'a very mean opinion of it'.[43] Pope 'refuses to follow Statius into what he considers instances of bathos, or of extravagant hyperbole'. In a word, Pope's rendering of Statius presents the *Thebaid* as though its poetic were in close proximity to the greater 'old Latin poets', especially Virgil and Ovid. As the Twickenham editors' notes indicate, it owes more frequent debts to Dryden's *Aeneis* than to any other poem, and Pope 'also, in the turns and ingenuities of his language, often recalls Ovid'.[44]

Yet this is not by any means simply to say that Pope misrepresents Statius, just as he does not simply misrepresent Homer; for the *Thebaid* itself is, and was in Pope's time, well recognized to be heavily allusive (especially in descriptive passages and similes), and the writers most heavily alluded to are probably Virgil and Ovid. Close local comparisons of a kind beyond the scope of the present discussion would be needed to explore this area fully where Pope's translation is concerned.

41. See recently on this assimilation the discussion of other areas of Pope's Statius translation in Sowerby (2006), 209–27, esp. 222–7.

42. Elwin is categorical: 'The notion … that the published translations are a true index of Pope's skill at fourteen, will not bear investigation … the whole represents the powers of the man who completed the task, and not of the boy who commenced it' (Elwin and Courthope (1871–89), I, 45–7). For the nature of the revisions see Pope (1939–69), I, 346–7. I have doubts about the conclusions of the only full-scale article published on Pope's translation, Aden (1973), that although Pope first undertook the translation 'out of motives exclusively literary', his revisions reflect 'the pressure of the political' (729).

43. These passages should follow lines 562 and 209 of Pope's text respectively. For decorum in Pope's *Iliad* see Mason (1972), Ch. 5. The Pope quotations are from Pope's letter to Cromwell of 22 January 1708/9, Elwin and Courthope (1871–89), VI, 74. In the editions of the translation Pope issued after 1712 which included the matching Latin text, the 73-line excision is made there too, marked by no more than a dash at the end of the line preceding.

44. Pope (1939–69), I, 352. For one example of a borrowing from Dryden's Ovid in line 5, not recorded by the Twickenham editors, see Maxwell (1964).

But, because we reach here another respect in which the special qualities of Statius' poetry impinge (or seemed to impinge) upon the central tenets of English neoclassical taste, contemporary critical comment again provides relevant documentary material. In the notes to his *Iliad* Pope often draws attention to Statius' success in imitating Homer – to copy Nature is, of course, to copy him. At the close of Book 23, however, comes a note in which it is Statius' *failure* to copy Homer that Pope remarks upon. Although, Pope writes, Book 6 of the *Thebaid*, on the funeral games in honour of Opheltes, is 'by much the most beautiful Book of that Poem', and Statius has 'follow'd' Homer and Virgil 'through the whole Course of his Games', yet 'in the particular Descriptions of these Games this Poet has not borrow'd from either of his Predecessors, and his Poem is so much the worse for it'.[45] If we wonder exactly how Statius may be said to have failed and Virgil to have succeeded in imitating Homer, and Nature, we may discover the answer in Bishop Hurd's 'Discourse on Poetical Imitation' (1751), which at one point draws on this note of Pope's. The difference between Statius and Virgil is that Virgil was 'too jealous of the honour of that character, which is peculiarly his own, to hazard it for the sake of acquiring the false fame of originality'. For Virgil, Hurd continues, the subject of the games 'admitted not any material variation: I mean in the hands of a judicious copier of nature'. Hurd then clinches his point by citing (anonymously) Pope's note just quoted:

> so impossible it is, without deserting nature herself, to dissent from her faithful copiers, that the main objection to the sixth book of the *Thebaid* hath arisen from this fruitless endeavour of being *original*, where common sense and the reason of the thing would not permit it. 'In the particular descriptions of each of these games (says the great writer before quoted, and from whose sentence in matters of taste, there lies no appeal) *Statius* hath not borrowed from either of his predecessors, *and his poem is so much the worse for it*'.[46]

A small spate of Statius translations follows Pope's publication, with six further renderings of parts of the *Thebaid* in the next 25 years; my Appendix enumerates them. As already noted, several of the translators are Pope's followers or protégés. This is the first time, too, that translators tackle individual passages or episodes, as opposed to specimen Books, in quantity. As well as the contemporary popularity of the miscellany format, encouraging short poetic publications, Pope's printed and unprinted opinions on Statius may lie behind this; the well-known Preface (1715) to his *Iliad* characterizes Statius as a writer in whom the poetical fire 'bursts out in sudden, short, and interrupted Flashes'. Jabez Hughes, a minor writer almost certain to have been socially acquainted with Pope, is plainly sub-Popean

---

45. Pope (1939–69), VIII, 533.
46. Hurd (1751), 169.

in his single rendering of a short passage from Book I already referred to.[47] However, passages such as the two englished by Henry Travers in 1731, the House of Mars and the House of Somnus in Books 7 and 10 respectively, had long been regarded together as set pieces. Walter Harte, very much Pope's protégé from about 1724, took the process of imitation still further in his *Thebaid* 6 by actually inserting four lines of Pope's *Windsor Forest*, lines he says Pope adapts 'almost verbatim' from the passage he is translating. 'I thought fit to transfer them hither', Harte's notes modestly explain, 'rather than expose my own weakness'.[48] Pope subscribed for four copies of the volume in which Harte's translation appeared. Christopher Pitt, best known for his *Aeneid* (seriously compared with Dryden's by Johnson), wrote congratulatory poems on Pope's *Iliad* and on Spence's essay on Pope's *Odyssey*, and as Johnson notes: 'as he wrote after Pope's *Iliad*, he had an example of an exact, equable, and splendid versification'.[49]

Given these translators' relationships to him, Pope must also be at least partly responsible for another decision taken by some, if not most of them; we might also wish to explain it partly in terms of a wider movement towards 'fluency' in translation.[50] Pope himself describes his practice with Statius in his letters to his friend Henry Cromwell (which would of course have become well known through the published collections of Pope's correspondence) in terms of trying to 'soften' the 'particulars blameworthy in our author'.[51] Harte is explicit about having taken freedoms with Statius that he would not with others:

> If a translator can leave out such similes (or other passages) in Statius as are not proper, without violating the context: or if he can supply any of their defects in a very short compass, I think he ought. Though these liberties are not to be taken with more correct writers.[52]

47. Compare, for example, from Hughes's translation:

> The Beasts and Birds were hush'd; and quiet Sleep
> On Cares began indulgently to creep,
> And Toils of anxious Life in sweet Oblivion steep
> (3–5; Hughes (1737), 37)

And Pope's Statius:

> All Birds and Beasts lye hushed; Sleep steals away
> The wild Desires of Men, and Toils of Day,
> And brings, descending thro' the Silent Air,
> A sweet Forgetfulness of Human Care.
> (478–51)

48. Chalmers (1810), XVI, 345.
49. Johnson (1905), III, 279.
50. For the rise of 'fluency' in eighteenth-century translation see Venuti (1995), Ch. 2.
51. 10 June 1709; Elwin and Courthope (1871–9), VI, 80.
52. Chalmers (1810), XVI, 341.

The last sentence may suggest this practice is not explicable purely in terms of general trends in translating procedures; certainly Dryden opposes 'improvement' of this kind where translation of Ovid is concerned only a few decades previously.[53] Lewis, who is in Harte's debt for notes and other material, explains his somewhat more conservative practice thus:

> It is hoped ... the liberties which are taken will not be deemed too great, nor the deviations from the original too many. In the main parts of the poem, such as the fable, manners and sentiments, omissions and contractions are altogether unpardonable; but in others less essential, where the variation does not exceed one word, as the substituting another epithet to strengthen the idea, it is presumed, no man of candour will be offended.[54]

Gray's three short versions take considerable liberties, as editors have noted: the most substantial of them is 'unusually free' and 'renders but vaguely the paradoxical hyperbole of the original'.[55]

Gray's 99 lines of translation from three segments of Book 6 in the 1730s are usually seen as examples of experimentation with a particular poetic style, one of several cases within a certain early period in the poet's development. Mason commented that Gray was 'imitating Dryden's spirited manner' in his Statius, and it is indeed Drydenian in texture whereas Harte (who translated the same passages in his complete Book 6) is Popean.[56] However, so too is Gray's apparently near-contemporary translation from Tasso. One of Gray's three Statius passages may have been a school exercise; a short portion of Dante was undertaken in apparently similar fashion while he was learning Italian.[57] None of these translations was published in Gray's lifetime and in this case it is apt to describe the renderings as apprentice-work. They are Drydenian pastiche, and reveal little about Gray's notion of Statius; the very selection of passages may derive from a prescription. Nor does Statius figure again in Gray's poetic career.

---

53. Dryden's comments on respecting the source-text's 'sense' (as opposed to 'expression') begin: 'The sence of an Authour, generally speaking, is to be Sacred and inviolable. If the Fancy of *Ovid* be luxuriant, 'tis his Character to be so, and if I retrench it, he is no longer *Ovid*'. Preface to *Ovid's Epistles*, Dryden (1956–2000), I, 118.
54. Chalmers, XX, 568
55. Gray (1966), 230.
56. Mason is quoted from Gray (1966), 230. There are verbal echoes of various Dryden texts. Lytton Sells (1980), 217, however, calls Gray's style here 'hardly distinguishable from that of any imitator of Pope'. See Gray's praise of Dryden's diction near the date of these translations in his letter to West of April 1742, Gray (1909), I, 98.
57. See Gray (1966), 231; Lonsdale (1969), 23, 277. Lonsdale also notes that Gray's two passages from *Theb.* 6 may originally have been linked by another 24-line section of the translation which has not survived.

Hughes' and Travers' selections, already mentioned, need no special explanation, reflecting the same appreciation as Dryden seems to have had, and was widely shared, for Statius' descriptive verse. We can also infer what drew Lawrence Eusden and Christopher Pitt to Statius. Unlike Gray's, each of their versions takes its place in a published collection of miscellaneous poems and translations and is intended to stand up as a self-contained piece. Eusden's 1714 work selects part of the preparations for the expedition against Thebes in Book 4: the description of the young Parthenopaeus, king of the Arcadians, and his mother Atalanta's entreaties not to embark. The episode is of a strongly Virgilian cast. Atalanta's feelings of foreboding and abandonment, her reproaches, and her desperate petitions urging her son's indebtedness to her, are all reminiscent of Dido's last scenes in the *Aeneid*; and Eusden attempts if anything to make the emotional tenor of the scene more Virgilian than it already is. Statius also owes specific debts here to *Aeneid* 8.514ff., in which Evander commits his son Pallas to Aeneas' charge as they depart for the war against Turnus.[58] Pitt's 1727 translation from Book 2 is the narrative in which Laius' shade disguised as Tiresias visits the sleeping Eteocles at Jove's behest, to sow discord. As Warton noted,[59] this is modelled on the episode in *Aeneid* 8 in which Juno sends Allecto, disguised as a priestess, to poison the sleeping Turnus' mind against Latinus. These translations, then, further reinforce the point that the eighteenth-century appetite for Statius was in fact for the most Augustan aspects of Statius, and that these aspects were heightened by the translators. The fact that one of the translators, Eusden, was by no means of the school of Pope, further implies these attitudes were those of an era, not of a single group.[60]

William Lillington Lewis's *Thebaid* of 1767 is a substantial piece of work, with a long preface and copious annotations as well as a complete translation. It belongs to a different generation from that of Pope's immediate successors of the 1720s and 1730s, and appears well over the 100 years I have specified after Thomas Stephens's first steps, but a few more words about it will serve to conclude this tour. Hardly anything is known of Lewis other than what he tells us himself. His still attractive *Thebaid* is the first production of a young hand, a hand, as it turned out, responsible for no further published books.[61] The translation and especially the notes are deferential to Pope, so that, for example, Pope's own *Thebaid* 1 is taken as indicative of Statius' merits and demerits. Of the long passage excised by Pope at 1.408–81, Lewis writes: 'It is remarkable, that Mr. Pope has omitted the

---

58. See Vessey (1973), 202.

59. Warton (1763), III, 229 (*ad Aen.* 8.525).

60. Eusden's Statius was published in 1714, before Pope's name had become famous (and before Eusden became Poet Laureate); Pope was later scathing about Eusden in *The Dunciad*, 'The Art of Sinking in Poetry' and the *Epistle to Arbuthnot*.

61. Lewis died before reaching the age of 40: see Tissol (2004), who credits his *Thebaid* as 'one of the best eighteenth-century translations'.

whole in his translation of this book: in my opinion, the strongest proof of its unreasonable insertion.' While feeling it necessary to acknowledge Pope's importance, however, Lewis actually places a higher value on Statius than he does. In this case he limits his criticism of the passage to the point that it 'should not have had a place … at this juncture', rejecting the idea 'that the piece itself … is destitute of merit'.[62] Though like Harte Lewis goes so far as to insert phrases from Pope poems into his translation,[63] he often finds himself contradicting or qualifying Pope's more negative comments on the *Thebaid*. *Pace* Pope's remarks in his Homer, Lewis avers, Statius *does* imitate Virgil in the games of Book 6; Tydeus gnawing his enemy's head is *not* less tolerable than Achilles wishing to do so; and Statius' heroes are *not* more monstrous than Homer's – Pope's observation to that effect only shows 'to what lengths a predilection for his author will carry a translator'.[64] By half a century after his *Thebaid*, Pope seems to have helped create a taste for Statius by which he himself stands reproved.

Appendix

English Translations of Statius, 1648–1767: A Checklist

An Essay upon Statius; or, the First Five Books of Publ: Papinius Statius his Thebais done into English Verse by T[homas] S[tephens] with the poetick history illustrated (London, 1648).

Sir Robert Howard, *P. Papinius Statius his Achilleis, with Annotations* in Howard, *Poems* (London, 1660).

[John Potenger], translation of 'To Sleep' (*Silvae* 5.4), in *Poems by Several Hands, and on Several Occasions. Collected by N. Tate* (London, 1685).

Alexander Pope, *The First Book of Statius his Thebais* in *Miscellaneous Poems and Translations* (London, 1712).

Laurence Eusden, *Theb.* 4.246–83 and 4.309–40 in Richard Steele, *Poetical Miscellanies, Consisting of Original Poems and Translations. By the best Hands* (London, 1714).

Anon., *Theb.* 9.570–907 in Steele, *Poetical Miscellanies* (above).

---

62. Chalmers (1810), XX, 578.

63. For example, Lewis renders the line in the *Thebaid* which Dryden applied to Statius' impetuous poetic character as 'A thousand steps are lost before they start'. This adapts *Windsor Forest*, 154, 'And ere he starts, a thousand Steps are lost'. Lewis's notes explain: 'Now it is clear that – Pereunt vestigia mille | Ante fugam, – are the very words of Statius; and indeed they were so very literally translated by [Pope], that I could not help rendering them in his own words'. Chalmers (1810), XX, 640.

64. Chalmers (1810), XX, 645, 674, 729.

Christopher Pitt, 'Part of the Second Book of Statius' (*Theb.* 2.55–133) in Pitt, *Poems and Translations* (London, 1727).

Walter Harte, 'The Sixth Thebaid of Statius' and 'The Army of Adrastus … from the 4th Thebaid' (*Theb.* 4.16–37) in Harte, *Poems on Several Occasions* (London, 1727).

Henry Travers, 'The House of the God of War' (*Theb.* 7.42–62) and 'The House of the God of Sleep' (*Theb.* 10.84–117) in Travers, *Miscellaneous Poems and Translations* (London, 1731).

Thomas Gray, translations of *Theb.* 6.646–88, 6.704–24 and 6.319–26, written 1736 and probably earlier, published 1775 and later in editions of Gray's letters and poems.

Jabez Hughes, 'The Description of a Storm, from the First Book of Statius's Thebais' (*Theb.* 1.336–63) and 'Stella and Violantilla, An Epithalamium' (*Silvae* 2.2), in Hughes, *Miscellanies, in Verse and Prose* (London, 1737).

William Lillington Lewis, *The Thebaid of Statius, translated into English Verse, with Notes and Observations, and a dissertation upon the whole*, 2 vols. (Oxford, 1767).

7

Classical Translation and the Formation of the English Literary Canon

In Chapter 6 we saw how translations can promulgate, and perhaps even help establish, an aesthetic, as well as reflect one. Chapter 7 considers another way in which translation can impact on a literary culture. If we look back also to Chapter 3, on the Renaissance, we may begin to speculate that translation has as much potential as any other kind of writing to exert pressure on such a culture and to redirect it. The emphasis there was on how writers saw their surroundings – how, for example, translations forged (as I put it) a new past for English poetry. A canon is never constructed by writers alone, and we move in what follows between writers' perceptions and those of readers.

Here I will suggest that at the time the modern English poetic and dramatic canon was emerging, perceived relationships between English and classical poetry were the crucial ones, and that translation mediated between the two. As we would expect to find, the vernacular canon appropriated some of the prestige of the classics. But the classical canon was reciprocally affected by such developments. Hence I will touch also on the contribution of, for example, Pope's work to the growing status of the Homeric epics. Even today, the shape of classical literature looks different from different geographical standpoints around the globe. The reasons are of course many, but among them, it could easily be argued, are the respective vernacular translations of the past which became, and those more recent vernacular translations which are still becoming, part of the experience of classical texts in different world cultures. In Chapter 10 I will suggest how much more than occasionally translations have mediated ancient texts to readers, to writers, and even to classical scholars.

◆　　◆　　◆

Today, we tend to see translation as a secondary, subordinate activity, less creative than original composition, less an art than a craft, and we tend to suppose the

English Translation and Classical Reception: Towards a New Literary History, First Edition. Stuart Gillespie.

purpose of a translation is to provide a guide to its original. Yet Matthew Prior (writing in 1725) suggests through his caricature of contemporary attitudes that translations may in some circumstances actually be preferred to their sources:

> Hang HOMER and VIRGIL, their Meaning to seek,
> A Man must go poke in the LATIN and GREEK;
> They who love their own Tongue, we have reason to hope,
> Have read them translated by DRYDEN and POPE.[1]

Though he implies the commonsense reason that it is easier to read English than learn another language, Prior also hints, more interestingly, that readers' national pride, 'love [of] their own Tongue', is involved. In fact, Prior's expressions ('Hang HOMER and VIRGIL') do not suggest the use of translations as utilitarian cribs to revered ancient classics, but as altogether superior alternatives, allowing readers to feel they can dispense with those classics. And his examples of translations which are preferred to their originals – Dryden's Virgil and Pope's Homer – are a reminder that over very long stretches of English literary history, writers of the very highest stature routinely devoted their best energies, and many years of their creative lives, to work of this kind. The obvious clashes implicit here between eighteenth-century assumptions (even allowing for Prior's comic overstatement) and our own are among the themes of this chapter.

Samuel Johnson's 1755 dictionary definition of a 'classick' is 'an author of the first rank: usually taken for ancient authors'. In the long eighteenth century, although a 'classick' need not be a Greek or Latin author (or work), so powerful is the sway of the Greek and Roman literary heritage that English poetry normally aims at an imitative relationship to it. This period is seen as crucial for the establishment of an English literary canon,[2] but such a canon emerges as a separable entity only as it becomes apparent that English writing need not be viewed exclusively as a subordinate branch of the classical line. 'By the early eighteenth century,' according to Richard Terry's recent account of the formation of an English canon, 'it had become possible to think that English or British literature might be successful in terms other than those laid down by the classics.'[3] That is, this was previously unthinkable. Where poetry and drama were concerned, the rest of the century saw this changing only very slowly.

Whether translations are undertaken for reasons of temporary expediency or in the most self-conscious homage to a revered model makes little difference to their capacity to reorient the way the native literary tradition is seen, and ultimately its future direction. For example, theatre translations of the 1660s were in part a response to the lack of suitable material in the existing English repertoire at the

---

1. 'Down-Hall; A Ballad', 10–13; Prior (1959), I, 551.
2. For an extensive recent analysis based on publishing history, see Bonnell (2008).
3. Terry (2001), 102.

Restoration. But in such fashion were generated the first two English translations of Corneille, translations which inevitably began to suggest comparisons between French tragedy in its heyday and the achievement of contemporary English playwrights. Such comparisons would very shortly be taken up by Dryden in *Of Dramatic Poesy*, 1668, or later and more invidiously by Thomas Rymer in *Tragedies of the Last Age Considered*, 1678 – both essays manifestly constituting attempts to influence perceptions of the English dramatic canon in terms of its overall status and its particular shape. Further, one of the 1660s Corneille translations, by Katherine Philips, had success with the new heroic couplet which helped popularize that verse form for stage tragedy, and thence more widely.

The stage was also a place where attitudes towards the emergent central icon of English literature, Shakespeare, were being consolidated in the eighteenth century, offering an example of the relevance to canon-formation of translations of 'non-creative' works such as literary criticism. The effects on English perceptions of the canon of Nicolas Boileau-Despréaux's *Traité du sublime* – a translation itself, first translated into English in 1680 – were profound. They can be traced in the progressively more marked application to Shakespeare of the terms in which 'Longinus' praises Homer, and in the 'applications' of Longinus to examples of historical English literary texts and authors – notably Shakespeare – in the course of the new translations of Longinus published in 1712 and 1739, respectively. In other words, Shakespeare's stature in the eighteenth century as a whole was seriously affected by translation of a single classical work, the *Peri Hupsous*.[4]

Translations and imitations of a work do not merely *reflect* its status: they often establish it, or consolidate it, or contribute to the process. This is by no means incidental to their purpose. As was pointed out in Chapter 1, and as was fully understood in the eighteenth century, Pope's Horace, Pope's Homer and Johnson's Juvenal were not produced merely to allow readers to understand the text of an established 'classic' more easily. In fact, a reader who expected Pope's *Imitations of Horace* to explain the meaning of the Latin would be sadly misguided. These translations aim not to 'copy' but to set a new stamp on their objects. Even a superficial survey of the reputation and readership of these classical authors over the course of the eighteenth century, and the contribution made by Dryden's, Pope's and numerous other English versions, shows their status is far from settled over time. Remarkable fluctuations take place over relatively short periods in the qualities for which ancient authors are valued, in what parts of their corpus are most prized, and indeed in their overall standing (during the eighteenth century Homer comes to be preferred over Virgil, an unprecedented ranking since ancient times).[5] The only permanent thing about their place in the canon, it would seem,

4. For full discussion, see Hopkins (2004).
5. The standard study is Simonsuuri (1979). For Virgil's changing status over the course of the eighteenth century, see Caldwell (2008).

is the requirement to re-examine and reassess it; and in this process translations can play, and can be shown to have played, a key role.

But translations, as has just been suggested with the example of Corneille, do not only affect the canonicity of the particular work translated. In his essay 'Tradition and the Individual Talent' T. S. Eliot outlines how a significant new work's arrival in a literature causes a reassessment of a large number of previous works both closely and more distantly related to it. Eliot was referring to original works in English, but translations can have this effect too.[6] This is at its most obvious in cases where the work has not been translated previously. The appearance in the 1760s of Macpherson's versions of the Gaelic bard Ossian had far-reaching consequences: for the established hierarchies of poetry (promoting simple ballads over sophisticated odes, demoting 'pagan' epic against quasi-Christian epic); for the ancestry British poets felt able to claim ('Ossian as a civilized primitive Homer parallels artful civilized Milton', observes Howard Weinbrot),[7] and, quite directly, for views of the British literary canon. Shakespeare can now be thought of as a 'countryman' of Ossian's, as John Ogilvie expressed it in 1765. Weinbrot explains: 'Even those Britons who thought Ossian suspect were encouraged to examine presumably ancient poems and their contexts', so that eventually 'Ossian ... liberates his later countrymen by expanding their canon.'[8]

It might be argued that Ossian is a special case, because the works Macpherson ascribed to him had been neither previously translated nor available to readers in the original. With an ancient Latin or Greek text this would not usually apply in this period. However, even to achieve a wide readership for a Latin or Greek work (let alone for it to become influential or canonical), an English translation is often required. Even where a work has been previously translated, a fresh version can place it in a strong new light, and thus have an equally pronounced effect. Pope's *Iliad* was not the first in English,[9] but from the start, readers clearly looked to it for things they did not find, or had not found, in previous versions. Still more pertinently in the present context, they looked to it for things they did not find in native English poetry. Pope's translations expressed the ideals and passion which Augustan literature found it impossible to realize successfully in any other literary form. Or, as John Barnard puts it, 'the *Iliad*'s intellectual energy, its heroic scope, and its epic grandeur provide the positive scale in Pope's imaginative world'.[10] Johnson records how the *Iliad* 'took possession of the publick ear; the vulgar was enamoured of the poem, and the learned wondered at the translation'.[11] Its far-

---

6. See pp. 23–4 above for the suggestion that Eliot's essay makes the poet's task seem to resemble that of the ideal translator.

7. Weinbrot (1993), 544.

8. Weinbrot (1993), 544, 547; see this discussion as a whole for the relationship of these developments to changing conceptions of the nation and nationhood.

9. Chapman's full text of 1611 was the first complete English version.

10. Barnard (1973), 12.

11. Johnson (1905), III, 238.

reaching effects on perceptions of the English canon included, for example, an upturn in the value of Milton's stock, as Pope's text and notes revealed strong affinities both local and general between the leading Greek and the leading English epic poet. Its far-reaching effects on future English writing are also glanced at by Johnson, who observes (*ibid.*): '[Pope's] version may be said to have tuned the English tongue, for since its appearance no writer, however deficient in other powers, has wanted melody.' Johnson's remark is a nutshell containing 'a short history of eighteenth-century poetry through Gray, Collins, Smart, Goldsmith, Johnson himself, early Wordsworth, [and] Wesley'.[12]

How much importance did this period attach to classical translation and translators in its views of English literary history, and how far were they included within the emergent canon? A small guessing game can (thanks to my deletion) be played with the following eulogy by the obscure Samuel Cobb of a certain great English poet-translator:

> But smile, my Muse, once more upon my Song,
> Let … be numbred with the Sacred Throng:
> Whose daring Muse could with Manilius fly,
> And, like an Atlas, shoulder up the Sky.
> He's mounted, where no vulgar Eye can trace
> His Wondrous footsteps and mysterious race.
> See, how He walks above in mighty strains,
> And wanders o'er the wide Ethereal Plains!
> He sings what Harmony the Spheres obey,
> In Verse more tuneful, and more sweet than they.
> 'Tis cause of Triumph, when Rome's Genius shines
> In nervous English, and well-worded Lines.[13]

This poem is not a dedicatory epistle or one penned by a friend of the subject; it was not even written during the subject's lifetime, so personal loyalties cannot explain the warmth. The passage in fact concerns a seventeenth-century English writer who receives no entry in the current *Oxford Companion to English Literature*: Thomas Creech, the author of no noted original works, but the translator of Manilius, Lucretius and Horace. The passage is a reminder that in this period translators and translations were by no means automatically relegated to secondary status in the pantheon. It also reminds us that the crucial relationship in perceptions of the canonical was between English and classical poetry.

Cobb's poem first appeared in 1707. A glance at three or four later documents will allow us to see the wider picture to the end of the century and beyond. In Johnson's *Lives of the Poets* (1779–81) classical translation is viewed as one of the glories of recent English poetry: 'The affluence and comprehension of our

---

12. Tomlinson (2003), 1.
13. *Of Poetry*, Cobb (1710), 219.

language,' Johnson declares, 'is very illustriously displayed in our poetical translations of ancient writers: a work which the French seem to relinquish in despair,
and which we were long unable to perform with dexterity.'[14] It is taken for granted
that the translations for which the English poets were responsible are every bit as
much a part of their *œuvres* as the rest of their work, and some of the very highest
praise to be found in Johnson's criticism is reserved for them. Pope's *Iliad* is 'the
noblest version of poetry which the world has ever seen'; a 'great work', a 'poetical
wonder', 'a performance which no age or nation can pretend to equal'. Johnson
had his friend Hester Thrale transcribe excerpts from one of Pope's manuscripts
in the British Library so that he could reproduce them in his 'Life of Pope' in
order to gratify 'every man who has cultivated poetry' with a practical way of
understanding how Pope's *Iliad* came to be composed.[15] Nicholas Rowe's 1719
Lucan is, quite simply, 'one of the greatest productions of English poetry'.[16]
(Joseph Warton thought this translation 'better than its original' and gave Pitt's
Vida as an example of the same thing.)[17] More than this, Johnson takes it as axio-
matic that the English poets *are* translators, so that there is something remarkable
about any who have risen to eminence without being so. Of Matthew Prior he
writes: 'Scarcely any one of our poets has written so much and translated so little.'[18]

Two large-scale, widely read, and enduring library editions of the English poets
took as their basis the volumes within which Johnson's *Lives* originally formed the
critical and biographical prefaces, quoting or reprinting his notices but supplementing his poetry texts, particularly with more up-to-date poems.[19] Robert
Anderson's 14-volume *Works of the British Poets* of 1792–5 contains as a matter
of course the translations of all the 114 poets printed in Volumes 1–11 – a substantial proportion of the work of such writers as Pope (even ignoring his Homer)
and a predominant proportion of several, such as Christopher Pitt and Alexander
Broome. Anderson laments in his preface that diligent search has not procured
him more: a copy of Surrey's *Aeneid* Books II and IV was wanting.[20] The final
three volumes (12–14) are then given over wholly to translations: (1) of Pope's
Iliad and *Odyssey*, Gilbert West's Pindar, Dryden's Virgil, Persius and Juvenal,
Christopher Pitt's *Aeneid* and Nicholas Rowe's Lucan; (2) Thomas Cook's Hesiod,
Francis Fawkes's Theocritus, Anacreon, Bion, Moschus, Sappho, Musaeus and
Apollonius Rhodius; *The Rape of Helen*, Creech's Lucretius and Thomas Grainger's
Tibullus; (3) Philip Francis's Horace, Samuel Garth's Ovid and William Lillington
Lewis's Statius. A few years later in his similar collection of *English Poets from*

14. Johnson (1905), I, 306.
15. Johnson (1905), III, 119, 236.
16. Johnson (1905), II, 77.
17. Warton (1822), VII, 139
18. Johnson (1905), II, 204–5.
19. For a fuller investigation of the English poetry collections published in the later eighteenth century,
see Bonnell (2008; brief listing 10–11).
20. Anderson (1792–5), I, 5.

Chaucer to Cowper, 1810, Alexander Chalmers also gave over three volumes (2,300 double-column pages) wholly to translations, adding a handful of modern European classics to Anderson's exclusively Greek and Latin items. By this date, evidently, not only were classical translations established as an integral part of the English poetic canon: a canon of major translations was also emerging and expanding.

◆   ◆   ◆

Canons by definition are public and not private constructs, and writers have always been well aware of the three-way relationship between their own work, the canon to which they aspire, and the public. Dryden makes it obvious that his own translations aim not only to promote the ancients, but in so doing to promote his own and his contemporaries' work too:

> What *English* Readers unacquainted with *Greek* or *Latin* will believe me or any other Man, when we commend those Authors, and confess we derive all that is pardonable in us from their Fountains, if they take those to be the same Poets, whom our *Ogelby's* have Translated?[21]

'Classical and contemporary canons,' Paul Hammond writes, were in Dryden's time 'each being reshaped by a process of interaction and reciprocal criticism.'[22] Knowledge of the vernacular canon could offer a newly diversified reading public some of the cultural capital previously bound up with literacy in the 'learned' languages. Reciprocally, that canon's construction and recognition were dependent on its appropriation of some of the prestige of the classics. Translation was thus naturally at the centre of these developments.

Translators found it necessary to defend themselves against the charge that their work merely pandered to an ignorant audience. The classical scholar Richard Bentley's patronizing attitude towards Pope's Homer, and Thomas Warton's claim that public taste was vitiated by translations, seem of a piece. Bentley, at least in the popular version, told Pope that his *Iliad* was 'a pretty poem … but you must not call it Homer'.[23] Warton wrote:

> the original not only begins to be neglected and excluded as less easy, but also to be despised as less ornamental and elegant. Thus … the genuine model is superseded,

---

21. Preface to *Sylvae*, 1685; Dryden (1956–2000), III, 4. The name of John Ogilby, who published his English *Iliad* in 1660, was more than once taken in vain by Dryden.
22. Hammond (2002), 407.
23. This is the version Johnson gives in his *Life of Pope*, but what sounds a more likely account is printed in the *Gentleman's Magazine*, October 1773, in which Bentley is given the words 'Why … the lines are good lines, the translation is a good translation, but you must not call it Homer, it is a good translation of Spondanus.'

and gradually gives way to the establishment of a more specious, but false, resemblance. Thus, too many readers, happy to find the readiest accommodation for their indolence and their illiteracy, think themselves sufficient masters of Homer from Pope's translation.[24]

Dryden wanted the audience for his translations to think of itself as composed of people 'who tho they are not Scholars are not Ignorant: Persons of Understanding and good Sense'.[25] In fact, he tasks scholars and classical specialists with lacking this 'good sense' – commentators (especially the Dutch ones whose editions he often uses) can be 'pedants'.[26] Moreover, such specialists have no claims to expertise when it comes to modern poetry – and modern poetry in English is now a force to be reckoned with. Cultural literacy for the first time demands knowledge of both classical and vernacular traditions.

'Dryden's classicism', William Frost has observed, 'dominated the succeeding decades. For the generation of Pope (born 1688) and Richardson (born 1689), it is hardly too much to say that Dryden's conception of satire *was* satire, that Dryden's Virgil *was* Virgil.'[27] But his authority was derived from his exemplary synthesis of classical and modern, through translation – through a principle of living reciprocation between writers of the past and present. His *Fables* of 1700 have been well said by James Winn 'to establish a kind of simultaneity linking the ancients, the (medieval) moderns, and Dryden himself'.[28] In the dedicatory poem of this, his last published volume, and perhaps most ambitious collection of translations, the circling tenses of the opening lines are one of the ways in which the 'simultaneity' is generated, in linking Chaucer, Homer and Virgil:

> The Bard who first adorn'd our Native Tongue
> Tun'd to his British Lyre this ancient Song:
> Which *Homer* might without a Blush reherse,
> And leaves a doubtful Palm in *Virgil*'s Verse:
> He match'd their Beauties, where they most excell;
> Of Love sung better, and of Arms as well.[29]

The rest of the *Fables* collection offers translations from Chaucer, Homer, Ovid and Boccaccio, together with several original poems, in such a fashion as to carry on a dialogue between these four ancient, modern, English, foreign classics and Dryden himself.

24. 'Observations on the Faerie Queene'; Warton (1762), I, 197–8.
25. *Discourse Concerning Satire*; Dryden (1956–2000), IV, 87.
26. Preface to *Sylvae*; Dryden (1956–2000), III, 4.
27. Frost (1988), 142.
28. Winn (2001), 158.
29. Dryden (1956–2000), VII, 48.

The character of this dialogue is hinted at in Dryden's expansive preface. Dryden has, he says, found numerous similarities of situation and of style between the poets he has translated. Starting with Homer, he proceeded to the passage in Ovid's *Metamorphoses* explaining the causes of the Trojan War; other parts of Ovid, he found, lay 'next in my way', so 'I could not balk 'em'. It then 'came into [his] mind' that Chaucer 'in many Things resembled' Ovid. And Boccaccio has several things in common with Chaucer, 'who was not only his Contemporary, but also pursu'd the same Studies'; both 'refin'd their Mother-Tongues'. Dryden is thus led to meditate on the affinities between writers at large:

> *Milton* was the Poetical Son of *Spencer*, and Mr. *Waller* of *Fairfax;* for we have our Lineal Descents and Clans, as well as other Families: *Spencer* more than once insinuates, that the Soul of *Chaucer* was transfus'd into his Body; and that he was begotten by him Two hundred years after his Decease. *Milton* has acknowledg'd to me, that *Spencer* was his Original; and many besides my self have heard our famous *Waller* own, that he deriv'd the Harmony of his Numbers from the *Godfrey of Bulloign*, which was turn'd into *English* by Mr. *Fairfax*.[30]

The language of literary paternity was a generic one for Dryden's time, though he seems to have used it in particularly significant ways.[31] More extraordinary is the trope of metempsychosis, as Dryden alludes to Spenser's claim to have possessed Chaucer's 'soul' or spirit (in the *envoi* to *The Shepheardes Calender*). Dryden himself, he says, has found he 'had a Soul congenial' to Chaucer's. What view of a literary tradition is being implied here?

The tropes of literary paternity and transmigration were the means by which the English Augustan poets expressed the living nature of the tradition they belonged to. One of the key terms they deployed was 'transfusion' – 'that the soul of *Chaucer* was transfus'd into his Body'. Dryden also uses the word 'traduction', technically the notion espoused by Hippocrates that the parent engenders the child's soul as well as its body.[32] Poets of the past, then, were envisaged as animating living poets, and accounts of the *Fables* Preface have rightly stressed Dryden's use of these metaphors. There is, however, another way of looking at these transactions between poets living and dead. It is one that Dryden is hardly in a position to mention himself in this context, but which is of no less interest as a way of expressing how translations contribute to forming canons. This is that living poets animate dead ones – an idea expressed by Congreve in his poem commending Dryden's 1693 translation of Persius. It is addressed to Dryden ('you'):

---

30. Preface to the *Fables*, Dryden (1956–2000), VII, 25.
31. See Terry (2001) 145–56.
32. For both terms in the eighteenth century, see Terry (2001) 161–2; for metempsychosis as a trope for poetic tradition, see Gillespie (2010).

> For still Obscure, to us no Light he gives;
> Dead in himself, in you alone he lives.[33]

Under what circumstances did this animation of 'dead' poets occur? Most of all, under those of translation and imitation. George Granville, Lord Lansdowne, also writing to Dryden ('On his several excellent Translations of the ancient Poets'), supplies a more explicit statement of how these arts can effect the 'transfusion' of the 'spirits' of dead poets:

> As Flow'rs transplanted from a Southern Sky,
> But hardly bear, or in the raising die,
> Missing their native Sun, at best retain
> But a faint Odour, and survive with Pain:
> Thus ancient Wit, in modern Numbers taught,
> Wanting the Warmth with which its Author wrote,
> Is a dead Image, and a senseless Draught.
> While we transfuse the nimble Spirit flies,
> Escapes unseen, evaporates, and dies.
> Who then to copy Roman Wit desire,
> Must imitate with Roman Force and Fire.

In Dryden, according to Lansdowne, 'ev'ry Genius was reviv'd' (the noun has the force of 'guiding spirit');[34] and he goes on: 'Thy Trumpet sounds, the Dead are rais'd to Light, | Never to die, and take to Heav'n their Flight.'[35]

It is in this light that Dryden's remarks in the Preface to *Fables* should be understood. 'Dryden,' William Frost remarks, 'wrote his translations and many of his original poems as part of a tradition of resumed continuity in civilization, a tradition stretching from Chaucer in the fourteenth century to Pope in the eighteenth, and well beyond. For Dryden, these bones lived.'[36] In fact, while Dryden is probably the first major writer to be fully conversant with the content of the English poetic tradition that precedes him, the mystical line of poetic descent in which he offers to take his place is importantly not a purely English one. It goes back all the way to the start of the western canon in Homer, whom, against all expectation, Dryden has found 'more according to my Genius' than Virgil, and translations from whose *Iliad* are given pride of place in his collection.[37] And the metaphors of transmigration and transfusion are most often used in this period, as by Lansdowne, in connection with cross-cultural, especially classical-vernacular, exchange.

---

33. Dryden (1693), A2ᵛ.
34. Hopkins (2001), 145.
35. Lansdowne, 'To my Friend. Mr JOHN DRYDEN', 1–11; Granville (1736), I, 121–2. The poem originally accompanied Dryden's 1697 Virgil; a revised form is preferred here.
36. Frost (1988), 145.
37. Preface to the *Fables*, Dryden (1956–2000), VII, 28.

Where does all this leave the poetic canon? Dryden's own translating work, he makes clear, has led him to conceive differently of both the ancients and the moderns: Chaucer *vis-à-vis* Boccaccio, Homer *vis-à-vis* Virgil, or (another kind of example) Chapman, earlier disparaged by Dryden as a translator of Homer, but who, contrastingly, Dryden draws upon in his late Homeric excerpts.[38] These perceptions are embodied and expressed in his translations, a body of work which will be read and reprinted throughout the eighteenth century, which readers regularly describe as eye-opening and which has the strongest possible effects on succeeding English writers. In sum, as a modern successor, Charles Tomlinson, has remarked, this greatest of English translators, 'through his versions of Ovid, Homer, Chaucer, Lucretius, Juvenal, and Virgil, permanently changed the scope of English poetry itself'.[39] To take these claims seriously is to entertain the notion that in this period the activity of translation, especially from Latin and Greek, is quite expressly the animating power in the English poetic tradition, and the decisive influence on canon formation.

38. Dryden's borrowings from Chapman's Homer are noted in Dryden (1956–2000), VII, 731 and notes following.
39. Tomlinson (2003), 3.

8

Evidence for an Alternative History: Manuscript Translations of the Long Eighteenth Century

English literature's history can, of course, be recounted in a variety of ways. To emphasize the English classical translating tradition with which this book is concerned is just one possibility. But all histories of modern western literatures have one thing in common, which also tends to differentiate them from all histories of pre-modern literatures: they are histories of major printed works. We would do well to remember that this is not an inclusive category even post-Gutenberg. Some writers did not print their compositions because they wrote only for their own circle, or their own purposes (educational, devotional, whatever), or chose not to expose themselves to much public attention. Other works did not see print for accidental reasons – an untimely death, a rival publication which happened to pre-empt them. The fortuitousness, and the sometimes fine line between one outcome and the other, is a reminder of the contingency of all history. Such circumstances have sometimes presented opportunities for narrative or dramatic treatment too, often in romantic tales of the tenuous survival of a unique manuscript.

Unprinted works, if they survive in some other form, may have plenty to tell us. In fact, some kinds of manuscripts reached a sizeable audience long after the printing press's arrival: 'publication' and 'printing' are not, after all, synonyms, and print was not always the only way, not always even the usual way, for current writing to be distributed. Manuscript circulation took various forms in the seventeenth and early eighteenth centuries. Manuscripts could be passed around within a closed circle, such as an extended family or a group of students, or be made available commercially to any paying customer. Texts could be copied out by individuals for their private use, or for the use of others, as a business operation. Sometimes professional scribes worked in a kind of factory, called (after the monastic institution) a 'scriptorium', to produce collections of unprinted texts to order

English Translation and Classical Reception: Towards a New Literary History, first Edition.
Stuart Gillespie.

from available stock, such as a set of songs, or poems by a range of authors in the same genre or on the same subject. Single works, whether short or long, could, on the other hand, be copied by individuals who had borrowed an existing copy, usually into their own collections or commonplace books, sometimes expressly for the benefit of other friends and acquaintances.[1]

Manuscript publication was for practical reasons (such as the ease of copying out short texts) especially suitable for verse. It was especially appropriate too for certain categories of writer – or to put it the other way round, print publication was felt inappropriate for some types of writer. From the sixteenth century on, those who liked to think of themselves – or merely liked to present themselves – as above commercial gain often saw it as beneath their dignity for their verses to be handled by a printer and sold by a bookseller. Women writers, even if so circumstanced as to have access to the press, often felt their work would be made too conspicuous and, in an 'unwomanly' way, too public, if it reached the bookseller's shop[2] – or so the standard story goes. But doubt has been cast on the assumed upper-class disdain for print.[3] In any case, the scope of manuscript culture was not determined entirely by class and gender. The story of manuscript circulation in the Sidney circle, as recently studied by Henry Woudhuysen,[4] combines the usual class and gender dimensions for the Elizabethan era. But on the eve of the eighteenth century, neither is relevant to those Margaret Ezell names as 'poets whose public reputations as writers were based on manuscript circulation': the professional poets and/or middle-class writers Granville, Garth, Talbot, Somers and the Bishop of Rochester. Pope too (as Ezell further brings out), unexpectedly in view of our usual idea of him as a pioneer of professional publishing, 'retained an allegiance to the practices of manuscript culture'.[5]

One reason why we should take an interest in all this in the present context is that circulation by manuscript gives real insight into how reception works. In the seventeenth and eighteenth centuries it was perfectly possible for a foreign-language text to become well known long before it reached print; moreover there were reasons why certain works might not appear in print even in the long term. An example is Machiavelli's *Il principe*, published in Italy in 1532, then in England in French translation in 1553 and in the original Italian in 1584, but not printed in English until 1640. We can infer that the English book trade felt it necessary to disguise its part in printing even Italian-language editions: London booksellers used false foreign imprints when issuing them. These circulated widely, together

1. See Love (1993) for a full treatment of the range of possibilities, extending beyond literary texts and concentrating on the period to 1700. For a taxonomy (authorial publication, entrepreneurial publication, user publication), see pp. 47–89.
2. A good starting point on women writers in this context is Ezell (1993).
3. A well-known critique of the notion of the 'stigma of print' is given in May (1980).
4. Woudhuysen (1996).
5. Ezell (1999), 81, 83. For further discussion of the significance of manuscript circulation in the seventeenth century, see Love (2002); Beal (1998); Hammond (2006).

with print copies of Latin and French translations. But so too, to judge by their survival rate, did manuscript English versions by a number of different translators.[6] The picture reflects what was understood to be Machiavelli's republican agenda under the Tudor and Stuart crowns.[7] But in spite of the evidently anticipated official disapproval, a wide acquaintance with Machiavelli's *Prince* in Britain is to be presumed, and texts in French, Italian, Latin and English all figure in its reception.

Thus manuscript circulation may be one of the ways in which a translated work first starts to make its appearance. Far from being a dead-end or a throwback to the antiquated practices of medieval times, manuscript translations can in the long eighteenth century be pilot projects which lead to further interest, further translation, and eventually the full-scale arrival on the scene of the work concerned, in other, perhaps more professional, English versions. The unprinted parts of John Evelyn's early but abortive *De rerum natura* look to have played a part in Dryden's selected renderings of Lucretius of 1685, which stand among the most powerful verse he ever wrote.[8] Only Book 1 of Evelyn's version was ever issued in print (in 1656), but Dryden seems to have read the rest of Evelyn's rendering in a manuscript copy, because he recalled phrasing from it in his own excerpts.[9] In the same decade as Dryden's there appeared the first full English version of the *De rerum natura* from the hand of Thomas Creech, a young Oxford don. In Creech, similarly, have been identified borrowings from the unprinted portion of Evelyn's Lucretius, as well as (less securely) from Lucy Hutchinson's manuscript translation of the 1650s.[10] It is unlikely to be a coincidence that John Wilmot, Earl of Rochester, who translated Lucretian passages at an unknown date in the 1670s, was related to Lucy Hutchinson. In 1676 both she and the Rochester family were the house-guests in Oxfordshire of the Earl of Anglesey, to whom Hutchinson had sent, and dedicated, her manuscript text in the previous year.[11] Creech, celebrated by the Town for his complete Lucretian translation of 1682, was shortly thereafter introduced to Dryden (then Poet Laureate) by their mutual publisher Jacob Tonson, and proceeded to become a member of the circle on which Dryden and Tonson drew in collecting translations for their miscellanies of the 1680s and beyond. In the second of these, in 1685, were first published, alongside some of Creech's new classical translations, Dryden's Lucretian excerpts.

◆   ◆   ◆

6. For some surviving examples, see Raab (1964), 52–3, and, presenting transcripts of two complete manuscript texts, Petrina (2009).

7. See here Donaldson (1988), 86–100.

8. A full text of Evelyn's Lucretius is available in Repetzki (2000). The verse of Dryden's Lucretius is characterized by Jones (1985); Hopkins (2007).

9. See Hopkins (2003), 116–18, including notes on personal connections between Evelyn and Dryden which could have facilitated an exchange of manuscript material.

10. Real (1970), 163–5, 161–2. See also Creech's 1682 letter of thanks to Evelyn (169).

11. De Quehen (1996), 12.

In this chapter, which may be the first critical discussion of its kind – of a range of surviving manuscript English translations of classical literary texts – I cannot hope to do more than begin to indicate the interest and the implications of the type of material involved. I shall draw on several published articles in which I have myself presented transcriptions of individual translated texts.[12] In order to achieve at least minimal continuity, I shall focus on one genre which Restoration and eighteenth-century writers took particularly to their hearts: formal verse satire. The manuscripts discussed all have something to tell us about the reception of a classical work, about the reception of earlier translations, and/or, comparatively, about the characteristics of more familiar translations. A subtext will gradually become more prominent: my examples go to suggest how Pope's *Imitations of Horace* (1733–8) grew out of, and were then received into, the translating tradition in Roman satire. Or, we might say, how the style of a widely acclaimed masterpiece of English verse takes its place within a series not of original English poems but of classical translations.

A survey of unprinted translations available in the anglophone world's repositories would show significant differences in scope and emphasis from material falling within the printed record. For example, a high proportion of translation was carried out for educational purposes, especially the teaching and learning of modern languages. Some translation, however, is apprentice-work by aspiring poets. No less distinguished a figure than Pope acquired much of his art by imitating and translating classical and modern verse, as is well known.[13] Pope mostly conducted his lessons for himself, but in one form or another translation had been a standard part of school training since before the time of Shakespeare, as we saw in Chapter 3. The other main difference from many other aspiring writers is that the precocious Pope was later able to publish some of these early translations and imitations, often after polishing them in more mature years – his Statius being one example, as noted in Chapter 6. Again, a high proportion of unprinted translations in such a survey would be devotional in character: one need only glance at the lists of English psalms in manuscript catalogues to see how frequently translation was resorted to as a vaguely improving pastime (and how little interested the writers were in print publication).[14] On the other hand, the results of such a survey would also reflect the way that anything unprintable for reasons of taste or tact is also destined to remain in manuscript. Satires involving contemporary figures, for instance, are often more frank and outspoken than their printed counterparts,

---

12. See the bibliography *s.v.* 'Gillespie'. The editorial matter of these articles may be consulted for further contextual and expository detail.

13. For the place of translation in Pope's early (self-)education, see Pope (1939–69), I, 329–31.

14. The list of psalm translations is longer than that for any single translated author in, for instance, Bodleian manuscripts (Horace being *proxime accessit*): Crum (1969), II, 1252. Translation here will, of course, normally be from the Latin, and sometimes the texts will simply rework previous English psalm translations. Most such translations are to be distinguished from the more strenuous, and more continental, procedures of penitential exercise through the making of psalm versions.

which to avoid recriminations could not afford to offend too seriously. Manuscript satires, circulated among acquaintances, with the author's name omitted or at least optional, required less discretion.

One case will suggest immediately how understanding such points can make a difference to the way we see the past, which here means the way we see key classical translations and, beyond them, the classical texts to which translations have given, and still give, most readers access. After Dryden inscribed a copy of his translation of Juvenal in 1693 'For his true Friend Mr Tho: Monson', the said Mr Monson (or perhaps another hand) was able to add several passages totalling 16 lines to the printed text of Dryden's Satire 6. First given full scholarly attention in 1972 (Monson's copy is now in the Beinecke Rare Book and Manuscripts Library at Yale), they have been accepted as authentically Drydenian; they also appear, in a later hand and with slight variations in wording, in the endpapers of another copy of the same volume now in the Huntington Library.[15] The first of the passages consists of two couplets translating the following lines on Messalina –

> tunc nuda papillis
> Constitit auratis, titulum mentita Lyciscae,
> Ostenditque tuum, generose Britannice, ventrem.
> Excepit blanda intrantes, atque aera poposcit:
> Et resupina jacens multorum absorbuit ictus.[16]

as follows:

> The fair unbroaken belly lay displayd
> Where once the brave Brittanicus was layd.
> Bare was her bosome, bare yᵉ feild of Lust
> Eagre to swallow Evry sturdy Thrust.

There has been speculation about the reasons for the composition and then omission of these and the other dozen obscene lines involved (since it is highly plausible that Dryden devised them): Was it on account of a publisher's decision? The translator's second thoughts? A choice made under the pressures of contemporary debate? But a completely different issue might be raised from the point of view

15. The first presentation of the lines, from the Huntington Library copy, was in Carnochan (1972), but the Monson copy's peculiarities were previously remarked by Osborn (1965), 250. For further discussion, see Dryden (1956–2000), IV, 781–2; Hammond and Hopkins (1995–2005), IV, 42–3. The dedication happens to point to another sometimes hidden side of Dryden's life and work: it has not previously been noted that Lionel Monson, Munsen, or Anderson is identifiable as an English Dominican priest suspected of involvement in the Popish Plot and sentenced to death in 1680, subsequently pardoned and exiled for life.

16. Juvenal 6.122–6; text from Dryden (1956–2000), IV. This text is from Prateus' Paris 1684 edition, and is also the source for quotations below from Juvenal 6.

of reception, namely, can Dryden's translation be said to include these lines or not? Since they were first fully documented in 1972, different editors have taken different views. Walker (1987) prints them within his text of Dryden's *Sixth Satire of Juvenal*, while Dryden's next editors, Hammond and Hopkins, print them only in their footnotes, on the grounds that 'the lines' circulation seems to have been strictly limited'.[17] Fascinatingly, the issue is tied up with the status of Juvenal's own text at this point, because the really offensive line in the Latin, 'Et resupina jacens multorum absorbuit ictus', has itself had its authenticity disputed. The decisions of Dryden's recent editors echo those applied before Dryden's day to Juvenal's text by the seventeenth-century editors whose work Dryden used. Pratus and Schrevilius, considering the line a late interpellation, omit it, whereas Henninius prints it. Even in our own time, in a series admittedly designed for educational purposes, the Loeb Classical Library text current from 1918 to 2003 omits the line, while numbering subsequent lines as if it were present. Its successor of 2004 prints the line, but in square brackets, and does not translate it.[18]

This is a special case of how manuscript evidence not only shows us material omitted from the printed record, but poses questions about the status of what may seem firmly settled texts by canonical English authors – and about how their translations represent classical texts. Juvenal's vocabulary itself may be bland – modern Juvenal commentators have concluded that he 'did not use the basic obscenities [and] for the most part favoured bland euphemisms'[19] – but it can be argued all the same that the toned-down Dryden text actually published 'both misses Juvenal's sharp irony and lacks the vigour of Dryden's imaginary brothel'.[20]

Raising these issues is far from being the only thing manuscript evidence can show us about this satire. Let's move to Dryden's version of Juvenal 6 as a whole. Here is the opening of Juvenal's satire on women in Dryden's 'massive, truculent English':[21]

> In *Saturn's* Reign, at Nature's Early Birth,
> There was that Thing call'd Chastity on Earth;
> When in a narrow Cave, their common shade,
> The Sheep, the Shepherds and their Gods were laid:
> When Reeds and Leaves, and Hides of Beasts were spread
> By Mountain Huswifes for their homely Bed,
> And Mossy Pillows rais'd, for the rude Husband's head.
> Unlike the Niceness of our Modern Dames
> (Affected Nymphs with new Affected Names:)
> The *Cinthia's* and the *Lesbia's* of our Years,

17. Hammond and Hopkins (1995–2005), 43.
18. Ramsay (1940), 92 (following line 125); Braund (2004*a*), 244 (line 126).
19. Adams (1982), 221.
20. Braund (2004*b*), 147.
21. Carne-Ross (1990), 106.

> Who for a Sparrow's Death dissolve in Tears:
> Those first unpolisht Matrons, Big and Bold,
> Gave Suck to Infants of Gygantick Mold;
> Rough as their Savage Lords who Rang'd the Wood,
> And Fat with Akorns Belcht their windy Food.
> For when the World was Bucksom, fresh, and young,
> Her Sons were undebauch'd, and therefore strong;
> And whether Born in kindly Beds of Earth,
> Or strugling from the Teeming Oaks to Birth,
> Or from what other Atoms they begun,
> No Sires they had, or if a Sire the Sun.[22]

Dryden's Juvenal – he translated Satires 1, 3, 6, and 16 himself and helped commission the rest from other hands – is usually felt to have no serious rival among historical English treatments other than Samuel Johnson's extremely powerful, though very differently tackled, imitations of 1738 and 1749.[23] Johnson's work extended only to Satires 3 and 10 (it is unthinkable that he might have produced an imitation of Juvenal 6). This would seem to imply that Dryden's is the definitive English version; and it is certainly impressive, quite apart from the overall weight, sonority and confidence to which Carne-Ross alludes. Dryden, we note, happily adds colour to Juvenal. In the line

> And Mossy Pillows rais'd, for the rude Husband's head

there was nothing in the Latin to supply 'mossy', 'rais'd' or 'rude' (Dryden is assimilating the passage to a traditional poetic lexis of the 'primitive': 'mossy' is a Spenserism, and 'rude husbandmen' are regular visitors to such scenes). Dryden is perhaps not always economical: the four lines on 'Modern Dames' stand for less than two in Juvenal ('haud similis tibi, Cynthia, nec tibi, cujus | Turbavit nitidos extinctus passer ocellos'). But the comedy ('And Fat with Akorns Belcht') and the wondrous fecundity ('strugling from the Teeming Oaks') consort together in the most satisfactory way. The first matrons and the bounteous natural world they live in are closely linked by many devices, such as the adjective 'bucksom': 'blithe, gladsome, bright, lively', but also, and 'chiefly of women', 'full of health, vigour, and good temper; well-favoured, plump and comely'.[24]

Yet Dryden's Satire 6 is not altogether in a class of its own, even if other printed translations seem so to place it, for his closest peer in the translation of Juvenal was for 250 years lost to view. William Popple, known as a minor dramatist of the

---

22. Lines 1–21; Dryden (1956–2000), IV, 149.

23. Though in assessing Dryden's Juvenal in the 'Life of Dryden' Johnson suggested it might at some future date be improved upon, Sowerby (1994), 364, is not unusual in presenting Dryden's as 'the best English version in his or any age'.

24. *OED*, 'buxom', *a.*, 3, 4.

1730s,[25] carefully prepared his translations of Horace (complete) as well as Juvenal (Satires 6 and 10) in the 1750s, but for uncertain reasons they never reached the bookseller's shop.[26] Popple's unprinted work has, however, been preserved in manuscripts in Oxford, in London and at Yale. Accordingly, we are in a position to compare the opening of his Juvenal 6 with Dryden's:

> It has been fabled (and it may be so,)
> That *Chastity* resided once below;
> But t' was when *Saturn* o'er the World had sway,
> And *Men* in subterraneous Caverns lay;
> Where, with their House-hold Gods, they Cattle kept,
> And under one dark Roof together slept.
> When the Goodwife – (what different cares engage
> The *Cynthias*, and the *Lesbias*, of our age,
> Who, if a *Sparrow* or a *Monkey* dies,
> With Tears efface the lustre of their eyes)
> When the Goodwife, on barren Mountains bred,
> With skins of Beasts and leaves prepared the bed;
> And at her prominent, unwieldy Breast,
> Of bulk much fitter to be tapp'd, than prest,
> With ever-running streams of wholesome food,
> Nourish'd with pleasure her *Gigantic* brood;
> Whilst by her side (tho' hideous to the sight)
> Her windy Husband belch'd and snor'd all night.
> But then, indeed, the World was fresh and young,
> The Sky above Men's heads but lately hung;
> For whether on the teeming *Oak* they grew,
> Or from the quick'ning *Mud* existence drew,
> No *Sires* they had, no *Laws* their steps to guide,
> *Nature* and common *Reason* both supplied.[27]

That takes a few lines more, but perhaps there is little to choose between 21 and 24 lines to Juvenal's 13 here. Popple's opening couplet is wittier, his parenthesis pausing to register the possibility that chastity is altogether a myth, whereas Dryden's 'that Thing call'd Chastity' implies only its unfamiliarity in later times. Popple's humour gets broader than Dryden's – 'Of bulk much fitter to be tapp'd, than prest'; 'hideous to the sight' – but then, the exact mood of Juvenal's passage could be debated. The second of these expansions is part of the way Popple turns the cave into a small dramatized scene (the night is passing) where Dryden does

---

25. See Rogers (2004) in the *Oxford Dictionary of National Biography*. This entry has subsequently been revised in the online edition to take account of recent findings.
26. Popple died in 1764. For the datings, see Gillespie (2006), 47–8. Popple's intention of printing his translations is established in Gillespie (2007*b*), 206–7.
27. Gillespie (2006), 51.

not go as far. Popple and Dryden both register Juvenal's new ('fresh', 'young') world, but only Popple the new sky Juvenal mentions ('Quippe aliter tunc orbe novo, coeloque recenti, | Vivebant homines', 11–12). Both depart from the Latin to arrive at their closing lines, Dryden (whether appropriately or not) veering towards Lucretius, Popple manoeuvring wittily together the grammatical subjects and objects of his couplet (he has the advantage of familiarity with Pope). Popple gives Dryden a run for his money here and elsewhere in his translation. He has plainly used Dryden's version, but used it creatively and in some ways perhaps succeeded in improving on it.[28]

Let us stay with Popple's unprinted translations, for the case is quite different with his Horace. The four-volume manuscript of Popple's poetical works, apparently a presentation copy of a text prepared for printing, collects his previously published poems (a translation of Horace's *Ars poetica* and an original satire, *The Age of Dulness*) together with unprinted translations including those discussed here. Two of the four volumes are occupied by Popple's Horace, a complete translation of the corpus explicitly inspired by Pope's *Imitations of Horace* (1733–8). Pope and Popple were near-contemporaries. Popple was by twelve years Pope's junior, but, by the date he was writing, had outlived him (Pope died in 1744). In a preface written to introduce his complete *Works of Horace* to the reader when, as he evidently intended, the collection was printed, Popple explicitly avers his intention to adopt Pope's approach, and to extend it to the rest of the Horatian corpus (Pope's *Imitations* cover only a selection of Horace's satires):

> The first effect, which the Reading this Part of Mr Pope's Works, had upon me, was Pleasure mixed with Admiration, to hear *Horace* speak the English Tongue, with such Perspicuity, Grace, Freedom and Ease, having till then only heard him, in the best of our English Translations, speak his own Sense without any of the Graces that accompany him in the Original, and which, where they can, should be preserved, and where they cannot, imitated.
>
> The next Effect (for which I expect the Censure of half Critics) was *Emulation*. This put me upon trying if it was within the Compass of possibility, to attemp [*sic*] the same Thing in the same Manner, with any prospect of Success. In order to try the Experiment, and to try it in the most difficult way, I resolved to begin with those which Mr Pope had gone thro'. I had two Reasons to induce me to make this Trial; the first was, the Advantage of having Mr Pope immediately under my Eye, from whom I might catch fire as I went on; and the other, an opinion, that if I would succeed in these, I should have the less Reason to apprehend Success in the remaining. What I understood by Succeeding, was, to be read without creating a Disgust in the Reader or a Contempt in the *Imitator*.

---

28. Popple himself suggests the likely reason: he was working without a library in the Bermudas, where he was Governor from 1745. See Gillespie (2007*b*), 206.

Popple lays particular stress on Pope's 'manner':

> As the design of this *Imitation* is to make Horace better known to the bulk of English
> Readers than the bare rendering him in English Prose or Verse can do, and as I am
> convinced that Mr Pope in the few pieces he has done, has contributed more to it
> than any literal Translation ever did or can, I had no Choice left as to the *manner*
> of executing my Purpose. He had pointed it out so strongly, that to have affected
> another Manner, for the sake of varying from him or for fear of Comparison, wou'd
> have been frustrating my whole Design at once.[29]

Popple's *Works of Horace*, then, excerpts from which were first published in 2007,
has quite striking implications for our view of one of Pope's mature poetic achievements. Popple uses Pope's 'manner' to generate a complete, not (like Pope's) a
selected, set of imitations of Horatian satires (and eventually a complete English
Horace). Popple's work, albeit hidden from view for so long, thus represents direct
testimony to the creative effect (in the terms I proposed in Chapter 2) of Pope's
Horace of the 1730s. Moreover Popple's own work, had it made its way in the
world, would in itself have represented a sizeable enough collection of poems and
translations to be recognizable as the work of a substantial mid-eighteenth-century
poet-translator, one specializing in classical translation and satire. Popple would,
that's to say, have continued the Popean tradition, and even emulated aspects of
the Popean career.

   In the case of Satire 1.10, Popple's Horace wittily uses Pope's manner against
him, so combining homage with mock-hostility. The opening lines may serve as
a sample of Popple's Popean Horace:

Horace Book 1st Satire 10th Imitated
To the Admirers of the late Mr *Pope*

Well! I have said it, and maintain it still,
That *Pope*, like other *Bards*, wrote sometimes ill;
That, striving with quaint words to mark the Line,
His *Verses* oft from *Harmony* decline;
Whilst rough harsh Numbers hobble into place,
And rob the Work of Elegance and Grace.
What fond Admirer, partial to his Fame,
Will not allow, ev'n *Pope* might merit blame;
Who will deny, but that sometimes his Pen
Play'd cruelly with *Characters* and Men?
Yet, tho' I charge him thus, I freely own,
In *Satire* and in *Wit* he stood alone.

29. Gillespie (2007*b*), 211, 212 –13.

> But granting this, it may be still deny'd,
> That he had ev'ry requisite beside;
> Reflected to the Mind, thro' this false Glass
> Ill-manner'd W—d for a Wit might pass,
> F—te wear the *Comic Wreath*, & Hilliad Sm—t
> Turn *Satirist* like *Pope*, and top his part.[30]

Popple, it's true, doesn't achieve here the density of Pope's verse textures, his wealth of implication and nuance. His work does, however, shine a strong light on the eighteenth-century reception of Pope's Horatian imitations – a topic on which the Pope *Critical Heritage* is strangely negative.[31]

The manuscript record, as well as showing us more about the place mainstream classical authors had in English writing, can also reveal new territory being opened up by English translators. The first printed English translations from Claudian belong to the seventeenth century: as has long been established, they are Leonard Digges's *Rape of Proserpine*, 1617, and various epigrams in Sir John Beaumont's *Bosworth-Field*, 1629. But it isn't until much later that Claudian's longer satires receive the attentions of translators, with *In Rufinum* receiving an English treatment from William King in 1712, then from Jabez Hughes (whom we met in Chapter 6) in 1737.[32] This showing makes Claudian the satirist appear a late acquisition, englished at a time when the only Latin texts remaining to be tackled by translators were second- or third-division material. For this reason alone, then, it seems worth recording that a full text of a translation titled *Cl: Claudian his first Booke against Eutropius, Anno: 1664* appears in a Bodleian manuscript, and that the translator, though unknown, was by no means a beginner.[33] Its context (is it in some way politically resonant?) is also obscure, but its degree of accomplishment can be inspected. Its 532 English lines correspond to 512 Latin ones, making the translation unusually condensed, and its crabbed, rebarbative style is somewhat reminiscent of the manner of Donne and certain other late sixteenth-century verse satirists.[34] The following sample concludes with Claudian's fantasia

30. Quoted from Gillespie (2007*b*), 219. Popple incorporates in Popean fashion the names of Leonard Welsted, Samuel Foote, and Christopher Smart (whose mock epic *The Hilliad* was printed in 1753).
31. Two of the main contemporary responses anthologized in Barnard (1973) are Thomas Bentley's satirical remarks (325–6) and Lord Hervey's attack (251–2).
32. There is also Ben Jonson's use of *In Rufinum* for the vivid account of mutilation by the Roman mob in his play *Sejanus* (1603).
33. Bodleian MS Rawlinson poet. 154, fols. 39–48. No translator is identified for *In Eutropium*, but following this translation, fol. 49ʳ carries in the same hand 'A Translation of Cl: Claudian his Panegyrick upon the fourth Consulship of Honorius. By J. H. Esq. [another hand adds 'Ætatis suae 60.'] Anno Domini 1665.' This text is no more than a twenty-line fragment, but the style is unmistakably identical with that of the longer *In Eutropium* translation. Hence it appears to supply the *In Eutropium* translator's initials and age.
34. This seems consistent with a translator born in 1605 who perhaps did not much develop his skills in later life; Donne and Jonson, both born in 1572, would have been at the height of their fame in his youth.

most familiar to readers of English satire from Pope's use of it towards the end of Book III of *The Dunciad* ('The forests dance, the rivers upward rise, | Whales sport in woods, and dolphins in the skies') – though there are strong ties to Horace and Du Bartas too:

> When fame his Treason through the Townes first brought,
> It vayne, unlikely, and rays'd in Jest men thought.
> As a light Rumor jeer'd it of strang things,
> Like Crowe with White, or Swann with Sable Wings.
> One gravely sayd, If we such monstrous Lyes
> Beleive as this, then sure the Tortoys flyes.
> Vulturs beare Hornes, the Rivers upstreame slyde,
> The Sun at Gades rising,'s Beames doth hyde
> With the Armenians. The Sea fruites doth beare,
> And Dolphins in the Woods theyr round Backs reare.
> Men stick to Shelfish, and the vayne things true
> Of India, which Jewes hangings painted shew.

The corresponding Latin runs as follows:

> Fama prius falso similis vanoque videri
> Ficta ioco; levior volitare per oppida rumor
> Riderique nefas: veluti nigrantibus alis
> Audiretur olor, corvo certante ligustris.
> Atque aliquis gravior morum: 'si talibus, inquit,
> Creditur et nimiis turgent mendacia monstris,
> Iam testudo volat, profert iam cornua vultur;
> Prona petunt retro fluvii iuga; Gadibus ortum
> Carmani texere diem; iam frugibus aptum
> Æquor et adsuetum silvis delphina videbo;
> Iam cochleis homines iunctos et quidquid inane
> Nutrit Iudaicis quae pingitur India velis.'[35]

What does J.H.'s work tell us? Partly because it achieves a certain density and conviction *qua* English verse (carrying it out was evidently no mere training exercise), it tells us that Claudian's reception in Britain looks different from what we previously thought.[36] It tells us, as already noted, that late Latin verse commanded more attention than the record of printed translations indicates. It tells us also that *In Eutropium* was felt by one seventeenth-century translator likely to answer his purposes (satirical, stylistic, whatever), and to be worth trying to represent in English form. More time and space would be needed to make good further

---

35. Quoted from the contemporary text in Claudian (1650), with contractions expanded.
36. The standard study is Cameron (1970), but this is largely concerned with later eras.

observations that might go beyond the purely historical, such as, for instance, that it suggests a species of seventeenth-century English couplet verse can be plausibly offered as an equivalent for Claudian's vigorous hexameters, or that Claudian can sound something like Donne, Marston or Hall in their roughest satirical modes.

Persius' reputation has since the Renaissance been slow to rise to anything like a level comparable with Juvenal's, but today it stands higher than at any previous date.[37] Dryden's much-reprinted complete version of 1693, which for the first time paired Persius with Juvenal in a new English translation,[38] and accompanied the poems with an eloquent discussion in Dryden's essay known as the *Discourse Concerning Satire*, must be supposed part of the story of Persius' rehabilitation, even if critics today do not always rate Dryden's Persius as highly as his contemporaries did.[39] But how influential was it? Did it become the last word on Persius for English readers who were not classical scholars – and for English poets? No other complete verse translation of Persius was printed between the first, by Barten Holyday in 1616, and Thomas Brewster's of 1741. Single-satire verse translations from Persius were likewise rarely printed in this era,[40] though Persius' reputation for difficulty and obscurity is not, incidentally, enough to explain this dearth; he was, after all, set for translation in school Latin classes.[41]

But this is not the whole story. Contrary to what we might expect, the appearance of one successful new translation often has the effect of encouraging other translators to try their hands. Sometimes this effect can be readily seen in publishing activity: in the 50 years preceding Dryden's 1697 *Works of Virgil* there had appeared only one previous complete *Aeneid* translation in verse, that of John Ogilby in 1649, whereas the following 50 years saw four more.[42] With Persius such an effect is not apparent in the publishing record, which after 1693 is largely confined to cribs and teaching materials such as the complete prose versions by Henry Eelbeck (1719) and John Senhouse (1730, with Latin). The next full translation with any literary pretensions takes almost 50 years to appear (Thomas Brewster's of 1741). Manuscript evidence, on the other hand, suggests that Dryden's Persius translation did, in fact, elicit other treatments. We happen to

37. Two powerful recent advocates are Henderson (1999) and Hooley (1997). For a conspectus of twentieth-century critical views see Sullivan (1972).
38. Barten Holyday's Persius of 1616 was eventually reprinted together with his posthumous Juvenal in 1673, but the edition carries separate title pages, indicating that this was an afterthought, and there were no further printings.
39. For some modern estimates of Dryden's Persius, see Nisbet (1963); Sullivan (1972).
40. Relevant to what follows is that between 1616 and 1740 the record for Satire 1 shows only a single partial rendering, by Charles Gildon (in his *Miscellany Poems*, 1692).
41. Dryden himself in the headnote to his version recalls translating Persius 5 as a Westminster School exercise. Houghton MS Eng 899 is a complete Persius by the 17-year-old Robert Southwell (1635–1702), later Secretary of State for Ireland, dedicated to his 'honoured master'.
42. These were Lauderdale (1709), Brady (1714–26), Trapp (1718–20) and Pitt (1736–40); John Davidson's (1743) is a prose crib.

know that an unattributed translation of Satire 1 in the Bodleian Library follows Dryden's 1693 publication in time because one line is actually quoted from it (at a point where an example of contemporary verse is called for).[43] Stylistically the translation is in sympathy with Dryden's while remaining almost entirely independent of it. The anonymous translator spruces Persius up, imposing a glossier finish through free development and expansion of the often terse and sometimes unclear Latin – and in all this follows where Dryden had led. We cannot quite say why the translator attempted it, nor whether there is a motive of competition with the 'market leader' (Dryden's Persius was frequently reprinted).[44] It went unpublished, yet it is no amateur effort, and in fact the translation can, like Popple's of Juvenal, bear close comparison with Dryden's prior work. Which of the following seems the more sophisticated handling of the passage following the quotations from the modern poetasters whose talentlessness is the subject of the satire (Persius 1.103ff.)?

> These are all soft, sweet, pretty, labral rhimes,
> *Mœnas* and *Attys* quadrate with the Times:
> For these no Desk is bang'd, no Nails are bit;
> We write such Stuff with the same Ease we spit: 170
> But were our Ancestors from Death to rise,
> Would they like us such wretched Dogg'rel prize?
> **M.** Yet the Resentments of the Great are strong,
> And if they snarl, they snap before 'tis long:
> Hold in your Hand, avert the pointed Sting,
> Or you may chance to starve, if not to swing.
> **P.** For once to please you, then, I'll change my Note,
> All, all is fine! All admirably wrote!
> In some Museum, lodge the sacred Store,
> And paint two crossed Snakes above the Door,   180
> With this Inscription all around:
> *Urine not here: 'Tis holy Ground.*

Or this?

> Cou'd such rude Lines a *Roman* Mouth become,   200
> Were any Manly Greatness left in Rome?
> *Mœnas* and *Atys* in the Mouth were bred;
> And never hatch'd within the lab'ring Head.
> No blood, from bitten Nails, those Poems drew:

43. MS Ballard 50. For the dating and other details mentioned here see further Gillespie (2007*a*). A previous draft of this translation is extant, as Rawlinson poet. 172, but there are no indications of its circulation in the form of other copies, excerpts, etc.
44. As well as within editions of Dryden's works following his death in 1700, there were fresh issues of his Juvenal and Persius (together) in 1697, 1702, 1711, 1713, 1726, 1732 and 1735.

But churn'd, like Spittle, from the Lips they flew.
FRIEND
'Tis fustian all; 'tis execrably bad:
But if they will be Fools, must you be mad?
Your Satyrs, let me tell you, are too fierce;
The Great will never bear so blunt a Verse.   210
Their Doors are barr'd against a bitter flout:
Snarl, if you please, but you shall snarl without.
Expect such Pay as railing Rhymes deserve,
Y'are in a very hopeful way to sterve.
PERSIUS
Rather than so, uncensur'd let 'em be:
All, all is admirably well for me.
My harmless Rhyme shall scape the dire disgrace
Of Common-shores, and ev'ry pissing place.
Two painted Serpents shall, on high, appear;
'Tis holy Ground; you must not Urine here.   220

The first of the two passages went unprinted until 2007; the second is Dryden's.[45]
Dryden's expansive tendencies are very much in evidence here, but a mere eleven
lines of Persius lie behind both versions. These Latin lines are unpacked in two
different ways, and the translators construct the principal speaker differently. For
Dryden, the Persius figure is anxious about his own verses' survival; alternatively,
in the anonymous translation he makes no mention of it. For a brief illustration
of typical issues, take Persius' lines 107–10:

Sed quid opus teneras mordaci radere vero
Auriculas? vide sis ne majorum tibi forté
Limina frigescant: sonat heic de nare canina
Littera.[46]   110

(But what need is there to scrape delicate ears with biting truth? Take care the
thresholds of the great don't grow chilly towards you: this is where the sound of a
dog's snarl is heard.)[47]

Is it the powerful, or the poet, that is doing the snarling in 109–10? Modern
editors of Persius are still undecided on this point, and our translators go their
separate ways, Dryden towards the poet, his successor towards the patron (212,
174). Perhaps this tends to confirm William Frost's contention that Persius' dif-

45. They are quoted respectively from Gillespie (2007*a*), 82–3, and Dryden (1956–2000), IV, 273.
46. Persius is quoted from the Casaubon (1605, reprint 1647) text supplied in Dryden (1956–2000),
IV, 272.
47. Braund (2004*a*), 59, adapted.

ficulty gave translators a freer hand.[48] Again, leaving questions of accuracy aside, the anonymous

> you may chance to starve, if not to swing

is measured, where Dryden's corresponding line seems not to avoid redundancy:

> Y' are in a very hopeful way to sterve.

But elsewhere Dryden accommodates more of the possible nuances of the Latin. 'Pay' (213) is not his own idea: it comes from Schrevelius, who had suggested that Persius' 'Limina frigescant' (109) was a reference to the daily dole. His successor makes nothing of the doorway.

One might argue that Dryden has a better command of the flow and trajectory of the passage, or that Anon. takes fewer risks, or has benefited from Dryden's earlier work (as in the last line); or one could go on singling out local successes in each case. My point, as with Dryden's and Popple's Juvenal, is that in spite of the disparity in their status – in the one case we are dealing with the mature work of a canonical English poet, in the other a text hitherto totally unread and unknown – both translations are in the same league. The anonymous Persius, in fact, is far more impressive than a great many of the English translations which did achieve the dignity of print.

Dryden's reworking of the long pent-up outburst that begins Persius' first satire has been highly praised. Taking it as a second and last point of comparison will develop my observation that the anonymous translation is stylistically in sympathy with Dryden's. Persius' opening lines are hardly likely to be seen as candidates for close translation by any English writer. Both Dryden and the anonymous translator dispense with most of the names and are forced considerably to increase the number of words used, simply in order to clarify what they think Persius is saying. This again is the Latin text of the passage (as it stood in Dryden's time but with inverted commas supplied):

> O Curas hominum! ô quantum est in rebus inane!
> 'Quis leget haec?' min' tu istud ais? 'nemo Hercule.' nemo?
> 'Vel duo, vel nemo. turpe et miserabile.' quaere?
> Ne mihi Polydamas, et Troiades Labeonem
> Praetulerint. nugae. non, si quid turbida Roma   5
> Elevet, accedas: examenve improbum in illa
> Castiges trutina: nec te quaesiveris extra.[49]

---

48. Frost (1988), 73–4; 'Obscurity in a foreign poet … can prove a translator's opportunity: the fact that he is forced to interpret may be a stimulus to new creation.'
49. Dryden (1956–2000), IV, 258.

Here is Dryden's rather loose reworking:

> PERSIUS.
>> HOW anxious are our Cares; and yet how vain
>> The bent of our desires!
> FRIEND.   Thy Spleen contain:
>> For none will read thy Satyrs.
> PERSIUS.   This to Me?
> FRIEND. None; or what's next to none; but two or three.
>> 'Tis hard, I grant.
> PERSIUS.
>>   'Tis nothing: I can bear   5
>> That paltry Scriblers have the Publick Ear:
>> That this vast universal Fool, the Town,
>> Shou'd cry up *Labeo*'s Stuff, and cry me down.
>> They damn themselves; nor will my Muse descend
>> To clap with such, who Fools and Knaves commend: 10
>> Their smiles and censures are to me the same:
>> I care not what they praise, or what they blame.
>> In full Assemblies let the Crowd prevail:
>> I weigh no Merit by the common Scale.[50]

Recent critical attention has focused less on Dryden's relation to Persius than on the style which he seems to develop almost independently here. Emrys Jones has discerned in these lines what he calls 'a new Drydenian style', a style Jones relates to the ultra-sophisticated mode of Pope's later Horatian imitations, so admired, as we have seen, by William Popple:

> The features of this style are a clipped economy, a rushing speed of movement, and an implacable resort to emphasis, often shaped in cleaving antithesis and parallel constructions. Lines in which words or phrases are repeated mimic the insistent Stoic curtness, the uncompromising adherence to doctrine: 'Shou'd cry up *Labeo*'s Stuff, and cry me down'; 'I care not what they praise, or what they blame' ... Despite the un-Persian volubility, Dryden is inventing a fast and agile style, packed yet light, which is extraordinarily close to Pope's later Horatian manner ... It's hardly too much to say that Dryden has here invented the style of Pope's Horatian *Imitations*.[51]

It's striking, then, that our anonymous post-Drydenian Persius translator should have found this style equally attractive and sought to emulate it too. As has been noted, Dryden is an explicit presence in this translation through one quoted line. It's almost as though the anonymous translator had decided to attempt a version which would use the same style but not the same words:

50. Dryden (1956–2000), IV, 259.
51. Jones (2004), 136.

P. How vain is Man! How anxious his Designs!
M. Suppress thy Rage, for who shall read thy Lines?
P. Who shall!
           M. Not one.
                      P. Not one vouchsafe a View!   5
M. Not one, perhaps, or at the most but two:
Shameful indeed!
               P. Wherein consists the shame?
Let the vile Rabble mouth out *Labeo*'s fame,
And their Boy Tyrant crown him with the Bays:
I slight their Censures, as I scorn their Praise.
Persius the Claps of factious *Rome* disdains;
With him, their Judgement never once obtains: 10
He knows his own less liable to fail,
Nor weighs his Merit in so light a Scale.[52]

Even in so short a sample can be found many of the features Jones points out in the Dryden, all belonging to an implacable, emphatic mode no less marked than his: repetition ('Shameful … shame', line 7), parallel or antithetical constructions (line 8), the 'packed' yet 'agile' phrasing which the tongue must pick its way round: 'the Claps of factious *Rome*', 'his own less liable to fail'. If Jones is right, it would seem that the testing and development of what was to become Pope's Horatian style, as first generated by Dryden in responding to Persius, was a process carried forward specifically by translators.

◆   ◆   ◆

In previous chapters I attempted to bring out some of what it means to refer to an English classical translating tradition, and gave examples of cross-fertilization between translations and original English poetry. On the face of it, translations of Roman satire might not seem the likeliest place to look for such relationships, in that, with the exceptions of Johnson's and perhaps Dryden's, even those which reached print are so little known today that they are not usually thought of as part of the history of English verse at all. But as we have noted, they form a tradition nevertheless, and one of relevance to the wider history of English poetry. We have seen Popple responding, in the most engaged and energetic way, to Pope's Horatian *Imitations*. But is the English Persius, perhaps, too shallow a stream, or too remote a backwater, for us to expect it to relate directly to that wider current? Not so. From Dryden's time, William Frost firmly asserts, Persius 'becomes, in his English versions, part of a new literary tradition'. Frost's examples include Dryden's Persius itself borrowing from Denham, Pope borrowing from Dryden (for *The Rape of the Lock*), Sir William Drummond (in his 1797 Persius) drawing on Pope's

---

52. Quoted from Gillespie (2007*a*), 78.

Essay on Man and Johnson's *Vanity of Human Wishes*, and the use of Dryden's version by three later translators.[53]

Manuscript evidence thus supplements and modifies our sense of the place classical satire has in English poets' work. The texts thus recovered are part of the story of English literary translation, part of English literary history. They do not show only 'what might have happened': they did happen, and in several cases they throw a strong light on the reception of canonical English writers and works. Where literary history in a still wider sense is concerned, they help to demonstrate the existence of a manuscript writing culture of much greater reach and professionalism than we have been accustomed to imagine. My self-imposed restriction of these illustrations to the genre of formal verse satire should at this point be underlined: unprinted manuscript translations of classical texts belonging to shorter forms such as epigrams or Horatian odes are actually much thicker on the ground, at least in terms of surviving copies.

There is, of course, a connection between the length of time it has taken for these and other unprinted translations to be brought to light, and the secondary place translation has for so long been accorded in the *œuvres* of English poets. The high premium placed on both 'originality' and 'individuality' has a doubly depressing effect on valuations of anonymous translations in particular.[54] Looking in other directions, however, allows one to point to a range of positive developments. To go no further than one of the Latin sources mentioned above, the last 15 years have seen the first complete printings of the Lucretius translations of both Evelyn and Hutchinson, with a more elaborate edition of the latter to come.[55] Digitization facilitates fuller cataloguing of English literary manuscripts and the online presentation of manuscript material.[56] We may hope that these straws in the wind will precede substantial further work in other genres, periods, and repositories than those this chapter has visited.[57]

---

53. Frost (1988), 92–3, 232.

54. The possible functions, and often deliberate election, of anonymity within manuscript circulation in the Tudor-Stuart periods are discussed in North (1982).

55. For Evelyn, Repetzki (2000); for Hutchinson, De Quehen (1996), with her Oxford University Press *Works* under the general editorship of David Norbrook appearing shortly, including her *De rerum natura* edited by Reid Barbour.

56. Those interested might like to investigate further the *Catalogue of English Literary Manuscripts 1450–1700*, an online record of surviving manuscript sources for over 200 major British authors; and the Perdita Project, cataloguing and presenting early modern women's manuscript writing, hosted by Warwick University.

57. Readers might wish to note the availability of a field for 'Translation' in the searchable Union First-Line Index of manuscript poetry hosted by the Folger Shakespeare Library (http://firstlines/ folger.edu). This online resource was first made available in 2010, and undoubtedly harbours many unexplored texts across the still expanding range of British and American repositories it covers. The repositories were at the time of writing: Beinecke (Osborn Collection), Bodleian, British Library, Folger, Harvard University, Huntington, and Brotherton Collection (University of Leeds).

9

Receiving Wordsworth, Receiving Juvenal: Wordsworth's Suppressed Eighth Satire

We move now from a linked selection of classical translations that went unprinted (no doubt for a range of reasons) to a single case of a deliberately suppressed translation which, I shall argue, has the power to affect the way we see the more prominent of its two authors, Wordsworth; beyond him the literary history of his era; and beyond both the satires of his original, Juvenal. In Chapter 8 formal verse satire was used as an example of one genre among others in which there is an impressive showing of unprinted translations for the long eighteenth century. In that sense verse satire is not a special case, but I added that it was 'one genre which Restoration and eighteenth-century writers took particularly to their hearts'. As will be seen, this is highly relevant to the Wordsworth text we are about to examine, because that text, composed but not completed 1795–7, is on the cusp of two eras in English literary history as conventionally narrated. Thus the place of satire within the output of the 'Romantic' generation is one of my concerns here; but the priorities of our own time, including our own understanding of how satire works, are another. Our reception of Wordsworth's reception of Juvenal, if that inelegant expression will pass, can inform our understanding of Juvenal (and other satirists) too.

Since Wordsworth's Juvenal translation appears in full only in one modern edition, and that a library edition likely to be on the shelves of few readers of this book, a reference text is supplied in an Appendix at the end of this chapter.

◆   ◆   ◆

Though the fact is felt of too little consequence to be recorded in many works of criticism or reference, in his mid-twenties Wordsworth was the co-author of a

English Translation and Classical Reception: Towards a New Literary History, First Edition.
Stuart Gillespie.
© 2011 Stuart Gillespie. Published 2011 by John Wiley & Sons, Ltd.

translation or imitation of Juvenal's Eighth Satire. It was not published in his lifetime and was not even partly printed until 1907, in an edition of Wordsworth family letters.[1] Ernest de Selincourt used the manuscripts then at hand to present a text in his Oxford Wordsworth edition of the 1940s, but only about half of the work was at that time available.[2] It was not until the 1990s that a letter of Francis Wrangham's containing the first 145 lines was discovered in the National Library of Scotland, following which, as recently as 1997, a near-complete printing of the imitation was issued for the first time, in the multi-volume Cornell edition of Wordsworth.[3]

The shadowy status of this translation in the Wordsworth corpus raises questions about the reception of both Juvenal and Wordsworth. What difference might it have made to Juvenal's reception had it been published? What difference does it make now? And how, on the other side, does it affect our understanding of Wordsworth and of the literary history of his era? These are different but related questions. If today we call Wordsworth a 'Romantic', a member of a school we oppose to that of his 'neoclassical' predecessors, one reason is that, perhaps partly following his own lead, we have been willing to play down his links to classical Greek and Roman poets (the latter being the stronger). No effort was needed to overlook his work on Juvenal: its demotion in his lifetime and its obscurity ever since is an orientation of the record which in later life he himself wished when he asked for the manuscripts to be destroyed. But it remains the case that over a period of around two years at a crucial point in his development, Wordsworth was apparently planning to appear in print as an imitator of Juvenal, as a Juvenalian satirist.

Let us first rehearse a little of what we know about Wordsworth's responses to the classics. As well as of Juvenal, Wordsworth is a translator (in some cases at length, in others only briefly) of Catullus, Horace, Lucretius and Virgil, though one is most unlikely to see any of these translations figuring in modern selections of his verse or in syllabi for courses on it. He claimed Horace as his 'great favourite' among classical poets, referred to him explicitly in 'Departing Summer' and

---

1. Knight (1907), I, 92–8. Down to 1930 these printed fragments had been 'almost completely ignored by critics, though … written in an important but obscure period of the poet's life', in the words of Tuckerman (1930), 209–10. Critics cannot be said to have paid much more attention since.

2. De Selincourt (1941–9). Incredibly, De Selincourt relegates it to his Appendix of 'Juvenilia', even though Wordsworth commenced it at the age of 25 and was 27 by the time he had finished with the text.

3. Within Landon and Curtis 1997 (hereafter 'Cornell'), which remains the only full edition of the text. A total 306 lines in final or near-final form, plus some draft material, is available. The ending once existed and is now lost, but beyond this the level of completeness is not entirely clear: the imitation's loose correspondence to the Latin makes it impossible to say how many further lines falling between the main passages available would have been composed (and are missing), and how many would have been freely omitted.

'Liberty', and drew on him allusively in other poems such as the sonnets on the River Duddon.[4] Beyond his translations of them, Lucretius and Virgil are presences in his work from early until late.[5] He remarked in later life that his 'long acquaintance' with Virgil, Horace, Lucretius and Catullus was an 'intimate' one.[6] Similarly, where Juvenal is concerned, it would be quite mistaken to imagine Wordsworth's acquaintance was limited to a single encounter as a translator. Wordsworth's long-term familiarity with Juvenal, as with many other Latin classics of verse and prose, can be taken for granted.[7] It would also be wrong to assume this familiarity had no identifiable effect on Wordsworth's own poetic output. That Wordsworth is not known as a verse satirist does not prevent him responding to Juvenal in his verse itself. To go no further than *The Prelude*, Juvenal's descriptions of Rome had long been prototypical for all such cityscapes, and some of the well-known depictions of the hustle and bustle of London life in Book VII draw more or less inevitably on Satires 1 and 3.

We can also go well beyond these canonical Latin poets in summarizing Wordsworth's classical affiliations. For instance, Wordsworth read extensively, up to and including his university years, in both Roman and Greek historians – he refers in letters to a wide range, and owned copies of their works.[8] Many of the editions of Greek and Roman texts he owned or consulted have been identified – for the Romans he often had Latin editions and used English translations too, whereas he knew the Greeks only in translation.[9] And so we could continue, partly because for anyone undergoing education at secondary or tertiary level in the eighteenth century, immersion in Latin culture was inevitable.[10]

This information is not obscure; nor would it be true to say that literary historians have ignored or overlooked it. The received account is that it is simply of limited significance: these points of contact represent early educational or self-educational exercises, or reflect transient early tastes, rather than Wordsworth's 'real' affinities. The received account is, in fact, that as a poet Wordsworth, in one brief recent formulation, 'had to move away from the classics before finding his

---

4. Knight (1907), II, 318: 'Horace is my great favorite: I love him dearly.' For a brief account of Wordsworth's transactions with Horace, see Graver (1986*a*).

5. For Wordsworth and Lucretius, see Chapter 10; for the ambitions of Wordsworth' *Aeneid* translation, see Chapter 10; for Wordsworth and Virgil, see, synoptically, Portale (1991), 131–55.

6. Letter to Walter Savage Landor, 20 April 1822; De Selincourt (1978), 125.

7. For one example of the assimilation of Juvenal into the poetic tradition active in and around Wordsworth's time, see the discussion in Lindop (2001) of how the *Prelude*'s Alpine episode (Book VI) relates to Satire 10 on Hannibal's crossing of the Alps.

8. For the historians and others, see Worthington (1970).

9. The standard reference for Wordsworth's reading is Wu (1993–5).

10. Juvenal played a significant part in Wordsworth's university education. Wordsworth was examined in Satires 3–15 at St John's College, Cambridge, in June 1790: see Schneider (1957), 167. The thoroughness of Wordsworth's classical training at Hawkshead School and Cambridge University is emphasized by Clancy (2000), 3–63.

own voice'.[11] Yet these engagements (such as Wordsworth's extensive 1823 translation from the *Aeneid*) persist well into the poet's maturity. It is unclear, too, why Wordsworth's 'own' voice must be contradistinguished from classical voices: some recent criticism has, on the contrary, suggested how classical voices may be said to *merge* with Wordsworth's voice.[12] What Wordsworth 'moves away from' is less classicism than the neoclassicism of eighteenth-century English poets, and even this is seriously qualified in practice, as we shall see in both this chapter and the next. Yet the received account prevails; in Robin Dix's words, 'there is still a reluctance to abandon the notion that Wordsworth challenged the classicizing tendencies of his predecessors'.[13]

The circumstances in which Wordsworth's Juvenal took shape now need some exposition.[14] It was while living in London in the summer of 1795 that he visited Francis Wrangham, a Cambridge friend who was by this time a curate in Surrey. Wrangham, as well as steadily advancing in the Church throughout his life, was later to carry on correspondences with such figures as Byron, Hunt and Scott, to become a prolific editor of both ancient and modern authors, and to publish translations from Homer and Virgil as well as French and Italian poets. At this point, in Surrey in 1795, the two young men, according to Wrangham's much later narrative, 'employed a fortnight's leisure ... in attempting a modernization of Juvenal's Eighth Satire ... on the plan of Johnson's Third and Tenth'.[15] With limited progress made, Wordsworth's plans took him away from London, but the two men continued to exchange passages they composed by post, in letters dated over the following two years or so, until the imitation (Wordsworth's usual word for their work; Wrangham's is 'paraphrase') had more or less been assembled. We know of Wordsworth's keenness on the project from a letter of 1796 assuring Wrangham that he did 'not mean to drop the Juvenal scheme' but was 'on the contrary ... determined to bring it to a speedy conclusion';[16] he was still sending Wrangham new material in February 1797. Publication plans had not been developed, however, and at this time the text's physical existence was, so far as is known, confined to these letters and the drafts previously made in Surrey.

This was where matters rested until a decade later, in 1806. Now, on receiving fresh proposals from Wrangham regarding publication, Wordsworth wrote to ask his collaborator to destroy the portions for which he had been responsible.

11. Kenneth Haynes, in Haynes and France (2006), 155.

12. For example, Bruce Graver's demonstration of 'how specific passages of Virgil's [*Georgics*] were translated, retranslated, combined, and finally adapted into Wordsworth's own poetry'. Graver (1991), 138. See also more recently Patterson (2007).

13. Dix (2002), 25.

14. I draw on three sources here: Cornell, Tuckerman (1930); Curtis (1997).

15. Francis Wrangham to William Blackwood, 25 July 1822; National Library of Scotland MS 4009, fols. 280–1.

16. Letter to Francis Wrangham, 7 March 1796; De Selincourt (1935), 153.

Ostensibly, his qualms are about 'personal satire', though he commends Wrangham's portions, which are of a piece with his own in this respect; perhaps his real motives are hidden. He adds that he would not have prevented Wrangham from publishing the whole as his own, but his (Wordsworth's) part in the project was too well known – an observation tending to confirm Wordsworth's public acceptance of his incipient role as Juvenalian satirist in the preceding years.[17] Wrangham held on to the material nevertheless, and many years later, in 1822, sought to publish the imitation, or selections from it – apparently including many of Wordsworth's portions as well as his own – in *Blackwood's Magazine*, without, it seems, contacting Wordsworth further. He sent Blackwood a text and was still reminding him of the idea two years later in a letter of 1824, but for reasons unknown, Blackwood seems to have taken no interest in publishing it. It is in a letter of Wrangham's to Blackwood of 1822, now in the National Library of Scotland, that the first 145 lines of the imitation were discovered. Parts of the finished text we now have are in Wordsworth's hand, parts in Wrangham's, but the covering letters usually indicate who composed what.[18] Sometimes it is a joint effort, and at one point, we are told, Robert Southey contributed two lines (the best two, according to Wordsworth, though dissimilar to most of his own input, as we shall see): 'Heavens! who sees majesty in George's face | Or looks at Norfolk and can dream of Grace?'

The ostensible style, as it were, of this work, like other Juvenal imitations of this date, is very clearly English Augustan. Its form is the heroic couplet; it is not just 'on the plan of Johnson's Third and Tenth' Juvenal Satires (respectively *London*, 1738, and *The Vanity of Human Wishes*, 1749), but often in their idiom, as for example here:

> Still prompt alike to teach and to defend,
> Be of the infant thou, and poor, the friend:
> Severely faithful to the empire's trust,
> On dubious points a witness sternly just.
> Though at thy back frown terror's threatening tribe,
> And Power's stern lictors perjury prescribe,
> Unmoved behold the dungeon and the wheel;
> No falsehood utter, and no truth conceal:
> Nor dare the spotless spirit to survive,
> And forfeit every end of life – to live.
>
> (75–84)[19]

---

17. Wordsworth to Wrangham, 7 November 1806; De Selincourt (1937), 72.
18. The only passage for which Wrangham appears to have been solely responsible is ll. 96–135 (or perhaps 96–145); more than half looks to be Wordsworth's work alone.
19. Line numbering is throughout from Cornell; for the basis of the text itself see the Appendix to this chapter.

The latinate syntactical inversions, the abstractions, the placing of the caesurae: all have the Johnsonian stamp, and are even stiffer than much contemporary verse of the late eighteenth century. This is the corresponding passage from an anonymous version of Juvenal 8 published in 1783, again in rhyming couplets but looser in syntax and more fluid metrically (most lines are not strictly iambic):

> Should Heav'n benignly grant a private sphere,
> May each domestic virtue centre there.
> Dear to your friends, dependants, children, wife,
> Reap the sweet, social charities of life.
> In Terror clad, let stern Oppression frown,
> And dictate falshood: Truth is still your own.
> Smile at her menace; on the torture smile;
> And, when her vengeance labours, mock the toil:
> Life, thus protracted, bears a price too high;
> Lose not the ends of being – dare to die.[20]

In fact, there is one occasion on which the Wordsworth–Wrangham imitation actually absorbs lines from the classic 'Augustan' English rendering of Juvenal 8. This is made evident by the manuscript's quotation marks surrounding the couplet in question:

> 'Erroneously we measure life by breath:
> They do not truly live, who merit death.'
> Though Luxury for their daily feast combine
> Whate'er is rare, from Lapland to the Line;
> For them though all the portals open stand
> Of Health's own temple at her Graham's command;
> And the great High Priest, baffling Death and Sin,
> Earth each immortal idiot to the chin:
> Ask of these wretched beings, worse than dead,
> If on the couch celestial, gold can shed
> The common blessings of a peasant's bed.
>
>   (85–95)

The first couplet is slightly adapted from what was known throughout the eighteenth century as 'Dryden's Juvenal', the famous translation by several hands first published in 1693 under Dryden's editorship (and sampled in Chapter 8). The version of Juvenal 8 in this collection is by the minor poet George Stepney, who at this point had offered:

---

20. Anon. (1783), 14–15 (lines 83–92).

> 'Improperly we measure Life by Breath;
> Such do not truly Live who merit Death;'[21]

The precise reason for the introduction of Stepney's couplet here is uncertain, but its seamless continuity with the ensuing lines demonstrates the stylistic affinities of Wordsworth's work in this passage. The final triplet, as much as anything else, evokes the Drydenian manner.

The stylistic congruity of Wordsworth and Wrangham's composition with the earlier eighteenth-century tradition represented, as far as Juvenal is concerned, by Samuel Johnson's two famous imitations *London* (1738) and *The Vanity of Human Wishes* (1749) is clear. Wordsworth and Wrangham's work is far from unique in this: Juvenal was very much an available model at this date, and his imitators have a strong tendency to adopt the formal couplets and many other qualities of his eighteenth-century English followers. Satires in the style of Juvenal, often specifically imitations or modernizations of individual Juvenal poems, are produced throughout the second half of the eighteenth century, climaxing in a surge over the years from the French Revolution to 1820. A similar surge affects the figures for translations of Juvenal, of which the best complete ones in the period are William Gifford's of 1802 and Francis Hodgson's of 1807. But no full-length imitations of Juvenal seem to have been published in the decade from 1822 to 1832, and indeed satire in general begins a slow decline as an independent genre not many years into the nineteenth century, almost disappearing towards the latter date.[22]

I want now to complicate the picture by outlining a number of further ways in which Wordsworth's imitation of Juvenal 8 stands at significant intersections in literary history and prompts questions about the received account of this period. All the terms here – 'imitation', 'Juvenalian', 'satire' – refer to phenomena our understanding of whose place in Wordsworth's era has been determined by the forces of reception, and one might say the same applies to our sense of the shape and significance of Wordsworth's work itself.

We might begin with translation and imitation. Wordsworth is known for neither, and they are usually understood to be much more of a neoclassical habit (Dryden, Pope, Johnson) than a Romantic one. Yet a survey of Greek and Latin translations and imitations published in the decade of Wordsworth's Juvenal, the

---

21. Dryden *et al.* (1754), 122. The inverted commas appear thus in Stepney also. The reason Wordsworth took over his couplet may be that he gave up trying to make sense of Juvenal at this point: Stepney's note *ad loc* informs us that 'This and the seven following Verses are a sort of Paraphrase … because the Sense of the Author is too close and obscure.'
22. I draw here and in what follows on the principal reassessment of satire in the Romantic period to date, Dyer (1997). See p. 43 for some statistics on Juvenalian translation and imitation in Dyer's period. For the second half of the eighteenth century, see Whitford (1928), 9–16.

1790s, would show an extensive output of varied kinds, from pedagogical aids, through hugely popular performances like Tom Moore's Anacreon (1800), to works still being read today such as Cowper's Homer (1791). Virgil was in this decade translated into English twice entire, and there were further separate translations of the *Aeneid*, of the *Georgics* and two of the *Eclogues*.[23] As for Juvenal, the decade previous to Wordsworth's first work on Satire 8 saw the appearance of two complete translations.[24]

Or we might ask about satire. Although the output of satire starts to decline not far into the nineteenth century, the underplaying of Romantic satire in literary-historical narratives has been remarkable. As Marilyn Butler has wryly observed, 'the so-called Romantics did not know at the time that they were supposed to do without satire', even if 'future generations have become convinced that the Spirit of the Age was very different'.[25] Hundreds of satirical works were in fact published in the era, in both verse and prose; in verse at least they make up a very considerable proportion of new titles published.[26] Nor are their authors by any means always minor writers. The downplaying of all this material set in as early as the Victorians, for whom, according to Gary Dyer, the appeal of satire was restricted 'in particular by the ideology of the ever-growing middle-class Dissenting and Methodist subculture'; 'members of this subculture preferred to avoid "personal" attack because it caused pain and arrogantly usurped God's privileges'.[27]

Within the possible generic range of satire, the choice of Juvenal as a model for imitation in 1795 is also significant, because Juvenal occupied a certain place in the literary culture of the mid-1790s. The very act of imitating Juvenal in itself positions Wordsworth and Wrangham with respect to predecessors and contemporaries – we have already seen a simple illustration of Wrangham's awareness of this, in his reference to Johnson's Juvenal as furnishing their 'plan'. Their informal diction and lightness of tone tell us that reformist authors like Moore or Leigh Hunt tend as satirists to work in the Horatian mode. Juvenalian satirists such as William Gifford, who in 1802 became the next English Juvenal translator, on the other hand, deploy formal rhetoric and heroic couplets. Juvenalian satire had conservative associations, partly because of its nostalgic tendency (it typically tilts at innovation in order to save an institution presented as ruinous), partly because

---

23. Details in Gillespie (2009), 222–3.

24. Edward Owen, *The Satires*, 2 vols (London, 1785, reissued 1786); Martin Madan, *A New Translation of Juvenal and Persius*, 2 vols (London, 1789, reissued Dublin, 1795). For a full listing of classical translations in English for the century, see Gillespie (2009).

25. Butler (1984), 209.

26. For some statistics see Dyer, 12. He claims (with some caveats) that 30 satirical poems in book form were issued in 1812, against 134 volumes of original poetry of any kind; in 1820, 60 out of 201.

27. Dyer (1997), 6, citing Jane Taylor's *Essays in Rhyme, on Morals and Manners* (London, 1816).

it was normally realized in English verse of a type perceived as traditional, and partly even because writers who adopted its mode usually had strong ties to the upper classes.[28]

If the choice of Juvenal as a satirical model is significant, so too, of course, is the choice of Juvenal's Eighth Satire. Earlier priorities for Juvenal's English imitators and translators had been different. Satire 6, on women, had been an especially popular choice for them in the seventeenth and earlier eighteenth centuries; then from the mid-eighteenth century, partly no doubt on grounds of decorum, versions of it seem to have appeared solely within complete translations. But among 15 full-length imitations of one or other of Juvenal's 16 satires which belong to the years 1789–1832, we find a wholly disproportionate number, fully a third, are versions of Satire 8, on the degeneracy of the Roman nobility.[29] Wordsworth (not included in this figure) was not alone. Indeed, his is not the most impressive of the versions, though it might have become so with further polish.[30]

Wordsworth himself, and the place of his work in our narratives of an era, is the final reception issue here, and what may strike us most when we contemplate such accidents as the survival or non-survival of manuscript compositions is the sometimes quirky nature of history's choices. Wordsworth has for a long time been established as the representative poet of his age. This is not accidental, but accident has played its part, and if Byron or Coleridge had been accorded this role, how different literary history would seem. Deliberate as well as unconscious manipulation of the record has had its effect. For example, Wordsworth scholars have long been aware of the loss of *The Somersetshire Tragedy*, Wordsworth's poem describing the brutal murder of a retarded woman by her husband. One manuscript was deliberately destroyed by Wordsworth's early editor William Knight (n. 1), and the only other known copy also ended up in a grate in 1931.[31] The custodians of these manuscripts could not reconcile this poem with the Wordsworth they recognized. Any other Wordsworth has been that much harder to imagine ever since.

The outlines of the corpus would also look different if Wordsworth had made his appearance in the otherwise unproductive (for him) 1820s as a published Juvenalian satirist, with what, if Wrangham had had his way, would have been a fully polished version of our text, and as a translator of Virgil. Only one 100-line segment of his *Aeneid*, a translation which took Wordsworth through the first

---

28. Dyer (1997), 53–5, elaborates on all three points.

29. Dyer (1997), 179–80 n. 32 for statistics, and further contemporary use of Satire 8. Dyer's figures for versions of Satire 8 are if anything an underestimate.

30. The wittiest though not necessarily the most Juvenalian of the Satire 8 imitations is the anonymous *High Birth* (London, 1821), evidently written by a Whig with an intimate knowledge of the milieu he was satirizing. Thus for 87–8 we get: 'If the long-wished for, long-expected call | At length shall hail thee, Viceroy of Bengal ...'.

31. Knight (1892–9), I, xxxvii. See for further discussion Gill (1998), 226, 309.

three Books of the epic in 1823, was published in his lifetime, in a short-lived journal.[32] Again, the whole text did not appear until De Selincourt's Wordsworth of the 1940s. Yet this imitation is the longest new composition for which Wordsworth was responsible after the publication of *The Excursion*, and it drew the interest and respect of every classical scholar to whom the poet showed it. As for Juvenal, notwithstanding Wordsworth's rejection of his plans, Wrangham appears to have been prevented only by Blackwood's lack of interest from publishing most if not all of the imitation. Had Blackwood responded otherwise in the 1820s, Wordsworth might have tried to disown the composition, but the record would inevitably read differently – with effects not only on Wordsworth's reception both contemporary and subsequent, but potentially on the literary history of his period more widely, as narrated over the next two centuries.

◆   ◆   ◆

And today? All the dominant schools of English Romantic scholarship have for decades now been historicist, especially New Historicist.[33] Scholars and critics have made deliberate and extensive efforts to implicate writers of this era in the social and political world of their time at every level, often with clearly fruitful results and sometimes with highly questionable ones. Wordsworth, for example, has been presented in one recent study as having operated as a government spy.[34] If the young poet's possible role as a subcontracted messenger for the secret service in Hamburg holds any real significance for his writings, Wordsworth's major work potentially turns into farce: how is it possible to compose an epic on the growth of the poet's mind if the poet is a spy, an impostor?

These are not the only terms on which we can read Romantic literature, and a modernized version of a Juvenalian satire is an especially rich context in which to examine our expectations. This is because of the diverse views that may be taken of Juvenal's relation to the social and political materials with which his satires seem filled. It is evident that in Wordsworth's time Juvenal was regarded, as we would probably no longer choose to regard him today, as an earnest moral crusader, deeply enmeshed in the decadent Roman world of his era. 'His great aim,' wrote the French revolutionary Jean Dusaulx approvingly, 'was to alarm the vicious, and if possible, to exterminate vice.'[35] Wordsworth's understanding of Juvenal's motives may well have been along these lines. But although a translator is not bound to work under the sway of (or even to form) an overall view of the source author's

---

32. For details and fuller assessment of the translation see Graver (1986*b*) and pp.152–4 below.

33. Chandler (1999) exemplifies the new historicist approach applied to Romanticism. For a critical overview of its strengths and weaknesses, see Brannigan (1998).

34. Johnston (1998); Johnston has since retracted his claim.

35. Gifford's translation, quoting Dusaulx in the 'Essay on the Roman Satirists' which prefaces his Juvenal; Gifford (1802), liii.

moral priorities, he is forced to pay close attention to his author's techniques and to decide, in thousands of instances, how to represent them coherently.

In order to accomplish whatever purpose he may have (be it reforming, entertaining or otherwise), Juvenal rarely attacks vicious or foolish contemporaries, telling us in a prominent passage in Satire 1 that he prefers to turn his attention to the dead.[36] Satire 8 mentions many names, but they are mostly the family names (*cognomens*) of the Roman nobility. Are we then to read him as targeting particular contemporary individuals by implication (if not by name), or is his eye on something other than the contemporary scene? Either way, would an imitator have to follow the same course? As a translator, Gifford was concerned to insist that his 1802 rendering contained 'no allusions, covert or open, to the follies and vices of modern times'.[37] But Wordsworth and Wrangham were engaged upon something different in precisely this respect: an imitation, meaning, in effect, 'modernization'. Just how implicated in 'modern times' is their work?

Wordsworth and Wrangham's modern editors, whose activity in the last decade of the twentieth century forms one of the latest phases in the reception of Wordsworth's Juvenal (and indeed of Juvenal too), are in no doubt of the answer to this question. The imitation, they suppose, was for Wordsworth 'a Juvenalian attack on the social and political leaders of the country' motivated by 'contempt for abusers of privilege and power'. They go further: 'The wit and ingenuity that the two poets displayed in finding moral equivalents for the persons and situations in Juvenal's satire contribute much to the interest of their *Imitation*, and their own savoring of this aspect of their work emerges tacitly alongside their moral purpose' (Cornell 791, 787). Accordingly, the Cornell edition very directly and very consistently presents the text in this light.

The opening of the imitation is construed as being directed towards two individuals. In this passage (jointly by Wordsworth and Wrangham) a side interest is the gothic cast the verse takes on at this early point, qualifying the overall adherence to Augustan norms. But we shall focus on the asterisks:

> What boots it, * * , that thy princely blood
> Has pour'd through time's dark waste it's glittering flood?
> That the huge tree within thy banner'd hall
> Spreads it's luxuriant arms athwart the wall;
> And with fantastic fruit profusely blooms –
> Dukes, Bishops, Masters of the Horse, and Grooms?
> What boot thy galleries, whose grim warrior train
> Have frown'd on time and hostile brooms in vain:[38]

36. I. 150–71, on which see further below.
37. Gifford (1802), lxiv.
38. 'Brooms' is for Juvenal's *uirga*, 7, making the translated line refer to a cleaning implement. Most translators, however, take *uirga* to refer to the 'branches' of the family tree.

> Or, blazon'd on yon monumental pile,
> That signs armorial mock the herald's toil;
> Where cross-legg'd knights by broken shields repose,
> Some without ears and more with half a nose?
> If near that fane (where, breathing Virtue's praise,
> In marble live the Good of former days)
> With ready voice, as place or passion leads,
> You vote, and Nature at each artery bleeds?
> If from gay rooms, where speaking pictures tell
> How Douglas conquer'd and how Falkland fell,
> Worn by the dice to slumber you repair,
> Just when their trumpets roused the morning air?
>
> (1–20)

Who is being addressed here? Juvenal's Ponticus, named in line 1 of the Latin, is a generic figure, though not exactly a fictional one. The name suggests someone with a noble ancestor who had triumphed in Pontus (in Asia Minor), and various individuals with that cognomen are known from the historical record. But none of them is hidden behind the name, because Juvenal blurs the singular (the individual) with the plural (the family), as John Henderson explains: 'the bearer of the name *Ponticus* is, in principle, just one "still" in the full-length feature-film of the *Pontici*, a would-be extra in a crowd of doubles'.[39] Juvenal's referent is not an individual Roman contemporary. That means an imitator need not fix on any particular target, and this may seem to be exactly why Wordsworth/Wrangham's asterisks are introduced here.

The Cornell editors think differently. For them, this passage 'seems to reflect the characters and status of two leading members of the nobility: Charles Howard (1746–1815), eleventh Duke of Norfolk … and Hugh Percy (1742–1817), second Duke of Northumberland'. They are forced to concede that they do not know how two different names could be represented by one set of asterisks, but, on the other hand, the apparent inappropriateness of either figure as an exemplar of a young blade who, for example, stays up all night playing dice (both these men would have been about fifty in 1795) is not seen as an obstacle to their hypothesis. Copious annotations to these opening 20 lines show beyond a doubt that Charles Howard and Hugh Percy (or at least members of their families) threw parties, played at dice and cards, and owned pictures. To these proofs of identity are added some specifics on their family chapels: Robert Southey once remarked the Percys' folly in displaying their family tree in the chapel (but the 'tree' of line

---

39. Henderson (1997), 33, who adds that the name frequently appears in satirical contexts in Martial. The question of whether Martial might have been referring to a real-life figure a generation previously is a different one.

3 is in the hall), and the Norfolk chapel was damaged by the Roundheads (but the damaged statuary in lines 11–12 is mounted externally on the house – 'on yon monumental pile' – and not internally within the chapel). Beyond this, a claim is advanced that Norfolk had 'touched [Wordsworth's] life in important and lasting ways'. This turns out to refer to Wordsworth's uncle having been a 'supporter' of Norfolk, which 'may have contributed to' the reluctance of his 'Tory rival' Lord Lonsdale to pay a debt he once owed Wordsworth's father (Cornell 787n.). Clearly, none of this evidence has supportive force for either identification, but at least it does not undermine them. A further detail, however, seems to tend in just this direction. The two family names 'Percy' and 'Howard' are explicitly deployed shortly hereafter, at line 44 ('Thou more than Percy, more than Howard, hail!'), which corresponds to Juvenal's 'salve Gaetulice, seu tu | Silanus' (26–7), two names signifying high virtue – 'If you prove yourself genuinely virtuous,' say Wordsworth and Juvenal, 'then I shall hail you by comparing you to such as these.' How this can be squared with the reading of the asterisks which the Cornell editors set out to establish is not a matter of which they undertake clarification, but it may explain why these names first swam into their view.

In this case the Grub Street asterisks (used at two or three other points in the imitation as well) seem to the Cornell editors to sanction their speculations. Let us next consider the use not of asterisks but of actual names. Juvenal's satires are full of names, although (as noted above) he declares in the programmatic Satire 1 that he will not attack contemporaries, but instead 'experiar quid concedatur in illos, | quorum Flaminia tegitur cinis atque Latina' ('try what I may say of those worthies whose ashes lie under the Flaminian and Latin roads', 170–1). An interlocutor (1.153–68) suggests Lucilius, his predecessor in satire, was wrong not to care whom he attacked: not only can it be dangerous for the satirist, it inflicts hurt on the victims too. Juvenal replies (in Gilbert Highet's paraphrase): 'Then I shall use names drawn from the past': that is, 'The vice will be living, but it will wear a death-mask.'[40] And Juvenal's readers have often believed him on this point.[41] He is remarkable not for attacking contemporaries, but for representing long-dead historical figures as alive.[42] This means that there would, in fact, have been reason for Wordsworth and Wrangham to look elsewhere for a satirical model if one

---

40. Highet (1954), 57. Highet's wider discussion of names in Juvenal at 289–94 is still worth consulting, but for the naming of names in Satire 8 in particular see Henderson (1997), *passim*. I return to the issue of Juvenal's naming of targets below.

41. For recent scepticism about Juvenal's (or his persona's) claim, see among others Braund (1988), 201 n. 22.

42. Line 39 of Satire 8 is a good example. This passage is omitted in the Wordsworth–Wrangham imitation. Courtney (1980), 383, comments: 'virtually all the noble families named in this satire were by now extinct or in total obscurity ... yet see how Juvenal gives advice to one long dead at 39'. Henderson (1997), 31, argues that with the help of Juvenal's 'generalizing plural' such names attain to exemplarity.

of their principal aims was to name and shame, in Popean fashion, their contemporaries. Once again, we must judge by what actually happens.

Wordsworth's imitation, leaving aside the supplementary 28 lines printed at the end by our editors,[43] contains by my count 40 personal names, two of which are those of entirely fictional characters. Of the other 38, about three-quarters (27) belong to historical or occasionally mythical figures. In other cases, naturally enough in a poem dealing with declining families, the name (as we have seen with 'Percy' and 'Howard', 44) refers not to an individual but a family over a long period, very much in Juvenal's manner of alluding to ancient houses. Only eight names belong specifically to contemporary individuals, and of these, three are referred to positively or neutrally. Thus, in 278 lines, only five contemporaries appear to be satirically targeted by name. One of these is a quack doctor (l. 90). A total of four members of the nobility remain.[44] Clearly this imitation is in this respect a *Vanity of Human Wishes* and not a *Dunciad*.

A Juvenalian passage (182ff.) containing several proper names concerns degenerate practices associated with the stage and other public spectacles, and here the technique is typical of Juvenalian satire where names are concerned. Patricians, who once would rather have died, now appear in shameful roles in comedies;

> Nec tamen ipsi
> ignoscas populo; populi frons durior huius
> qui sedet et spectat triscurria patriciorum
> planipedes audit Fabios, videre potest qui
> Mamercorum alapas.
>
> (183–92)[45]

(Nor yet can you acquit the people themselves from blame, whose brows are hardened as they sit spectators of the buffooneries of patricians, listen to the Fabii barefoot, and laugh at the slaps on the faces of the Mamerci.)

The two ancient houses of the Fabii and Mamerci are supplied as the objects of the satirist's scorn here. Let us follow what happens to them in Wordsworth's (at this point unpolished) response:

---

43. Wordsworth himself doubted whether these lines of his were suitable for the imitation, noting in his covering letter to Wrangham that they contained 'not a syllable correspondent to … Juvenal' (Wordsworth to Wrangham, 20 November 1795). The passage names *inter alia* George III and the Duke of Norfolk, but these names occur within the couplet contributed by Southey (above).
44. These four are George III (named at 266), his second son the Duke of York (at 157), the Duke of Norfolk (211), and apparently – though the sense is not fully clear – one of the Percys (at 162).
45. Juvenal is quoted in this chapter from the text Wordsworth probably used (see Wu (1993–5), I, 80): Juvenal (1683), with contractions expanded.

> How throngs the crowd to yon theatric school
> To see an English lord enact a fool?
> What wonder? – on my soul 'twould split a tub
> To see the arch grimace of Marquis Scrub:
> Nor safe the petticoats of dames that hear
> The box resound on Viscount Buffo's ear.
>
> (184–9)

Wordsworth has used the names of familiar fictional characters. 'Scrub' alludes to the man-of-all-work in Farquhar's comedy *The Beaux' Stratagem*. The name of Buffo ('buffoon') can be found in more than one source, but the best known would have been Pope's *Epistle to Arbuthnot*. So much, one might suppose, for contemporary individuals. But our editors, nothing daunted, find one here all the same. They contrive to read lines 184–5, 'How throngs the crowd to yon theatric school | To see an English lord enact a fool', as a satirical reference to George Hobart, Earl of Buckingham, commenting that 'Hobart, before his elevation to the peerage, was "a conductor of the opera-entertainment," and in June 1795 he and his wife took part in amateur theatricals at Brandenburgh House.' But plainly, none of this offers support for the identification. Hobart was not 'an English lord' at the time he conducted operas. Wordsworth does not mention conducting but acting. No 'crowds' are present at private theatricals. A private house cannot be described by the term 'theatric school'.

Landon and Curtis, in the only complete edition of this poem ever made available to Wordsworth scholars, have been thorough in their trawling of contextual and collateral material from the years around 1795, and their presentation of Wordsworth's Juvenal in its light. They may have begun reading the imitation as what they call 'a Juvenalian attack on the social and political leaders of the country' because their training or the critical *Zeitgeist* predisposed them to do so, but the way they have attempted to develop and enforce that reading is through serious work. Nevertheless, theirs is clearly a reading which will in its turn be overtaken by another phase in the reception history of this imitation, because it is very easy to discern its bias. Their own annotations reveal that a high proportion of the persons and institutions 'boldly identified' (Cornell 797) belong to a point in time some decades (and regularly many centuries) in the past. They are forced to conclude that others cannot be securely identified at all. But where there seems the smallest scope for the kind of reading they want, it is exploited to the fullest.

They are, as we have seen, much exercised by the asterisks introduced by Wordsworth and Wrangham where proper nouns might be expected. But because they do not allow that the asterisks might represent no *particular* name, a certain awkwardness always tends to arise. The next point at which asterisks appear corresponds to the start of Juvenal's lively character sketch (lines 146ff.) of Lateranus, a dandy of Nero's reign (in the previous century); this must be a thrust at the frivolity of the scions of the ancient nobility. This is the Wordsworth/Wrangham version:

> Close by the dome, where * * sate, to awe
> The house of taxes, turnpike-roads, and law –
> With six-in-hand, to make the cockneys stare,
> His grandson whirls; in daylight's broadest glare
> Would meet without a blush e'en Wilberforce,
> And crack his whip, and whistle to his horse.
>
> (136–41)

William Wilberforce, the famous politician and philanthropist, is explicitly named here, but plainly as a type of the upright man of the public world – he lends no assistance in the quest for contemporary satirical targets. Landon and Curtis's interpretation of this passage is based instead on a few elements one might think generic enough: the ancestor (or grandfather) was a Member of Parliament; the young man drives the eighteenth-century equivalent of a Porsche, a six-in-hand; he is a braggart and he is brass-necked. Our editors, however, firmly identify the name behind the asterisks as 'Stanhope' and the scion as Henry Barry, eighth Earl of Barrymore. We can see that what set them off was probably a reference to 'six-in-hands' and 'four-in-hands' in some contemporary gossip on the Barrymore family. Their three notes (in full) inform us:

> The portrait is of Henry Barry (1770–1824), eighth Earl of Barrymore who succeeded his brother and fellow rake, Richard, in 1793. Both were noted "whips" (see John Robert Robinson, *The Last Earls of Barrymore* [London, 1894]).
>
> The asterisks must represent 'Stanhope.' Henry Barry's maternal grandfather William Stanhope, second Earl of Harrington, had been a member of Parliament, though possibly the reference here is to his more notable great-grandfather, William Stanhope, first Earl of Harrington, who, besides being a member of Parliament, had a distinguished military and diplomatic career.
>
> Richard Barry drove a six-in-hand, but after his death, Henry, succeeding to a depleted estate, apparently had to content himself with a four-in-hand. The *MP* of January 10, 1794, remarks, 'What a *blank* must that man's mind be, who conceived, that turning a corner neatly in a Phaeton and four is the greatest achievement of the age …,' and the same journal refers on February 12 to Lord Barrymore's being soon to drive a four-in-hand, adding an ironic comment on the "achievements of our young nobility." Robinson, cited above, quotes anecdotes that show the high-handed behaviour of both brothers toward anyone who might impede their progress along the road.[46]

Not the least of the problems here is that given the institution of hereditary peerage, one or both grandfathers of almost any young nobleman will tend to have been a Member of Parliament (that is, of the House of Lords), simply by virtue of having been himself a nobleman. The slippage in the evidence between the two brothers – it will be observed that the wrong one is said to have driven

---

46. Cornell, 803.

the six-in-hand – is a type of slippage familiar in New Historicist interpretation. The Wordsworth–Wrangham passage does not say that either brother was a bad or high-handed driver, so the last detail cannot help enforce the identification. But worst of all, sitting in 'the dome' (which goes curiously unglossed by Landon and Curtis) would imply that the ancestor was not a lord at all, but Dean of St Paul's.

I shall not dwell much longer on the Cornell Wordsworth, but what is most striking overall, beyond the ingenuity with which they prosecute it, is the extremely strong predisposition of Wordsworth's most recent editors to prefer this type of reading. Of their determination there can be no doubt. Who would imagine that Wrangham's line 123, 'In the red field of Hastings seek thy Sire', as well as alluding to the Norman origins of the English nobility, may harbour 'an ironical reference to Warren Hastings'? The supporting evidence is that 20 lines earlier Wrangham referred to 'Benares', a city whose overlord was 'heavily taxed by Warren Hastings ... the first British Governor General in India' (Cornell *ad* 123, 102). Who would guess that in the lines on a young dandy, 'Some spruce man-milliner, of the band-box fry, | Has wing'd the bot into a butterfly' (Wordsworth/Wrangham 144–5) there lurks a French pun? 'Bot' is in English a kind of parasitical worm, and this seems to fit rather well with the sense evidently required; but if we read it as a pun on the French word for 'club[foot]', we can turn the line into a further allusion to the clubfooted eighth Earl of Barrymore (Cornell *ad* 145). The self-evident far-fetchedness of these claims goes to show how much effort the editors had to put in to maintain their stance. What is most remarkable is the overwhelmingness of their predisposition.

The Wordsworth–Wrangham imitation of Juvenal 8 is certainly a modernization of the Latin poem. It is certainly outspoken and indignant. It does name a handful of extremely prominent public contemporaries. But the only currently available presentation of it, by turning it into a satire in which 'most of the figures are identified boldly by name or by implication' (Cornell 787), and much of the 'interest' of which in fact revolves around such identifications, has made it harder for us to hear Wordsworth's dialogue with Juvenal. Wordsworth's imitation has more to tell us about Juvenal than this, because it is in these respects much more like Juvenal than its editors allow. Here another Juvenal translator, Dryden, offers guidance.

Dryden's long essay prefacing his 1693 translations of Juvenal and Persius, the *Discourse concerning the Original and Progress of Satire*, 'still', as William Frost writes three centuries later, 'the chief discussion in English of satire in verse',[47] stresses that Juvenal's reluctance to criticize contemporaries can be seen as traditional and responsible, rather than, as it was sometimes seen, evasive and pusillanimous. Dryden first reminds his readers that, in Latin, 'satire' is not the same as 'invective'. Properly speaking, Dryden goes on, 'invective Poems', the sort

---

47. Frost (1988), 41.

of satire in which individuals are named and shamed, belongs to the genre of 'lampoon', which he characterizes as

> a dangerous sort of Weapon, and for the most part Unlawful. We have no moral right on the reputation of other men. 'Tis taking from them, what we cannot restore to them. There are only two Reasons, for which we may be permitted to write Lampoons; and I will not promise that they can always justifie us: The first is Revenge, when we have been affronted in the same Nature, or have been any ways notoriously abus'd, and can make our selves no other Reparation. And yet we know, that, in Christian Charity, all Offences are to be forgiven.

Naming and shaming are by no means securely permitted, for reasons of potential injustice to the victim. Dryden outlines another possible exception, applicable to Juvenal:

> The second Reason ... is when [a Person] has become a Publick Nuisance. All those, whom *Horace* in his Satires, and *Persius* and *Juvenal* have mentioned in theirs, with a brand of Infamy, are wholly such ... But how few Lampooners are there now living, who are capable of this Duty! ... good God, how remote they are in common Justice, from the choice of such Persons as are the proper Subject of Satire! And how little Wit they bring, for the support of their injustice! ... There can be no pleasantry where there is no Wit: no Impression can be made, where there is no Truth for the Foundation.[48]

Some of this sounds very like what Wordsworth wrote in his 1806 letter to Wrangham. Wordsworth too disavows personal satire, with the possible exception of individuals who have become 'public nuisances':

> I have long since come to a fixed resolution to steer clear of personal satire; in fact I never will have anything to do with it as far as concerns the *private* vices of individuals on any account; with respect to public delinquents or offenders I will not say the same; though I should be slow to meddle even with these.[49]

From this it emerges that what Dryden endorsed as Juvenal's stance was what Wordsworth subscribed to as well. Indeed, it is, if we are to give Dryden any credence, the traditional satirist's posture.

◆ ◆ ◆

To return, then, to my opening questions about what difference this imitation makes to the reception of Juvenal and of Wordsworth. In imitating Juvenal at all,

---

48. Dryden (1956–2000), IV, 59–60.
49. De Selincourt (1937), 72. It remains a puzzle that these principles are advanced as reasons for leaving the ten-year-old Juvenal imitation unpublished. Wordsworth's memory may have been hazy: he adds that since he has no copy of his own portions, he 'could not possibly judge of the effect of the whole' (*ibid.*).

in selecting a classical Roman model, Wordsworth presents by no means his most familiar face – but one we ignore at the risk of complacency. Since this imitation can be seen as the early manifestation of a long-term aspect of Wordsworth's work (his classicism), its appearance in print in or near his lifetime might very possibly have made the other manifestations fall into place within a coherent (and durable) new view of the corpus. While we sometimes speak casually of 'rewriting history', its concrete hardens quickly, and something like a full-scale paradigm shift can be required if categories as venerable as 'neoclassical' and 'Romantic' are to undergo any genuine reconsideration, however vaguely or pluralistically we use them.

In imitating Juvenal in this particular fashion, Wordsworth's version challenges us again, to say how we see Juvenal, and how we suppose Juvenalian satire works. Is it by lashing out at egregious individual exemplars, or by exaggeration to the point of fantasy, or perhaps more performatively, by creating strategies that force the reader's reflection or point at the reader's implication? The Wordsworth Juvenal imitation might not be a polished poem, but it is already more than a mere occasion to lampoon individuals by ventriloquizing Juvenal. That is to say, Wordsworth can be seen engaging in a dialogue with Juvenal, working with the conscious manoeuvres the Latin poem enacts. This makes the imitation, for us, a way of reading Juvenal.

Finally, the sudden, and therefore highly visible, assimilation of Wordsworth's Juvenal to currently dominant interpretative modes and models provides a consciousness-raising moment for all those ambitious of interpreting formal verse satires whether ancient or modern. In the previous chapter I tried to suggest how revealing the recovery of lost translations and imitations can be in itself. In this case, the reception such a recovered text has been accorded proves equally thought-provoking.

Appendix[50]

The Wordsworth–Wrangham Satire 8

What boots it, * *, that thy princely blood
Has pour'd through time's dark waste it's glittering flood?

---

50. The reference text of the imitation reproduced here is based on a fresh examination of the manuscripts, which has largely had the effect of confirming the accuracy of the Cornell editors' transcription work. My views on the ordering of the imitation's *disiecta membra* are also in close accord with theirs, including the impossibility of positioning the stray 28-line passage which is here printed at the end. Landon and Curtis (1997) remains the edition to consult for full details on such matters as apparent lacunae, and for details of manuscript readings silently adjusted below to accord with normal usage of this period in terms of punctuation, etc.

Between lines, asterisks indicate points at which surviving textual material has been conjoined.

That the huge tree within thy banner'd hall
Spreads it's luxuriant arms athwart the wall;
And with fantastic fruit profusely blooms –
Dukes, Bishops, Masters of the Horse, and Grooms?
What boot thy galleries, whose grim warrior train
Have frown'd on time and hostile brooms in vain:
Or, blazon'd on yon monumental pile,
That signs armorial mock the herald's toil; 10
Where cross-legg'd knights by broken shields repose,
Some without ears and more with half a nose?
If near that fane (where, breathing Virtue's praise,
In marble live the Good of former days)
With ready voice, as place or passion leads,
You vote, and Nature at each artery bleeds?
If from gay rooms, where speaking pictures tell
How Douglas conquer'd and how Falkland fell,
Worn by the dice to slumber you repair,
Just when their trumpets roused the morning air? 20

* * *

Go, plunge thyself in mausoleum glooms,
'Mid kindred 'scutcheons and recording tombs;
The phantoms of thine ancestry pursue,
Till the long line's first shade elude thy view:
Then let this truth sink deep into thy mind –
'The virtuous only are of noble kind.'
Be mild in manners, and in morals pure,
As Camden independent, firm as More:
Let these, before thee marching still take place
Of all the proud memorials of thy race; 30
Let these, or men like these, the seals precede,
And to the Law's unsullied temple lead.

O grant me, Deity, full power to scan
Th'eternal sacrifice man owes to man;
That sacred debt, which toil through every day
And thought through every night alone can pay.
Hast thou, through life, tenaciously referr'd
To truth and justice every deed and word?
Roused all thy faculties, and bade them tend
Right to the good of all, their one sole end – 40
Convinced that to thy kind belongs alone,
And not to thee, what most thou call'st thine own?
Then fear not aught be wanting in thy scale:
Thou more than Percy, more than Howard, hail!

So will I deem thee, of whatever blood;
Heaven made thee noble, when it made thee good.
Illustrious gift! A Nation at thy name
Spreads all her hands, and triumphs in thy fame;
And loud huzzas, for once with unbought sound,
To the glad Thames proclaim a Patriot found.   50

* * *

The lapdog sleek, my Lady's dearer mate,
That sleeps within her bed and feeds on plate,
Is Pompey, Caesar, or – if these appear
Accents too bloodless for a modern ear,
Suwarrow, Buonaparte, Robespierre.
Such the caprice of names! not such be thine,
Doom'd only by antithesis to shine.

* * *

For half a realm two rival Scots dispute,
And law rejoices in the endless suit.
A Samson in some Thurlow shall be found,   60
That law's eternal riddle to expound.
See ardent Wolfe to bleak St. Lawrence fly,
And brave with wasted form a polar sky;
Blest, as his standards wave on Abra'm's Height,
In victory's lap to close his lingering sight:
Whilst thou art but the tail of * *'s line,
Ape of thy barber's block – were barber thine:
In all, this parallel of heads is good,
Save that thine frowns in lead and his in wood!

* * *

  Would'st thou to Wisdom's genuine praise aspire,   70
That Wisdom ever backward to admire?
Like Howard, urged by energy sublime
Tempt and exhaust the rage of every clime:
Then from bright virtue's eminence &c.

* * *

Still prompt alike to teach and to defend,
Be of the infant thou, and poor, the friend:
Severely faithful to the empire's trust,
On dubious points a witness sternly just.

Though at thy back frown terror's threatening tribe,
And Power's stern lictors perjury prescribe,   80
Unmoved behold the dungeon and the wheel;
No falsehood utter, and no truth conceal:
Nor dare the spotless spirit to survive,
And forfeit every end of life – to live.
'Erroneously we measure life by breath:
They do not truly live, who merit death.'
Though Luxury for their daily feast combine
What'er is rare, from Lapland to the Line;
For them though all the portals open stand
Of Health's own temple at her Graham's command;   90
And the great High Priest, baffling Death and Sin,
Earth each immortal idiot to the chin:
Ask of these wretched beings, worse than dead,   ⎫
If on the couch celestial, gold can shed   ⎬
The common blessings of a peasant's bed.   ⎭

* * *

Less deep, poor India! were the wounds that gored
Thy bosom, recent from the Mongul sword.
For not at once Oppression's bloody goad
Drove joy and plenty from their long abode;
Or Mirth refused to wing the languid noon,   100
When on the rice-field beat the fierce monsoon.
The pilgrim, journeying to Benares' towers
Fearless outspread his stores by tombs and bowers:
Nor wanted wealth the pagod's inner pride,
That glitter'd frequent o'er the holy tide –
Shrines, where Devotion's pious hand had wreathed
Her countless gems; and hallow'd ivory breathed.

* * *

Prudence whispers that too sharp a thong
May scourge those shoulders, which though bare are strong.
Even Avarice, forced to leave the wretched soil   110
(For her own ends) its implements of toil,
Has learn'd to dread the vengeance lurking there,
Pikes in the scythe, and musquets in the share.

* * *

Be it thy care, with trusty friends and trie[d,]
O'er India's patient millions to preside;

No contract-thriving minion to oppress
Her meagre sons, and batten on distress;
While in gilt palanquin he sweeps the street,
With subject Nabobs crouching at his feet –
Then claim thou nearest kin with noblest line: 120
I own the link; thy bearings are divine.
If to remotest times thy mind aspire,
In the red field of Hastings seek thy Sire:
Through mustier annals dart thine eagle eyes,
And choose the warrior whence thy stem shall rise;
Nay soar to heavenly ancestry, and trace
Through Adam up to God thy genuine race.
But if thy fiendlike thirst of murther yell
'Whips, racks, and torture! Flog the scoundrels well!'
Till the scourge galls the beadle's hand, though rough;   130
And the life-poising surgeon cries, 'Enough' –
Then blasted by thyself, whate'er thy name,
Hengist nor Adam can redeem it's fame:
They but inflame thy guilt, that one so bred
With bastard blood should slur the virtuous dead.

* * *

Close by the dome, where * * sate, to awe
The house of taxes, turnpike-roads, and law –
With six-in-hand, to make the cockneys stare,
His grandson whirls; in daylight's broadest glare
Would meet without a blush e'en Wilberforce,   140
And crack his whip, and whistle to his horse.
At night how changed! Him haply has array'd
Some French friseur, all prattle and pomade:
Some spruce man-milliner, of the band-box fry,
Has wing'd the bot into a butterfly.
But whence this gall, this lengthened face of woe?
We were no saints at twenty – be it so.
Yet happy they who in life's latter scene
Need only blush for what they once have been
Who pushed by thoughtless youth to deeds of shame   150
'Mid such bad daring sought a coward's name.
I grant that not in parents' hearts alone
A stripling's years may for his faults atone.
So would I plead for York – but long disgrace
And Moore and Partridge stare me in the face.
Alas 'twas other cause than lack of years
That moistened Dunkirk's sands with blood and tears;
Else had Morality beheld her line
With Guards and Hulans run along the Rhine,

Religion hailed her creeds by war restored,   160
And Truth had blest the logic of his sword.
Were such your servant Percy! (be it tried
Between ourselves! the noble laid aside)
Now would you be content with bare release
From such a desperate breaker of the peace?
Your friend the country Justice scarce would fail
To give a hint of whips and the cart's tail,
Or should you even stop short of Woolwich docks,
Would less suffice than Bridewell and the stocks.
But ye who make our manners, laws, and sense,   170
Self-judged can with such discipline dispense,
And at your will what in a groom were base,
Shall stick new splendor on his gartered grace.
       The theme is fruitful, nor can sorrow find
Shame of such dye but worse remains behind.
– My lord can muster (all but honor spent)
From his wife's Faro-bank a decent rent,
The glittering rabble housed to cheat and swear,
Swindle and rob – is no informer there?
Or is the painted staff's avenging host   180
By sixpenny sedition shops engrossed,
Or rather skulking for the common weal
Round fire-side treason parties en famille?
How throngs the crowd to yon theatric school
To see an English lord enact a fool?
What wonder? – on my soul 'twould split a tub
To see the arch grimace of Marquis Scrub:
Nor safe the petticoats of dames that hear
The box resound on Viscount Buffo's ear.
But here's a thought which well our mirth may cross: 190
That Smithfield should sustain so vast a loss,
That spite of the defrauded Kitchen's prayers,
Scrub lives a genuine Marquess above stairs.
And they who feed with this Patrician wit
Mirth that to aching ribs will not submit –
Good honest souls! – if right my judgement lies,
Though very happy are not very wise,
Unless resolved in mercy to the law
Their legislative licence to withdraw,
And on a frugal plan – without more words.   200

But whence yon swarm that loads the western bridge,
Crams through the arch and bellys o'er the ridge?
– His Grace's watermen in open race
Are called to try their prowess with his Grace.
Could ought but Envy now his pride rebuke?

– The cry is six to one upon the Duke.
St. Stephen's distanced, onward see him strive
Slap-dash, tail foremost, as his arms shall drive.
With shouts th' assembled people rend the skies.
– His Grace and his protection win the prize.   210
– Now Norfolk set thy heralds to their tools,
Marshal forth-with a pair of Oars in gules.
– Though yet the star *some hearts* at court may charm,
The nobler badge shall glitter on *his arm*.
    Enough – on these inferior things:
A single word on Kings and Sons of Kings.
– Were Kings a freeborn work – a peoples choice
Would More or Henry boast the general voice?
What fool besotted as we are by names
Could pause between a Raleigh and a James?   220
How did Buchanan waste the Sage's lore!
– Not virtuous Seneca on Nero more.
A leprous stain! ere half his thread was spun,
Ripe for the block that might have spared his son.
For never did th' uxorious martyr seek
Food for sick passion in a minions cheek,
To patient senates quibble by the hour,
And prove with endless puns a monarch's power,
Or whet his kingly faculties to chase
Legions of devils through a key-hole's space.   230
– What arts had better claim with wrath to warm
A Pym's brave heart or stir a Hamden's arm?
But why for scoundrels rake a distant age,
Or spend upon the dead the muses rage?
The nations hope shall shew the present time
As rich in folly as the past in crime.
Do arts like these a royal mind evince?
Are these the studies that beseem a prince?
Wedged in with blacklegs at a boxers show,
To shout with transport o'er a knock-down blow,   240
'Mid knots of grooms the council of his state
To scheme and counterscheme for purse and plate?
Thy ancient honours when shalt thou resume?
Oh shame – is this thy service, boastful plume?
Go, modern Prince, at Henry's tomb proclaim
Thy rival triumphs – thy Newmarket fame –
There hang thy trophies – bid the jockey's vest
The whip, the cap, and spurs thy praise attest;
And let that heir of Glorys endless day
Edward the flower of chivalry! survey   250
(Fit token of thy reverence and love)

The boxer's armour – the dishonoured *glove*.

When Calais heard (while Famine and Disease
To stern Plantagenet resigned her keys)
That victims yet were wanting to assuage
A baffled Conqueror's deeply searching rage,
Six which themselves must single form a train,
All brothers, long endeared by kindred pain,
Who then through rows of weeping comrades went
And self-devoted sought the monarch's tent –   260
Six simple burghers – to the rope that tyed
Your vassal necks how poor the garter's pride!
Plebeian hands the [   ] mace have wrenched
From sovereigns deep in pedigree intrenched.
Let grandeur tell thee whither now is flown
The brightest jewel of a George's throne;
Blush Pride to see a farmer's wife produce
The first of genuine kings, a king for use.

_____

Let Bourbon spawn her scoundrels. Be my joy
The embryo Franklin in the printer's boy.   270

* * *

But grant [   ]
The bastard gave some favorite stocks of peers
Patents of Manhood for eight hundred years.
Eight hundred years uncalled to other tasks,
Butlers have simply broached their Lordships' casks.
My Lady ne'er approached a thing so coarse
As Tom – but when he helped her to her horse.
A Norman Robber then &c &c

Additional unplaced lines
Ye kings, in wisdom, sense and power, supreme!
These freaks are worse than any sick man's dream.
To hated worth no Tyrant ere design'd
Malice so subtile, vengence so refin'd.
Even he who yoked the living to the dead,
Rivall'd by you, hides the diminish'd head.
Never did Rome herself so set at naught
All plain blunt sense, all subtlety of thought.
Heavens! who sees majesty in George's face?
Or looks at Norfolk and can dream of grace?   10
What has this blessed earth to do with shame
If Excellence was ever Eden's name?
Must honour still to Lonsdale's tail be bound?

Then execration is an empty sound.
Is Common-sense asleep? has she no wand
From this curst Pharaoh plague to rid the land?
Then to our bishops reverent let us fall
Worship Mayors, Tipstaffs, Aldermen and all.
Let Ignorance o'er the monster swarms preside
Till Egypt see her antient fame outvied.   20
The thundering Thurlow, Apis! shall rejoice
In rites once offered to thy bellowing voice.
Insatiate Charlotte's tears and Charlotte's smile
Shall ape the scaly regent of the Nile.
Bishops, of milder Spaniel breed, shall boast
The reverence by the fierce Anubis lost.
And 'tis their due: devotion has been paid
These seven long years to Grenville's onion head.

10

The Persistence of Translations: Lucretius in the Nineteenth Century

In earlier chapters we have seen numerous examples of English poets assimilating, developing and creatively reusing vocabulary, verse forms and other elements first made available to them through classical translations. This chapter goes further. It suggests that the primary means of access English poets have to ancient writers *always* tends to be through the translations of previous English poets (rather than through Latin or Greek texts). Second, it proposes that historical English translations have been influential on interpretation of ancient works much more widely, inflecting readings by those we might assume, and who would themselves probably expect, to be capable of more independent responses, unmediated by translations of the past. In this chapter illustrations will be supplied from three kinds of 'respondent': one poet (Wordsworth), one poet-critic (Arnold) and one classical scholar (H. A. J. Munro). First, I take up Wordsworth once again.

◆　　◆　　◆

Wordsworth's interest in Virgil, the translations resulting from which were accorded at least the dignity of inclusion in one of the volumes of the Cornell Wordsworth edition in the 1990s,[1] at first sight looks considerably more sustained than his attention to Lucretius. Both are of interest here. Wordsworth became a Lucretius translator only briefly and informally, when in 1833 a passage in Book 5 of the *De rerum natura* (522ff.) was the basis of his poem to his daughter-in-law 'On the Birth of her First-Born Child'. Wordsworth's epigraph gives the first lines: 'Tum porro puer, ut sævis projectus ab undis | Navita; nudus humi jacet.' The passage, as it happens, had also formed part of Dryden's small selection of transla-

---

1. Ed. Graver (1998).

English Translation and Classical Reception: Towards a New Literary History, First Edition.
Stuart Gillespie.
© 2011 Stuart Gillespie. Published 2011 by John Wiley & Sons, Ltd.

tions from Lucretius' epic.[2] This is the first stanza of Wordsworth's five-stanza composition:

> LIKE a shipwreck'd sailor tost
> By rough waves on a perilous coast,
> Lies the Babe, in helplessness
> And in tenderest nakedness,
> Flung by labouring nature forth
> Upon the mercies of the earth.
> Can its eyes beseech? – no more
> Than the hands are free to implore:
> Voice but serves for one brief cry,
> Plaint was it? or prophecy
> Of sorrow that will surely come?
> Omen of man's grievous doom![3]

Wordsworth's memory of Dryden's translation kicked in no later than his third word (another of Dryden's words appears in Wordsworth's third line):

> THUS like a Sayler by the Tempest hurl'd
> A shore, the Babe is shipwrack'd on the World:
> Naked he lies, and ready to expire;
> Helpless of all that humane wants require:
> Expos'd upon unhospitable Earth,
> From the first moment of his hapless Birth.[4]

as may be seen by comparing the completely different vocabulary of Creech:

> A *Man*, when first he leaves his *primitive* Night,
> Breaks from his *Mother's womb* to view the Light,
> Like a poor *Carcass* tumbled by the flood,
> He falls all *naked*, but *besmear'd* with blood[5]

But although these verses form Wordsworth's sole translation from the *De rerum natura*, they by no means constitute his only recorded response to Lucretius, even if, as Robin Dix writes, 'modern critical constructions ... still struggle to accommodate without awkwardness [his] admiration' for the poem because 'Lucretian ideas and attitudes are often fundamentally opposed to our sense of what

2. Dryden translated five passages: the exordium to Venus, the opening of Book 2 (the 'detached spectator', 2.1–61), the Book 5 passage discussed next, and two longer excerpts: 3.830–1094 and 4.1052–287, which he titled respectively *Against the Fear of Death* and *On the Nature of Love*.
3. Ed. Curtis (1999), 252; lines 1–12.
4. Dryden (1956–2000), III, 66.
5. Creech (1700), 146.

Wordsworthian writing is really like'.[6] Wordsworth's esteem for Lucretius is apparent from a range of other contexts.[7] Wordsworth headed the early *Descriptive Sketches*, 1793, with an epigraph from Lucretius' evocation of pastoral simplicity, 'Loca pastorum deserta atque otia dia' (5.1387). He placed Lucretius first in his list of didactic poets in the Preface to *Poems, 1815*. But Lucretius evidently figured in Wordsworth's imaginative life at a level well beyond these formal salutes. Lucretius lies behind his uncompleted poem *Salisbury Plain* (1793–4), whose opening description of savage existence threatened on all sides by storms and wild beasts derives from *De rerum natura* 5,[8] as does the ensuing comparison with the present where 'Many thousands weep | Beset with foes more fierce than e'er assail | The savage without home in winter's keenest gale'.[9] His 1807 poem 'Elegiac Stanzas, Suggested by a Picture of Peele Castle, in a Storm' draws specifically on the well-known image of the 'detached spectator' at the opening of Book 2 of the *De rerum natura* to generate a poem on nature 'coded', according to Martin Priestman, 'in completely Lucretian terms'.[10]

But what form, so to speak, did Wordsworth's Lucretius come in? As we saw in Chapter 9, Wordsworth was trained in Latin to the comparatively high standards of university men of his time, and obviously considered himself competent to translate Virgil. Yet it seems not to have been primarily the Latin of Lucretius himself that was stored in his memory (though some of that may have stuck too). Instead, episodes like his poem on the newborn babe show that it was largely to Dryden's Lucretius that Wordsworth's thoughts turned – and in a long-term way.[11]

Wordsworth was not formally a translator of Lucretius, but his late, abandoned *Aeneid* translation was referred to in Chapter 8. This will enable us to inspect what is in some ways an even stronger demonstration of the 'persistence' of an earlier translation in the work of a later poet. Once again the earlier translation in question is Dryden's, and the reason the demonstration is so powerful is that it was precisely the aim of Wordsworth's fresh attempt on the *Aeneid* to avoid what he saw as Dryden's inappropriate approach to Virgil. Wordsworth's comments survive in a series of letters of 1823–4. 'When I read Virgil in the original,' he writes, 'I am moved; but not so much by the translations; and I cannot but think this owing to a defect in the diction; which I have endeavoured to supply.' He is anxious that

6. Dix (2002), 25.

7. Fuller treatments of Wordsworth and Lucretius are found in Kelley (1983); Spiegelman (1985); Priestman (2008), 292–5.

8. Lines 1–9 in the unfinished first version of *Salisbury Plain*; compare Lucretius 5.955–87.

9. *Salisbury Plain*, 34–6; compare *De rerum natura* 5.999–1000, 'at non multa virum sub signis milia ducta | una dies dabat exitio'.

10. Priestman (2008), 295; see his full discussion.

11. And on occasion to Creech's standard version too. For Wordsworth's use of Creech's Lucretius, see Dix (2002); the impact he identifies comes largely from Creech's commentary rather than Creech's translation.

his rendering 'should have far more of the *genuine* ornaments of Virgil than my predecessors', among whom he singles out Dryden, who 'has been very careless of these, and profuse of his own, which seem to me very rarely to harmonize with those of Virgil'. Not only has Dryden taken far too many 'liberties', he has failed to capture Virgil's 'tenderness'; Wordsworth aims, he says, to produce something 'to a certain degree *affecting*, which Dryden's [*Æneis*] is not to me in the least'.[12]

Bruce Graver showed convincingly in a 1983 article how in the early part of his translation Wordsworth embraces Latinate diction in an effort to avoid what he saw as Dryden's mistakes in handling Virgil's style.[13] But Graver's examples are almost all drawn from Book I. The further Wordsworth's three completed Books move forward, the more Drydenian the diction becomes, and this, very evidently, in spite of the author's own intentions. Wordsworth, it can be shown, had in front of him as he worked not only Dryden's *Aeneis* (1697) but also Ogilby's (Wordsworth used a 1650 edition), Pitt's (1728–40) and perhaps Trapp's (1731) *Aeneid* too.[14] Indeed, the manuscript of his translation (only one passage was printed in his lifetime) is prefaced by a note admitting a few borrowings:

> It is proper to premise that the first Couplet of this Translation is adopted from Pitt – as are likewise two Couplets in the second Book; & three or four lines, in different parts, are taken from Dryden. A few expressions will also be found, which, following the Original closely are the same as the preceding Translators have unavoidably employed.[15]

Wordsworth was deceiving himself, as simple comparisons establish. In the following passages translating part of Helenus' advice to Aeneas in Book 3, Wordsworth's lines are given first, followed by Dryden's, with my emphases indicating borrowed phraseology:

> **Arrived at Cumæ** and the sacred **floods**
> **Of black Avernus** resonant with **woods**,
> Thou shalt behold the Sybil where She sits
> Within her **Cave**, rapt in extatic **fits**,
> And words and characters **to leaves commits**.
> The prophesies which on those leaves the Maid
> **Inscribes**, are by her hands **in order laid**
> Mid the secluded **Cavern**, where they fill
> Their several places, undisturb'd and still.[16]

12. De Selincourt (1978), 235, 252, 253, 253.
13. Graver (1983).
14. Graver (1998), 156, gives details.
15. Ed. Graver (1998), 181.
16. Wordsworth's 3.610–18; ed. Graver (1998), 263–4.

> **Arriv'd at Cumæ**, when you view the **flood,**
> **Of black Avernus**, and the sounding **wood,**
> The mad prophetic sibyl you shall find,
> Dark in a **cave**, and on a rock reclin'd.
> She sings the fates, and in her frantic **fits**,
> The notes and names **inscrib'd, to leaves commits.**
> What she commits to leaves, **in order laid,**
> Before the **cavern's** entrance are display'd:[17]

I have not emphasized the word 'leaves', which does seem, as Wordsworth put it, 'unavoidable'; but every other element given in bold here is avoided by most or all of the other translations Wordsworth had available. The 'cave', for example, is a 'grot' in Trapp, a 'rock' in Ogilby. Wordsworth's rhyme 'maid'/'laid' is there in Pitt too, but the rest of Pitt's translation of this passage makes clear how small is Wordsworth's debt to him at this point:

> There when arriv'd you visit *Cuma's* Tow'rs,
> Where dark with shady woods *Avernus* roars,
> You'll see the *Sibyl* in her rocky Cave,
> And hear the furious maid divinely rave.
> The dark Decrees of Fate the Virgin sings,
> And writes on Leaves, Names, Characters, and Things.
> The mystic Numbers, in the Cavern laid,
> Are rang'd in Order by the sacred Maid.[18]

Many other passages would show exactly the same things. The reader may have noted, further, that Wordsworth not only finds himself absorbing Dryden's vocabulary, but at the same time developing and building on it. The 'extatic fits' of his Sybil are a response to Dryden's 'frantic fits' and perhaps an improvement on them – though Wordsworth's phrase is probably a conscious borrowing from Milton too.[19] His epithet in 'Avernus resonant with woods' develops out of Dryden's 'sounding wood'. Not only repetition but variation too can be a sign of a previous translation's background presence.

In describing Wordsworth's Drydenian Lucretius I wrote of the agency of memory. In working on a full-dress translation of an epic poem, memory will normally be less involved than methodical consultation: translators are apt to seek assistance from existing versions in their own language for solutions to individual problems of, say, prosody or rhyme. This is unexceptional, and it is in fact

---

17. Dryden is here quoted from the text Wordsworth used, Robert Anderson's twelve-volume collection of British poets (Anderson 1792–5); in modern editions of Dryden these are lines 3.561–8.
18. Pitt (1740), I, 123–4. It will be noted that Pitt is also indebted to Dryden's Virgil for several items of his phrasing.
19. 'The Passion', line 42.

what appears to be happening in Wordsworth's deployment of Ogilby or on other occasions of Pitt. It is the much more extensive appropriations from Dryden's *Aeneis*, and the way they contradict Wordsworth's stated aims in translating the Latin epic, that give pause for thought. We might adapt his words and say that what Wordsworth found 'unavoidable' was, in fact, Dryden's Virgil. The adjective can be used very seriously. Wordsworth was unpersuaded and unpersuadable that Drydenian diction was appropriate for his translation. It seems we must presume, then, that running counter to this belief was an ingrained sense, exerting itself progressively over the course of Wordsworth's work, that what the *Aeneid* sounds like is, in fact, Dryden's translation. That is to say, to imagine a Virgil unmediated by Dryden is at this date an impossibility for an English poet.

◆   ◆   ◆

Wordsworth was, of course, a national celebrity by the time of his death in 1850. Matthew Arnold had known him since boyhood as a neighbour at Fox How, the Arnold family's Lake District holiday house, but it was a more impersonal tribute the 27-year-old Arnold aimed at when he characterized the effect Wordsworth's work had had on his readers in his *Memorial Verses*:

> He laid us as we lay at birth
> On the cool flowery lap of earth,
> Smiles broke from us and we had ease;
> The hills were round us, and the breeze
> Went o'er the sun-lit fields again;
> Our foreheads felt the wind and rain.
> Our youth returned; for there was shed
> On spirits that had long been dead,
> Spirits dried up and closely furled,
> The freshness of the early world.[20]

It is acknowledged that Arnold drew in this eloquent poem on Lucretius 2.29–33; Wordsworth's Lucretian ties make this highly appropriate:

> cum tamen inter se prostrati in gramine molli
> propter aquae rivum sub ramis arboris altae
> non magnis opibus iucunde corpora curant,
> praesertim cum tempestas adridet et anni
> tempora conspergunt viridantis floribus herbas.

20. Arnold (1965), 228–9 (lines 48–57).

What should be added, however, is that Arnold remembered Dryden's Lucretius too:

> Yet on the grass beneath a poplar shade
> By the **cool** stream, our careless limbs are **lay'd**[21]

There is more than one surprise here, since the later Arnold is notorious for his coolness about Dryden as a poet. In famously calling Dryden and Pope 'classics of our prose', Arnold has been seen as setting in motion a devaluation of Dryden's work lasting for many decades thereafter.[22] Lucretius and Wordsworth will both come to claim highly significant long-term places in Arnold's literary life; the Drydenian associations which both must have had for him in 1850 suggest another dimension to those relationships.

But the earlier chapters of the present study have already provided examples of poets using the vocabulary of English classical translations in their original verse. To that extent, Arnold's diction is no more than a further case. More unexpected is that Arnold remembered Dryden's Lucretius not only when composing verse, but when writing of Lucretius in his capacity as a critic and cultural commentator. Arnold's poem *Empedocles on Etna*, his most extended 'creative' response to Lucretius, was first published in 1852.[23] But Arnold's fullest discursive treatment of the *De rerum natura*, of a piece with the suicidal gloom of *Empedocles*, comes in his 1857 lecture 'On the Modern Element in Literature'. Here Arnold presents Lucretius as a morbid atheist:

> Depression and *ennui*; these are the characteristics stamped on how many of the representative works of modern times! They are also the characteristics stamped on the poem of Lucretius. One of the most powerful, the most solemn passages of the work of Lucretius, one of the most powerful, the most solemn passages in the literature of the whole world, is the well-known conclusion of the third book. With masterly touches he exhibits the lassitude, the incurable tedium which pursue men in their amusements; with indignant irony he upbraids them for the cowardice with which they cling to a life which for most is miserable; to a life which contains, for the most fortunate, nothing but the old dull **round** of the same unsatisfying objects for ever presented ... there is no peace, no cheerfulness for him either in the world from which he comes, or in the solitude to which he goes ... Lucretius is, therefore, overstrained, gloom-weighted, morbid.[24]

---

21. Dryden's 2.33–4, my emphases; Dryden (1956–2000), III, 47.
22. 'The Study of Poetry', 1880. Arnold wrote: 'Dryden and Pope are not classics of our poetry, they are classics of our prose.'
23. Mackenzie (2005) is the most recent reading.
24. Arnold (1960), 32–4; my emphasis.

Once again it is Dryden's translation Arnold is recalling, in which the voice of Nature is given this memorable triplet:

> To please thee I have empti'd all my store,
> I can invent, and can supply no more;
> But run the **round** again, the **round** I ran before.[25]

Lucretius' Latin does not suggest the word 'round', and neither had other translators offered it. Creech supplied:

> nam tibi praetereae quod machiner inveniamque,
> quod placeat, nil est: eadem sunt omnia semper.

> My *Pleasures* always in a Circle run,
> The same *Returning* with the Yearly Sun[26]

Arnold attributes directly to Lucretius ('he upbraids them') the arguments Dryden had given to the personified voice of Nature who in *De rerum natura* Book 3 reproaches and hectors Man for his dissatisfaction with her bounteous gifts (there is, of course, no mention of the gifts in Arnold). Another triplet in Dryden's translation reinforces the effect, generalizing in the poet's own voice:

> Besides we tread but a perpetual **round**,
> We ne're strike out; but beat the former ground
> And the same Maukish joyes in the same track are found.[27]

where much less colourful language is found in Lucretius and in Creech:

> praeterea versamur ibidem atque insumus usque
> nec nova vivendo procuditur ulla voluptas

> Life adds no *New Delights* to those possest[28]

That Arnold remembered Dryden's translation does not necessarily mean Arnold's presentation of Lucretius is in harmony with Dryden's. What it does mean, when taken along with *Memorial Verses*, is something of perhaps greater consequence: that the words and cadences Arnold heard when the *De rerum natura* came to mind were those of the Dryden translation. Arnold was not a professional classical scholar, but he did not need to read Lucretius in English. He was, however, an

25. Lines 138–40; Dryden (1956–2000), III, 51; my emphasis.
26. Lucretius 3.944–5; Creech (1700), 96.
27. Lines 205–7; Dryden (1956–2000), III, 56; my emphasis.
28. Lucretius 3.1080–1; Creech (1700), 101.

influential cultural commentator. Dryden's translation, these echoes imply, was mediating Lucretius both as the *De rerum natura* presented itself to Arnold, and as Arnold presented it to his audience. In a moment we will see that other kinds of evidence also make this proposition appear entirely plausible.

What of Lucretius' nineteenth-century translators? There was no shortage – indeed, there was a remarkable level of fresh interest. This list of the published translations (except where stated, complete and in verse) incorporates brief descriptions of the translators' backgrounds:[29]

1799   Anon. [?John Nott, physician and classical scholar]. Book 1 only.
1805   John Mason Good. Physician, surgeon, linguist, scholar.
1808   William Hamilton Drummond. Irish Presbyterian minister, scholar, and poet. Book 1 only.
1813   Thomas Busby. Composer, musicologist, and satirist.
1850   Roscoe Mongan. Scolar of Trinity College Dublin. Book 1 only.
1851   John Selby Watson. Headmaster. Prose.
1864   H. A. J. Munro. Cambridge don. Prose.
1872   Charles Frederick Johnson. Classical scholar; translation dedicated to Munro.
1879   Sir John Trelawny. Politician and Member of Parliament. Book 1.
1879   Sir Robert Collier. Judge and Member of Parliament. Book 2. Printed with above.
1884   Thomas Charles Baring. Member of Parliament and Oxford don.
1889   F. G. Plaistowe. Tutor in Classics. Prose. Book 5 only.
1900   W. H. Mallock. Writer and polemicist.

For all this fresh activity, however, it is very much to be borne in mind that reprints of earlier English translations were going on throughout this period. The availability of earlier translations to readers of every period is something often overlooked in accounts of readerly experience: it is wholly exceptional to find that a new translation acquires more readers than existing translations in any given era. Nineteenth-century readers had at their disposal one existing translation of Lucretius in particular. Creech's English text was not reprinted after 1800, though his Latin notes were. But Dryden's Lucretius was printed more often than all these nineteenth-century translations put together, and would have reached a far wider audience.

Dryden's five Lucretius excerpts (totalling 762 lines) were too short ever to be published as a book in themselves. However, not only were Dryden's poetical works reprinted with very great frequency; their print-runs and their readership would have been much larger than those of the independent versions of Lucretius

---

29. For further bibliographical details of all these editions see Gordon (1962). For comment on the first three see Priestman (2008); on Munro and Mallock, Talbot (2006*b*), 190.

listed above.[30] Relevant are full-scale new multi-volume library editions of Dryden's works at the start of the nineteenth century by Edmond Malone (1800) and Sir Walter Scott (1808, 1821), and the later revision of Scott's work by George Saintsbury (1882–4). So too are the multi-volume collections of 'English' or 'British' poets in which Dryden's verse both original and translated always had a prominent place, such as Anderson's (1792–5; used by Wordsworth and Coleridge), Chalmers's (1810) and Park's (1813), with their reprints.[31] Then there are the numerous reissues of Samuel Johnson's *English Poets* and other later eighteenth-century compilations such as Bell's *Poets of Great Britain* (109 volumes, 1777–93). As well as all these heavyweight library editions, Dryden's *Poetical Works* were issued as a separate entity, often in one volume, practically throughout the nineteenth century, under the names of a long succession of editors. In several cases these editions were functional books printed in large numbers to achieve afford-ability, like Macmillan's Globe edition of 1874.

◆   ◆   ◆

But (it might be objected) Wordsworth was a poet, Arnold a man of letters. These were no professional classical scholars, living on intimate terms with ancient Roman literature in the Latin language. Nothing in this chapter's exposition so far has brought into question the ability of the great classical scholars of the past to read and interpret Latin texts without the intervention of English translators. Classical scholars may, it is true, be in some ways dependent on the scholarly tradi-tion for their insights, but that is a quite different thing from relying on the amateurish efforts of poets.

Few more admired nineteenth-century classical scholars could be produced than H. A. J. Munro. When his edition of Lucretius, with commentary and translation, was published in 1860–4, it was, in the words of J. D. Duff's *Dictionary of National Biography* entry on Munro, 'at once recognised by competent judges as the most valuable contribution to Latin scholarship that any Englishman had made during that century'. Munro (1819–85), Fellow of Trinity College, Cambridge, from within a year of gaining the University's First Chancellor's Medal upon his graduation, was a highly cultured man, deeply conversant with the lan-guages and literatures of France, Germany and Italy, as well as his native Britain. We know from his commentary on the *De rerum natura* that he was aware of the historical translations of Dryden, Creech, Hutchinson and Evelyn.[32] We might also

---

30. Of these, John Mason Good's remained available over a number of editions because it appeared alongside a prose translation in Bohn's Classical Library from 1851.

31. For the place of translation in such compilations see pp. 98–9 above.

32. Munro (1928), II, 20. It is of some interest that he does not refer to Hutchinson or Evelyn by name, assuming his readers will be able to identify them when he writes that Dryden and Creech were preceded as translators by 'one of the most accomplished cavalier gentlemen and by the most accom-plished of puritan ladies'.

suppose him to have read several of those more recent translations listed above. But we could also infer his knowledge of Dryden's from the way he hears Lucretius' voice.

We have already seen how Arnold recollected Dryden's supreme rendering of the speech Nature is imagined making to Man in Book 3. It is one of the Dryden passages that was memorable enough to play its part in Munro's work too, clearly enough so as to provide sufficient support for my point in itself. Sometimes, it is true, the evidence is slightly ambiguous. When Munro translates 3.961 *nunc aliena tua tamen aetate omnia mitte* as 'resign all things **unsuited** to thy age', he seems to draw on Dryden's 'Now leave those joys **unsuiting** to thy age'.[33] Yet this could be the result of Munro's use of his immediate predecessor Watson, whose 1851 prose version had offered 'resign all things **unsuitable** to thy age'.[34] But here is how Munro paraphrases a slightly earlier passage (3.931–77) in his commentary:

> If nature were to say to you or me 'why lament your death? if your life has been a **pleasant** one, why not go to rest satisfied with the feast? for I have **nothing new to give** you, if you were to live for ever': we must allow her words to be true: if an old man were to bemoan himself, would she not with justice thus **chide**? 'a truce with tears; the fault is your own, if you have not had enjoyment'; make way for others: they too will follow you, as you now follow those before you; **life is but** a limited tenure; what took place before our birth is nothing to us; **judge** from this of what the future will be after our death.[35]

I give the Drydenian source material in truncated form for reasons of space:

> For if thy life were **pleasant** heretofore ...
> Why dost thou not give thanks as at a plenteous feast
> Cram'd to the throat with life, and rise and take thy rest? ...
>   **life is** still **but Life**, there's **nothing new to give** ...
> Is Nature to be blam'd if thus she **chide**? ...
> Thus may'st thou **judge** the future by the past.[36]

Of course, certain words ('feast' and 'future' are two) are not distinctive, and turn out to be common to more or less all English versions. And of course, some of Munro's phrasing is original to him in this context. But of the phrasing in bold,

33. Dryden (1956–2000), III, 52 (line 161).
34. Watson (1851), 140. Other previous translators all treat this line differently, so that Watson is likely to be drawing on Dryden here, and Munro doing so either directly or indirectly. A systematic search for Drydenian influence on Watson's translation would produce further results. His introduction pays extensive attention to Dryden's account of Lucretius' poetic character.
35. Munro (1928), II, 219–20.
36. Dryden (1956–2000), III, 51–2 (lines 226, 130–1, 144, 163, 178).

all items can be found only in one translator, and only occasionally can an item be matched in another. Others offer, for example, in place of 'chide': 'reprehensions' (Hutchinson), 'nature complaines' (Evelyn), 'Reproofs' (Creech), 'reprove' (Good), 'upbraid and reproach' (Watson).[37] And for 'nothing new to give': 'no other pleasures' (Hutchinson), 'nought else to content thee' (Evelyn), 'no *New*, no *Fresh* Delight' (Creech), 'nothing further' (both Good and Watson).[38]

Such documentary detail as is required here is inherently awkward to amass and to present, but enough has now been produced, I hope, to show that Munro as well as Wordsworth and Arnold received Lucretius through the powerful English poetic handling of John Dryden.

◆   ◆   ◆

My examples in this chapter have spanned only about half a century, from Wordsworth to Munro. Perhaps contemporary tastes happened to combine with the priorities of the book trade to promote Dryden's classical translations – perhaps, in other words, the effect we have noted was temporary? While it's true that there was much publishing of the classics of English literature for the nineteenth-century market, what Arnold and Wordsworth have to say about Dryden critically would in fact imply the opposite: that it is despite and not because of the critical *Zeitgeist* that his influence exerts itself. Moreover, it can easily be shown that Dryden's shadow casts itself over much wider spaces. Another Virgilian example comes to hand. At *Aeneid* 3.690 Achaemenides is able to act as a guide for the Trojans because he has recently sailed the same seas. 'Talia monstrabat relegans errata retrorsus | litora Achaemenides', Virgil writes. Dryden translates Virgil's rare verb as 'tracing': 'This Passage *Achæmenides* had shown, | Tracing the Course which he before had run'.[39] Damien Nelis has recently pointed out how remarkably consistently twentieth-century Virgil translators have followed suit, and used a verb which slightly refines on this: 'retrace'. Nelis instances C. Day Lewis, Alan Mandelbaum, Robert Fitzgerald, Robert Fagles and Frederick Ahl.[40]

Peter Green, writing self-deprecatingly of his own paperback version of Ovid, says that translation 'remains, in the last resort, a *pis aller*', because 'those with the original do not need it'.[41] No doubt he is thinking of the use of translation as a mere aid to deciphering an original, and it goes without saying that translations

---

37. 'Iure, ut opinor, agat, iure increpet inciletque' (3.963); Hutchinson 3.1042 in de Quehen (1996), 109; Evelyn 3.994 in Repetzki (2000), 87; Creech (1700), 96; Good 3.1000 in Good (1805), I, 513; Watson (1851), 140.

38. 'Nam tibi praeterea quod machiner inveniamque, | Quod placeat, nil est' (3.961); Hutchinson 3.1022 in De Quehen (1996), 109; Evelyn 3.988 in Repetzki (2000), 86; Creech (1700), 96; Good 3.978 in Good (1805), I, 511; Watson (1851), 139.

39. Dryden (1956–2000), V, 447 (3.907–8).

40. Nelis (2010), 13.

41. Green (1994), viii.

intended to work this way are common. They should not be confused with translations which even those 'with the original' could not avoid even if they tried, and
whose 'need' for which is not the issue. The Drydenian cast of the *De rerum
natura* for nineteenth-century English readers, no matter how professional their
relation to Latin literature, is manifest. When a recent scholar claims Munro's
edition and prose translation were 'crucial' in 'making both Lucretius's poetry and
his philosophy more immediately accessible to a wider audience',[42] he is no doubt
thinking of the admiration Munro's work elicited. But there is a serious lack of
perspective here, because Dryden's excerpts had long ago familiarized Lucretius
to English-speaking readers, and continued to perform this function through the
nineteenth century. On the basis of what we have seen of that century in this
chapter we can go further still, and say that Dryden's Lucretius was an unavoidable
part of the experience of the *De rerum natura* for anglophone readers.

42. Holmes (2008), 266.

11

'Oddity and struggling dumbness': Ted Hughes's Homer

Ted Hughes is one of several poets of his generation to take a pronounced interest in translating ('adapting', 'imitating') the Latin and Greek classics of dramatic and non-dramatic verse. Before his time this had not happened on any scale in English poetry for many decades. But as we travel deeper into the twenty-first century, verse translation in English, from postclassical as well as classical sources, almost begins to resemble the English Renaissance translating tradition in its scope and scale. Not only does it connect senior figures such as Ciaran Carson, Tony Harrison, Seamus Heaney, Brendan Kennelly, Edwin Morgan, Peter Porter and C. K. Stead; from younger generations may be mentioned others: say, Liz Lochhead, Derek Mahon and Tom Paulin. I am thinking here not of specialist translators, but of writers whose *original* verse is normally considered their principal work – though in some cases, including Hughes's, translation seems increasingly to have become the main thing as their careers went on.[1]

Like many of these other figures, Hughes's classical translations were in the two fields of poetry and drama. While not best known for his contribution to the theatre tradition that has proved the most popular destination for many recent translators, that of Greek tragedy, his early Seneca (*Oedipus*, 1969) is recognized as 'outstanding in every way',[2] while his *Oresteia* and *Alcestis* (both 1999) remain to be further explored. His best-known classically inspired verse, in *Tales from Ovid* (1997), like most of the rest of this work, came late in his career. But Hughes was pervasively engaged at one level or another with classical poetry, drama and myth throughout his writing life, extending to the refracted use of classical material

---

1. Several of the writers mentioned here engagingly discuss their own use and translation of classical texts in Harrison (2009).
2. Burgess (2005), 358.

English Translation and Classical Reception: Towards a New Literary History, First Edition.
Stuart Gillespie.

in his version of Racine's *Phèdre* (1998), his play for children, *Orpheus* (1971), and the Greek mythology often near the surface in verse collections like *Gaudete* (1977) and *Cave Birds* (1978).

My purpose here is not to deal with Hughes's classicism in general.[3] Far less is it possible to address the recent classical translation boom at large. Instead, this chapter calls attention to another dimension of this enduring interest of Hughes's, his version of a passage from the *Odyssey* (Hughes's text is reproduced in the Appendix).[4] This translation, as far as is known, is Hughes's earliest completed translation of any kind, and it is certainly his sole translation of Homer. It remains remarkably little noticed, which can be explained entirely by its publication history – or lack of one. The appearance of Hughes's *Collected Poems* in 2003 made it readily available, but following its reading on BBC radio's Third Programme in 1960 there was no print publication either in Hughes's ensuing collections or at any other time during the following 42 years.

In previous chapters I have argued that English literary history should not confine itself to the record of familiar printed works because they do not reflect the full range of literary activity. Hughes's early Homer translation allows a demonstration that against the run of expectation (for who would suppose a substantial composition by one of our highest-profile contemporary poets would fail to achieve print publication for nearly half a century?) such a generalization can be valid for writing of very recent times as well as of the more distant past (Hughes died in 1998). Thus it presents a particular kind of reminder of the discrepancy between the place translation may have in the *œuvres* of well-known writers and in the histories we construct.

I have also previously observed that in the reception of ancient authors, changes of emphasis, and on occasion more radical repositionings, are always discernible over time. While Homer was a constant reference point for post-medieval English writers at large, perceptions of the *Iliad* and *Odyssey* and their significance have shifted constantly too. We have seen (in Chapter 7) how Dryden invokes Homer as a father-figure at a time when Virgil is officially considered the pre-eminent epic poet; we have noted (in Chapter 3; see also below) how Chapman's early translation is briefly eclipsed by Pope's, then revived in Keats's day, as the ethos of the Renaissance is equated with the perceived freshness of Homeric verse and as Hellenic cultural precedence is asserted across Europe. Homer's nineteenth-century prestige has been alluded to: what of his fortunes in the twentieth?

Finally, this chapter broaches a fresh issue, one concerning the options available to a translator. Hughes himself evidently tended to view the translator's choices, at the date of this work, in terms of the binary familiar since at least the time of Schleiermacher: translators can either stay put and pull the foreign text towards their own language and culture, or bridge the distance by moving as far as possible

---

3. Essays addressing much of the range of Hughes's classicism are found in Rees (2009).
4. It is reproduced there and quoted below from Keegan (2003), 93–6, its sole printing to date.

towards the foreign work.[5] Hughes's preference was for the latter; below I contrast his approach with that of Robert Fitzgerald, thus illustrating, I hope, exactly what effects it has for a translator to favour each tactic. But it should be added that there are perhaps no absolutes in this perennial debate. Hughes, as we shall see, is explicit that the reason for moving towards the foreign, even for embracing the 'oddity and struggling dumbness of a word for word version', is specifically to 'make our own imagination jump' and force us to leave behind 'our familiar abstractions'. Yet these are exactly the sort of reasons other translators would give for adopting the opposite approach, and making their author (as Dryden put it in connection with Virgil) 'speak such *English*, as he wou'd himself have spoken, if he had been born in *England*, and in this present Age'.[6] In Chapter 5 we examined in detail just such a translation by Dryden's hand.

◆   ◆   ◆

Because *The Storm* has so little 'prehistory' in what has been said and written about Hughes and his work of this period, I first outline its immediate context.[7] Its ultimate origins are obscurely connected with those of Christopher Logue's Homeric imitations (fresh instalments of which have continued to appear many decades later, into the twenty-first century). In the late 1950s, verse by the young Logue (then in his early thirties) was being broadcast on the BBC's Third Programme, but he had no training in Greek. Donald Carne-Ross (then working as a BBC producer) and his partner Xanthe Wakefield (the daughter of a Tory Member of Parliament) helped Logue acquire a commission which proved to be the beginning of *War Music*, his first volume of verse 'after' Homer. Logue recalls events thus in his biographical memoir *Prince Charming*:

> Donald gave me lunch at Broadcasting House and, at Xanthe's bidding, proposed I translated a sequence from Book XXI of the *Iliad*. To the question of my knowing no Greek Donald answered: 'Read translations by those who did. Follow the story. A translator must know one language well. Preferably his own.'
>
> …
>
> When 'Achilles and the River' was transmitted in June 1959 it interested a number of literary grandees. The broadcast was repeated; parts of it were televised; then it was published by *Encounter*, a serious non-specialist magazine. Finally, promoted by

5. Schliermacher expounded his thesis in his lecture of 1813 'On the Different Methods of Translating'. For relevant excerpts in translation, see Lefevre (1992); for discussion, Pym (1995).
6. *Dedication of the Aeneis*, Dryden (1956–2000), V, 330–1.
7. The principal source here is the commentary in Weissbort (2006), based on notes emanating originally from Anthony Thwaite. I am grateful to Alistair Elliot for supplementary information drawn from his recollections of participating in the series to which *The Storm* belongs (see below).

the grandees, I was given a grant by an American foundation to do more of the same.[8]

It seems to have been partly the interest Logue's work attracted that led to a series of translations of Homer being specially commissioned by the BBC from contemporary poets immediately after this point: twelve verse renderings of twelve different episodes in the *Odyssey*. The editors responsible were Louis MacNeice and Anthony Thwaite, for the BBC's Features Department. It was MacNeice who singled out the twelve episodes he felt would be most suitable. The translators – some with Greek and others, like Logue, without – included Alistair Elliot, Peter Green and Rex Warner. Like the other contributions to the series, Hughes's work was read for the broadcast by Patrick Garland.[9]

The episodes seem to have been allotted in something like the way the chunks of the *Metamorphoses* were apportioned in that later Hughes-related collection of classical translations by several hands, *After Ovid* – as the editors of the more recent compilation have described it.[10] In that case, the editors chose the writers and proposed the selection to them; the writers said yes or no. But things would seem to have been rather less flexible in the BBC venture. Alistair Elliot reports having had no choice about which episode to take on,[11] whereas in *After Ovid* there was negotiation and some of the contributors eventually supplied more passages than they were originally asked to translate. With the BBC project there were doubtless certain other guidelines, but specific forms were not suggested – Elliot remembers agonizing about the range of verse options (metre, rhyme). There was never any plan for print publication; in fact, Elliot possesses no copy of his own contribution. And contrary to what Anthony Thwaite seems to have suggested to Daniel Weissbort,[12] there was no attempt to cover the whole of the *Odyssey*, to translate all parts, which indeed could hardly have been a realistic objective within twelve segments of the size of Hughes's 100-line rendering.

So much for the context of the BBC commission; what of the context in Hughes's own work? Just one obviously Homer-inspired poem, 'Everyman's Odyssey', had preceded it. Though not published until *Lupercal* (March 1960), this was written in 1957.[13] 'Everyman's Odyssey' relates to the story of Odysseus' son Telemachus and his punishment of Penelope's suitors. It is about Telemachus' coming of age, metaphorically part of the 'odyssey' all men undergo. Like *The*

---

8. Logue (1999), 221, 224.

9. The broadcast date of 10 November 1960 is supplied by Keegan (2003), 1245, and Weissbort (2006), 14.

10. Hoffmann and Lasdun (1994), xii–xiii.

11. Elliot's recollections on this and other points were in the form of personal communications to the present author.

12. Weissbort (2006), 14.

13. Keegan (2003), 1243.

Storm it discerns in the experience of Homer's heroes the experience of mankind, but here the resemblance largely ends.

Hughes wrote more than once on the subject of translation in the 1960s, in editorials contributed to early issues of the journal *Modern Poetry in Translation* which he co-edited with Weissbort.[14] Perhaps his own experience of working on Homer itself helped him arrive at these views; in any case there is a good fit between his desiderata and the mode of the *Odyssey* translation. Hughes wrote in the first issue of *MPT* as an editor inviting contributions:

> The type of translation we are seeking can be described as literal, though not literal in a strict or pedantic sense. Though this may seem at first suspect, it is more apposite to define our criteria negatively, as literalness can only be a deliberate tendency, not a dogma. We feel that as soon as devices extraneous to the original are employed for the purpose of recreating its 'spirit', the value of the whole enterprise is called in question.[15]

By the third issue of the journal Hughes was developing the view that literalism will in itself lead to new possibilities of thought and expression:

> The first ideal is literalness ... The very oddity and struggling dumbness of a word for word version is what makes our own imagination jump. A man who has something really serious to say in a language of which he knows only a few words, manages to say it far more convincingly and effectively than any interpreter, and in translated poetry it is the first-hand contact – however fumbled and broken – with that man and his seriousness which we want. The minute we gloss his words, we have more or less what he said but we have lost him. We are ringing changes – amusing though they may be – on our familiar abstractions, and are no longer reading through to what we have not experienced before, which is alive and real.[16]

Quoting this passage in a recent account of Hughes's views at this date, Weissbort writes that Hughes 'adhered, even this early and well before it was identified by scholars, to a "foreignizing" tendency, a readiness to allow translation of foreign texts to alter English itself'.[17] This is indeed the implication of attempting the kind of literalism Hughes specifies here.

These are some of the wider contexts for *The Storm* in Hughes's work of the 1960s. Once we explore the texture of the translation closely, we shall see how some more strongly characteristic preoccupations of Hughes as poet may be discerned in it.

14. The two editorials quoted here were printed in Nos. 1 and 3 of *Modern Poetry in Translation* in the years 1965 and 1967 respectively. These unsigned pieces, according to Weissbort (2006), 200, express the 'views and intentions' of Hughes.
15. Quoted from Weissbort (2006), 200.
16. Quoted from Weissbort (2006), 201.
17. Weissbort (2010), 109.

◆ ◆ ◆

The passage – 111 lines in Homer (*Od.* 5.382–493), 94 lines in Hughes – comes from the point in Odysseus' story after Poseidon's earthquake has demolished his boat. Athene, his divine patroness, checks the storm, but Zeus having already ordained the period it will take for Odysseus to reach the Phaecians, the ship-wrecked hero floats and flounders in the still heavy seas for two days and nights. Even when he spots a coastline he can see nowhere to get ashore safely, but with the help of Athene, the exhausted Odysseus eventually makes land. When darkness falls he escapes the cold and his fatigue by finding a grove to sleep in. Here he creeps under a thicket of olive bushes and rakes together a pile of leaves, within which he nestles safely for the night.

In Homer this is a highly charged episode containing several distinct segments, each with something of its own mood. The moment of Odysseus' eventual emer-gence from the sea drew a memorable reaction from Keats when Charles Cowden Clarke read it to the poet in Chapman's translation (I quote from the latter's account):

> One scene I could not fail to introduce to him – the shipwreck of Ulysses, in the fifth book of the *Odysseis*, and I had the reward of one of his delighted stares, upon reading the following lines:
>
> > Then forth he came, his both knees falt'ring, both
> > His strong hands hanging down, and all with froth
> > His cheeks and nostrils flowing, voice and breath
> > Spent to all use, and down he sank to death.
> > *The sea had soak'd his heart through* ...
>
> Chapman supplied us many an after-treat; but it was in the teeming wonderment of this his first introduction, that, when I came down to breakfast the next morning, I found upon my table a letter with no other enclosure than his famous sonnet, *On First Looking into Chapman's Homer*.[18]

The immediately following segment of the narrative, containing the image of Odysseus lying exhausted under the leaves which closes Book 5, and involving a simile in which the safe preservation of the hero is compared to the careful guard-ing of a spark of fire by a man far from other men, has provoked a number of more recent writers to imitation or emulation. Perhaps most notably in recent times, Michael Longley, a poet who has been 'Homer-haunted for fifty years',[19] is

18. Quoted from Colvin (1917), 39–40. See further on the incident Bate (1963), 253.
19. Longley (2009), 97; this autobiographical piece reflects (97–104) on his poems' varied uses of Homer. On Longley's Homeric leanings see further Hardwick (2006); Taplin (2009).

responsible for a translation of this short excerpt (*Od.* 5.474–93) which is out-standing in its finely modulated simplicity:

A BED OF LEAVES

He climbed to the copse, a conspicuous place near water,
And crawled under two bushes sprouting from one stem (olive
And wild olive), a thatch so close neither gale-force winds
Nor sunlight nor cloudbursts could penetrate: it was here
Odysseus snuggled and heaped on his mattress of leaves
An eiderdown of leaves, enough to make a double-bed
In winter, whatever the weather, and smiled to himself
When he saw his bed and stretched out in the middle of it
And let even more of the fallen leaves fall over him:
As when a lonely man on a lonely farm smoors the fire
And hides a turf-sod in the ashes to save an ember,
So was his body in the bed of leaves its own kindling
And sleep settled on him like ashes and closed his eyelids.[20]

Conspicuous here is Longley's obsolete or dialect word 'smoors' ('smothers', line 10), which corresponds to an ordinary enough Homeric verb but is perhaps not inappropriate within a passage which contains several words unique either to Homer or to Greek literature.[21]

The moment when Odysseus relaxes exhausted into the pile of leaves features also in several poems by Peter Reading. One illustration, from the start of Reading's collection *Final Demands* (1988), must suffice. Here Odysseus is crossed with a man 'clearing the family's papers for next crowd's vacant possession':

Crapulous death-fright at 3 in the morning, grim fantasising …
Morphean, painless, idyllic expiry, easeful, Sabaean …
duvet and pillow-case metamorphose to sweet-smelling sered leaves,
thick-fallen under two olive boles grafted, canopied tightly,
such as the storm-wrecked Laertides, life-wracked, sunk in exhausted
snug at the end of Book V …

dreamingly crawls and his hands have now raked a litter together,
spacious and deep, for the leafage is lying in plentiful downfall,
lays him to rest in the midst of the leaves and piles them around him,
just as a man might cover a brand with char-blacked ashes,
guarding the seed of the fire for his tribe to use in the future,
so does he deeply immerse in the fall of past generations,

---

20. Longley (1995), 33. In the same collection Longley has also used Homer's lines 5.432–4, in the middle of Hughes's *Odyssey* passage, for an image of poetic tradition in the short poem 'Homer's Octopus'.
21. For examples, see Dawe (1993), 242.

litter of leaves, not from olives, but the sepia, brittle
leaves of the letters of lost correspondents, infinite, death-frail
      (Croxley, papyrus and bond), sinks in the lines of the dead.[22]

Varied as they are, these reactions to the *Odyssey* passage demonstrate that while the selection of lines for Hughes's translation exercise may have been externally imposed, it took him to a Homeric episode found suggestive and rewarding by other poets of his own time as well as other times.

His commission once accepted, how did Hughes proceed? Like Logue, he had little or no Greek and presumably he commenced, as Carne-Ross advised Logue, by 'reading translations by those who did'. This does not preclude word-by-word progress with a dictionary or perhaps a parallel text at the same time. But it may prove less productive to compare Hughes's work with the Greek than with the exactly contemporary translation of the *Odyssey* by Robert Fitzgerald, first published in 1961. Fitzgerald's was one of the most highly acclaimed translations of its era. It won the 1961 Bollingen Award for the best translation of a poem into English, was hailed in the *New Statesman* as 'the best poetic version of the *Odyssey* this century', and soon found its way onto innumerable 'great books' reading lists; it is still in print today.[23]

It is immediately apparent how Hughes's technique generates something of the quality of 'struggling dumbness' he associated with literal translation. Odysseus soon finds himself unable to make land:

Then the heart of Odysseus shrank and he groaned:
'Against hope, Zeus gives this glance of the land,
And I have managed my body over the gulf
Only to find no way from the water. Offshore, horns of rock,
Surf bellowing and mauling around them,
Behind them, empty cliff going up
And the sea crowding in deeply. Nowhere foothold
To step from disaster, but, in attempting,
A surge would uproot me and shatter me on rock-edges,
Sluicing my whole trouble to nothing. And if I swim on further,
Seeking the sands of a bay where the sea goes in more peaceably
Some squall will whirl down and drag me,
For all my protesting, out into depths and the maws of ravenous fish,
Or a god fetch something monstrous up from the pit to attack me –
One of the horde that feed at the hand of Amphitrite;
And I know too well how the Earth-shaker detests me.'

           (21–36)

22. Untitled; quoted from Reading (1996), II, 119.
23. The Fitzgerald text is quoted below from Fitzgerald (1965), 96–9. For further critical reaction to Fitzgerald's Homeric translations, see Carne-Ross (1974).

There is certainly 'oddity': 'to maul' has not previously been known as an intransitive verb (even supposing it is something surf is capable of doing), and the grammar of, for instance, the middle sentence ('Nowhere foothold ... to nothing') would not pass muster as strictly correct English, though it could not be said to be particularly Greek either. Fitzgerald is more idiomatic:

> No matter how I try it, the surf may throw me
> against the cliffside; no good fighting there.
>
> (415–16)

Overall, Fitzgerald's less coloured rendering, here as elsewhere, might be supposed on that account more faithful: is it Hughesian rather than Homeric violence and overstatement that leads to the 'ravenous fish' and the frighteningly overabundant progeny of nature (the 'horde that feed') in the last lines? In fact, these elements are present in the Greek. 'Some scholars,' Dawe notes, 'have rightly complained that things are overdone here.'[24] The Loeb crib offers 'lest some god may even send forth upon me some great monster from out the sea – and many such does glorious Amphitrite breed'.[25] It is Fitzgerald who fights shy of presenting these features, offering only 'Or then again, some shark of Amphitritē's | may hunt me, sent by the genius of the deep'. True, Fitzgerald is committed to rendering the Greek in the same number of English lines, and economy is a basic principle; but 'genius' looks a questionable choice for δαίμων, and 'shark' for the non-specific κῆτος.[26]

This is a passage of interior monologue (there are four in this episode). Narrative passages require different handling, and Hughes achieves a tumultuous effect over long stretches here, partly by adopting a simple iterative mode throughout – 'he felt', 'he groaned', 'it happened'. He can go further, too, into markedly asyndetic writing:

> But within hail of the land, heard sea rending on rock,
> Eruption of the surge, whitening over the land-face,
> Bundling everything in spray. No harbour fit for a ship and no inlet,
> But thrust prows of crags and spines of reefs under hanging walls.
>
> (17–20)

In these ways Hughes manages greater directness than Fitzgerald's more conventionally presented narrative, in which verbal markers like 'as', 'during' and 'when' are constantly organizing the material. Compare Fitzgerald's corresponding lines:

24. Dawe (1993), 243.
25. Murray (1919), 201, for *Od.* 5.421–2: 'ἠέ τί μοι καὶ κῆτος ἐπισσεύῃ μέγα δαίμων | ἐξ ἁλός, οἷά τε πολλὰ τρέφει κλυτὸς Ἀμφιτρίτη'.
26. A κῆτος could, according to Aelian (*NA* 9.45), be many types of sea monster. This is the *Odyssey*'s sole allusion to this danger, according to Huebeck *et al.* (1988–9), I, 285.

> But when he came in earshot
> he heard the trampling roar of sea on rock,
> where combers, rising shoreward, thudded down
> on the sucking ebb – all sheeted with salt foam.
> Here were no coves or harbourage or shelter,
> Only steep headlands, rockfallen reefs and crags.
>
> (400–5)

Some of Fitzgerald's verbs are energetic enough, but the overall effect is constrained by his decision to stick to fully grammatical sentences and introduce each new element with proper narrative *ordonnance*. Hughes aims rather for immediacy.

Near the start of the episode Fitzgerald has a couple of typical narrative lines:

> Two nights, two days, in the solid deep-sea swell
> he drifted, many times awaiting death
>
> (388–9)

These correspond to Hughes's:

> Two days and two nights he foundered in massive seas
> With the darkness of death breaking over and hollowing under.
>
> (6–7)

Hughes's second line strongly evokes the heavy sea-swell and the movement of the body rolling helplessly in it, which is to say that we are at least in the realms of poetry here, whereas with Fitzgerald this is scarcely so: we are informed that there was a 'sea swell', but there seems no attempt to summon one up. On the other hand, Hughes's adjective 'massive' is rather uncertain in its register, perhaps a little too informal for the surrounding material. It is notable that as he goes on, Hughes actually eschews adjectives whereas Fitzgerald tends to insist on them. I don't mean conventional or formulaic epithets like 'Owl-eyed Athene' (in Hughes's line 41), which he may have seen as more or less obligatory in a Homer translation, but rather the way in which, within the cut-and-thrust of the violent action, the head-on quality is attained partly by throwing the onus onto nouns and verbs, making them carry the weight directly:

> He plunged forward,
> Both hands grasped rock, and he clung there groaning
> As the mass ground over.
>
> (41–3)

But, where Hughes does permit himself more adjectival writing, his expressions again partake of that quality he was to claim translations need to achieve in his

MPT editorials, 'the very oddity and struggling dumbness of word for word version' which 'is what makes our own imagination jump'. The contrast with Fitzgerald could not be clearer in this respect; far from deploying the unexpectedly expressive word, the American translator tends towards stock phrases and even periphrasis.

> His flesh swollen and his heart swamped by the seas (Hughes 64)
> all vital force now conquered by the sea (Fitzgerald 451)

> A mounding wave heaved him (Hughes 37)
> a heavy surge | was taking him (Fitzgerald 425–6)

> calming the chop of its waves and smoothing a path (Hughes 62)
> the river god made quiet water (Fitzgerald 449)

Numerous other local felicities present themselves to the eye in Hughes's version. Toward the end he drops in and out of an alliterative technique suggestive of Old English poems like *The Seafarer* and *The Wanderer* – the same sound being used in the second half of the line as the first, and/or in the second of two adjacent lines:

> He ... **cl**imbed to a **cl**ump
> Of trees in a **cl**earing, near the water.
> It was an **o**live and a wild **o**live knotting so densely one with the **o**ther
> **N**either the stroke of the **n**aked sun
> **N**or **w**et sea-**w**inds **n**or the **n**eedling rain could enter ...
> **W**here dead **l**eaves **w**ere **l**ittered abundant enough
> To **w**arm two or three from the **w**orst of **w**inter.
>
> (80–4, 87–8; my emphases)

Some of Homer's commentators have found Odysseus distinctly valetudinarian at this point. If he stays in the open, he fears, the frost, dew, and wind might over-come him in his enfeebled state. Fitzgerald offers:

> how can I not succumb, being weak and sick,
> to the night's damp and hoar-frost of the morning?
> The air comes cold from rivers before dawn.

Hughes manages a voice of bitter experience rather than of grandmotherly caution:

> Clamping frost and the saturating dews, sea-sodden as I am now,
> Could be my death. And I know how bleakly
> Wind before dawn comes off the water.
>
> (73–5)

One could go on pointing out such successes,[27] but it is time to suggest (as proposed earlier) how this translation links with the rest of Hughes's imaginative life of the period in which it was composed.

The commentary on *The Storm* in Weissbort's *Selected Translations* is based on occasions on which Hughes mentioned Homer in interviews. In these contexts he referred to Homer as one of the 'poets of violence', and to the story of Odysseus, like those of other epics, as a sort of shamanistic flight. 'The shaman's dream,' Hughes is recorded as saying in the year he prepared this translation, 'is the skeleton of thousands of folktales and myths. And of many narrative poems, the *Odyssey*, the *Divine Comedy*, *Faust*, etc.'[28]

Hughes undoubtedly characterized *The Odyssey* in this way. But he only ever did so when speaking of it as one example among several of major poems that conform to some generalization he was making. These remarks seem to draw on his broader reading of the *Odyssey* more than his actual translating of this episode. And a broader reading of the *Odyssey* is something Hughes's work of these years reflects, as we have seen from the one use of the poem that most Hughes readers will recall, the short *Lupercal* composition 'Everyman's Odyssey'. Hughes, that is, had taken an independent interest in the Homeric epic, and that interest was not confined to shamanism.

Hughes's first translation reflects several characteristic interests and emphases. Physical struggle is prominent. There is violence. A number of gods are invoked or otherwise mentioned. But none of these things is as central as a more fundamental subject still: the existential plight of man. The Homeric passage is one, after all, in which Odysseus is brought, by a bitter combination of divine wrath and divine assistance, to his lowest ebb; as a modern commentary observes of this moment at the end of Book 5, 'it is the poet's wish that the recovery of Odysseus' fortunes shall begin from the lowest possible point'.[29] The great English Homer translator Alexander Pope appears to have found in Odysseus' situation here one of the character's principal claims to distinction over Virgil's Aeneas, to judge by one of the notes on this passage in his translation:

> The proposition of the Poem requires [Homer] to describe a man of sufferings in the person of *Ulysses*: he therefore no sooner introduces him but he throws him into the utmost calamities, and describes them largely, to shew at once the greatness of his distress, and his wisdom and patience under it. In what are the sufferings of *Æneas* in *Virgil* comparable to these of *Ulysses*? *Æneas* suffers little personally in comparison of *Ulysses*, his incidents have less variety, and consequently less beauty.[30]

---

27. For further comments, including the intriguing suggestion that this is a rare instance in Hughes's verse in which the formal elements of classical prosody seem to exert an influence on his own, see Talbot (2006*a*).
28. Weissbort (2006), 14–15.
29. Heubeck *et al.* (1988–9), I, 288.
30. Pope (1939–69), IX, 199 (*ad* 5.550).

One last comparison between Hughes and Fitzgerald will bring out the differences between their responses to this.

Halfway through the passage the exhausted Odysseus calls on the unknown god of the river in which he is attempting to swim to land. Fitzgerald and Hughes at this point offer respectively:

> O hear me, lord of the stream:
> how sorely I depend upon your mercy,
> derelict as I am by the sea's anger.
> Is he not sacred, even to the gods,
> the wandering man who comes, as I have come,
> in weariness before your knees, your waters?
> Here is your servant; lord, have mercy on me.
>
> (Fitzgerald 442–8)

> Whoever you are, king, hear my prayers, for I come
> Out of the sea's gape and Poseidon's anger.
> The everlasting gods give ear to the prayer of a wanderer,
> And a wanderer I come now, humbly to your waters,
> After hard sufferings. Pity me, king, and take me into your care.
>
> (Hughes 56–60)

For Homer, Odysseus is of course a stranger and a suppliant,[31] and some of the phrasing of both translators reflects this: both present a 'wanderer' who asks to be 'heard'. Fitzgerald also suggests something of the special status of the stranger in the antique Greek world; his 'sacred' (445) equates to Homer's ἱκέτης (447). But Fitzgerald has assimilated the episode overall to an obviously alien Christian ethos. Hughes envisages Odysseus offering 'prayers' to the unknown river-god; prayers are common to all religions. But the inescapably Christian, indeed quasi-liturgical vocabulary used by Fitzgerald's Odysseus, most egregiously in the final line, pulls the Homeric text into another orbit. To speak of oneself as god's 'servant' is the most traditional of Christian tropes. Homer's ἱκέτης (line 450) is a suppliant, a fugitive, and he stands in need not of 'mercy' (another Christianization) but of a protector who will undertake to apply the laws of hospitality to a stranger in an alien environment.

When Charles Lamb used Chapman's *Odyssey* as the basis for his prose retelling *The Adventures of Ulysses* (1808), he was advised to tone down his narrative and remove 'shocking' elements which might alienate some readers. Lamb defended what he had done, complaining of Homer translators who had taken that course. He wrote to Charles Lloyd the Elder, a member of his circle who was attempting

---

31. This supplication scene, which has a special form because Odysseus' circumstances do not allow him to follow the normal ritual, can be considered 'an anticipatory doublet of the two major "supplication" scenes to follow' in Books 6 and 7 of the *Odyssey*. Jong (2001), 146–7.

a new version: 'What I seem to miss [in your specimen translation], and what certainly everybody misses in Pope, is a certain savage-like plainness of speaking in Achilles – a sort of indelicacy – the heroes in Homer are not half civilised.' Lloyd's 'turn of mind', Lamb told him, 'would, I have no doubt, lead you to *civilise* his phrases, and sometimes to *half christen* them'.[32] This acute analysis helps us see why Lamb's generation prized Chapman and demoted Pope correspondingly. But the terms Lamb uses also suggest how the contrasting approaches of Chapman/Pope have played themselves out again in Hughes/Fitzgerald. If we see things Lamb's way, the courses taken by the two translators in each pair are antithetical. Fitzgerald places Odysseus in his world while Hughes aims for an imaginative jump into the Homeric world. Fitzgerald moves Homer towards him, while Hughes tries to allow Homer to exert the pull. Neither course is in itself a guaranteed route to success or failure, and it might be said that neither translator applies his procedure with complete consistency. (What is Hughes's alliteration but a 'device extraneous to the original', to quote his own *MPT* editorial?)

I have suggested in the course of this book that successful translations have the character of a meeting or dialogue between writers rather than of ventriloquism in either direction. What previous discussion there has been of Hughes's Homer seems to imply that Hughes fell into the trap of making Homer speak his own thoughts, whereas I'd say it's Fitzgerald who most seriously risks ventriloquy. The danger on the other side is that of failing to connect Homer to the present. But finally, and more widely, these two translations seem to show the permanence of this dilemma. We can recognize that, while still enjoying what both Chapman and Pope, both Hughes and Fitzgerald, have to offer.

Appendix

The Storm

from HOMER, *Odyssey*, Book V

And now Athene, daughter of Zeus, descended to change matters:
Reined back all blasts from their running and bound them in stillness.
Then called a smooth wind out of the North to flatten the mountainous water
Where the Zeus-born Odysseus laboured, and to help him to safety
With the Phaecians, those sea-farers.

Two nights and two days he floundered in massive seas
With the darkness of death breaking over and hollowing under.

---

32. 13 June 1809; Lamb (1975–8), III, 17.

Until, touched by the third dawn, all wind dropped of a sudden,
And in the airless after-calm
Craning around as the huge swell hoisted him upwards   10
He saw coast along the skyline. Then as children
See their father's life coming clear of the grip of an evil
That has stretched and drained him with agony long and binding,
And they rejoice that the gods have loosed him,
Odysseus exulted at his glimpse of the land and its trees,
And he drove through the waves to feel his feet upon earth.

But within hail of the land, heard sea rending on rock,
Eruption of the surge, whitening over the land-face,
Bundling everything in spray. No harbour fit for a ship and no inlet,
But thrust prows of crags and spines of reefs under hanging walls.   20

Then the heart of Odysseus shrank and he groaned:
'Against hope, Zeus gives this glance of the land,
And I have managed my body over the gulf
Only to find no way from the water. Offshore, horns of rock,
Surf bellowing and mauling around them,
Behind them, empty cliff going up
And the sea crowding in deeply. Nowhere foothold
To step from disaster, but, in attempting,
A surge would uproot me and shatter me on rock-edges,
Sluicing my whole trouble to nothing. And if I swim on further,   30
Seeking the sands of a bay where the sea goes in more peaceably
Some squall will whirl down and drag me,
For all my protesting, out into depths and the maws of ravenous fish,
Or a god fetch something monstrous up from the pit to attack me –
One of the horde that feed at the hand of Amphitrite;
And I know too well how the Earth-shaker detests me.'

A mounding wave heaved him from his deliberations,
Building beneath him it carried and crashed him onto the outworks.
There he would have been skinned in an instant
And the bones pestled within him,   40
But Owl-eyed Athene touched him. He plunged forward,
Both hands grasped rock, and he clung there groaning
As the mass ground over. So he survived it.
But, collapsing back, it stunned and tossed him far out into the sea.
Thickly as gravel crusting the suckers
Of some octopus plucked from its crevice
The rock tore flesh from his fingers.
And there wretched Odysseus, buried in the backwash welter,
Struggled with a death none had predicted
Till the Grey-eyed Athene found him.   50

Shouldering to air outside the surf and its wrack
He swam along watching the shore for a bay and quieter water.
Soon, off the mouth of a sweet river, saw landing,
Clear of rocks, and protected from the onset of open sea.
Feeling the shove of the current, he prayed in his heart to its god:
'Whoever you are, king, hear my prayers, for I come
Out of the sea's gape and Poseidon's anger.
The everlasting gods give ear to the prayer of a wanderer,
And a wanderer I come now, humbly to your waters,
After hard sufferings. Pity me, king, and take me into your care.'   60

Even as he spoke, the river stilled its momentum
And calming the chop of its waves and smoothing a path
Gathered the swimmer to safety. Now knees and thick arms folded:
His flesh swollen and his heart swamped by the seas
Odysseus slumped, unable to speak or move, and gulping at air
While sea-water belched from his mouth and nostrils.

Till his powers gathered and he stood. And unbinding the veil of the goddess,
Dropped it into the seaward river.
The weight of the current snatched it and in a moment Ino held it.
Then Odysseus turned from the river, kneeled in the reeds and kissing the
      earth   70
Groaned: 'What more misery now? And how shall a man get out of this?
What if I wait the night away, crouching here in the river-bottom?
Clamping frost and the saturating dews, sea-sodden as I am now,
Could be my death. And I know how bleakly
Wind before dawn comes off the water.

Or higher on the land, under the trees
And bedded in undergrowth, praying for the bone-chill
And fatigue to go from me, and praying for sleep to find me,
Maybe it will be the wild beasts that find me.'

Yet he took this last and climbed to a clump   80
Of trees in a clearing, near the water.
It was an olive and a wild olive knotting so densely one with the other

Neither the stroke of the naked sun
Nor wet sea-winds nor the needling rain could enter.
After his bitter ordeal, gladly royal Odysseus
Crept in under there and raked a bed wide
Where dead leaves were littered abundant enough
To warm two or three from the worst of winter.

Then he stretched out his body and heaped leaves over.
As one on a lonely farm and far from neighbours
Buries a live brand in black embers, preserving the seed of fire
Lest at need he be forced to go find fire elsewhere,
Odysseus hid under leaves. Then Athene ended his labours.
Covering his eyes, in sleep she released him.

12

Afterword

Considerable discussion has recently been devoted to what is called the 'invisibility' of the translator since the later seventeenth century. This has to do with the self-effacing approach that has become conventional, and with the way the translator's contribution to the translated material is, at least in the anglophone world, normally downplayed; it is understood as a commendation to say that a text 'does not read like a translation'. This book has engaged with a different subject. I have rarely been concerned with 'approach' in the abstract, at times indeed suggesting it is an ambition of doubtful value to identify the point at which 'translation' becomes 'imitation', becomes 'response' – and even suggesting that hard-and-fast distinctions between translated and original works may often be as inappropriate for English as for ancient writings. Instead, I have primarily addressed a different kind of blind spot. It would obviously seem very strange to suggest that a translator of the stature of Wordsworth is 'invisible'. But as we have seen, Wordsworth, like other translators whose *œuvres* contain non-translated work, is in fact largely unknown to literary history, and entirely unknown to students of literature in schools and universities, in that capacity. Thus the lacuna I have been pondering is not what is meant by the expression 'the translator's invisibility'. My concern here does not start with the seventeenth or eighteenth century, when the central place of translation in English literary culture was, as we have repeatedly noted, assured. The optical problem this book has explored seems rather to have developed in the course of the twentieth century, and it is a blind spot not primarily affecting writers and translators, but literary critics and historians. All the same, it is with us.

On the Classics side, while it is clear that translation can be well accommodated to the agenda of reception, it is less clear that translation is actually coming to

English Translation and Classical Reception: Towards a New Literary History, First Edition.
Stuart Gillespie.
© 2011 Stuart Gillespie. Published 2011 by John Wiley & Sons, Ltd.

take what I would see as its rightful place. We have begun to explore the dissemination of classical texts through creative responses of all kinds, especially in the culture of the English-speaking world; with translation as with other creative responses, there is scope for comparative scholarship too. But the basis for further progress is in some ways narrow, and the precedents unimpressive. The 'approved' translations for Classical Studies purposes have in the recent past been practical and prosaic ones (such as Lattimore's Homer), seldom 'creative' ones (too distant from the Latin or Greek, too likely to 'mislead' as to the 'sense'). That is, they are Gilbert Murray's descendants rather than Ezra Pound's, or (perhaps worse) the descendants of all those eighteenth-century classics 'literally translated into English prose'. They have seldom reached back in time; in fact, as far as their language goes, they have as 'modern' an idiom as can be managed, but their authors are never known for their writing, if they ever attempt it, in their own tongue. Looking back to the nineteenth century, Dryden's Virgil and Pope's Homer were still considered 'ways in' to the study of Virgil and Homer more than a hundred years after they first appeared. For example, a 700-page production under the title *Classical Manual; or, a Mythological, Historical, and Geographical Commentary on Pope's Homer and Dryden's Æneid of Virgil* appeared in 1827 and was reprinted in 1839. In our own time, in contrast, the fate of the excellent paperback series of selected English translations by diverse historical hands under the title 'Penguin Classics in English' points in the opposite direction. It ran from 1996 to 2005 over some 15 volumes extending to Homer, Virgil, Horace, Martial, Ovid, Catullus, Juvenal, Seneca, and beyond Greek and Latin to Baudelaire, Dante, Petrarch and other moderns, before the difficulty of selling the titles in North America led to its cancellation.[1] That difficulty was specifically related to the lack of adoptions on college courses, Penguin's aspiration for these titles, though the blame can be laid at the door of more college subjects than one.

These are some of the difficulties on each side – at bottom, it may be, reducible to a single problem, the canard of linguistic immediacy: 'There is no substitute for the original.' But the final emphasis should be on possibilities rather than limitations. The disciplines of Classics and English can come together in translation because it presents us with a transformative moment involving more than one culture. Eliot wrote in his review of Murray's Euripides of how 'we need a digestion that can assimilate both Homer and Flaubert'. 'How does classical literature look after English?' can be broken down into questions like 'How does Homer taste after Hughes, or after Chapman?' and 'How does Greek tragedy look after Shakespeare?' If we read classical literature at all, we cannot help but read through post-classical culture: these questions are inherent in the activity of reading ancient texts. We are already looking at Greek tragedy through Shakespeare, only we are not always conscious of it.

---

1. Or more precisely, as vouchsafed to the present writer by the series editor, the difficulty of selling further titles in the series to the Penguin's New York office for publication in the USA.

In his sprightly essay 'Why read the Classics?' Italo Calvino defines a 'classic' by reference to the marks previous readings have left upon it. 'The classics,' he proposes, 'are the books that come down to us bearing the traces they themselves have left on the culture or cultures they have passed through.'[2] This perhaps risks understatement – a 'trace' implies a small and maybe alien feature (as in a 'trace element') – but points helpfully to the two-sidedness of this exchange, and its effect upon the cultures through which the classics pass. For digestion is of course a process that transforms the eater as well as the eaten, so there are corresponding questions about the receiving culture: how do we feel about Wordsworth when his ties to Juvenal, or Virgil, or Lucretius, are adequately registered? How does Hughes's work look after his Homer translation has been recovered, or his Seneca, his Ovid and his Euripides given full weight? That is, how does English literature look after classical translation is accorded its due in the record? This book has argued that fully answering these questions would lead us into a literary-historical landscape looking very different from those which currently present themselves to the eye. A new planet might, indeed, swim into our ken.

2. Calvino (1989), 128.

References

Adams, J. N. (1982). *The Latin Sexual Vocabulary*. London.

Adamson, Sylvia (1999). 'Literary Language' (pp. 539–642) in Roger Lass, ed., *The Cambridge History of the English Language*, Vol. 3: *1476–1776*. Cambridge.

Aden, John M. (1963). *The Critical Opinions of John Dryden: A Dictionary*. Nashville, TN.

Aden, John M. (1973). '"The Change of Scepters, and impending Woe": Poetical Allusion in Pope's Statius', *PQ* 52: 728–38.

Anderson, Robert, ed. (1792–5). *The Works of the British Poets. With Prefaces, Biographical and Critical*, 14 vols. Edinburgh.

Anon. (1783). *Nobility: A Poem. In Imitation of Juvenal's Eighth Satire*. London.

Apter, Ronnie (1984). *Digging for the Treasure: Translation after Pound*. New York.

Archibald, Elizabeth (1991). *Apollonius of Tyre: Medieval and Renaissance Themes and Variations*. Woodbridge.

Armstrong, Richard (2007). 'Introduction' (pp. 1–10) in *Remusings: Essays on the Translation of Classical Poetry* (*Classical and Modern Literature*, 27/1).

Arnold, Matthew (1960). 'On the Modern Element in Literature' (pp. 18–37) in *Arnold on the Classical Tradition*, ed. R. H. Super. Ann Arbor, MI.

Arnold, Mathew (1965). *Poems*, ed. Kenneth Allott. London.

Ascham, Roger (1570). *The Scholemaster or Plaine and Perfite way of teachyng Children, to understand, write, and speake, the Latin Tong*. London.

Attridge, Derek (1974). *Well-Weighed Syllables: Elizabethan Verse in Classical Metres*. Cambridge.

Baldwin, T. W. (1944). *William Shakspere's Small Latine and Lesse Greek*, 2 vols. Urbana, IL.

Barber, Charles (1997). *Early Modern English*. Edinburgh.

English Translation and Classical Reception: Towards a New Literary History, First Edition.
Stuart Gillespie.
© 2011 Stuart Gillespie. Published 2011 by John Wiley & Sons, Ltd.

Barkan, Leonard (1986). *The Gods Made Flesh: Metamorphosis and the Pursuit of Paganism*. New Haven, CT.

Barnard, John, ed. (1973). *Pope: The Critical Heritage*. London and Boston, MA.

Bate, Jonathan (1993). *Shakespeare and Ovid*. Oxford.

Bate, Walter Jackson (1963). *John Keats*. Cambridge, MA.

Beal, Peter (1998). *In Praise of Scribes: Manuscripts and their Makers in Seventeenth-Century England*. Oxford.

Benson, Larry D., ed. (1987). *The Riverside Chaucer*, third edition. Boston, MA.

Boas, M. (1914). 'De librorum Catonianorum historia atque compositione', *Mnemosyne* 42: 17–46.

Bolgar, R. R. (1954). *The Classical Heritage and its Beneficiaries*. Cambridge.

Bonnell, Thomas F. (2008). *The Most Disreputable Trade: Publishing the Classics of English Poetry 1765–1810*. Oxford.

Bottkol, J. M. (1943). 'Dryden's Latin Scholarship', *Modern Philology* 40: 241–54.

Boutcher, Warren (2000). 'The Renaissance' (pp. 45–55) in *The Oxford Guide to Literature in English Translation*, ed. Peter France. Oxford.

Braden, Gordon (1985). *Renaissance Tragedy and the Senecan Tradition: Anger's Privilege*. New Haven, CT.

Braden, Gordon (2004). 'Plutarch, Shakespeare and the Alpha Males' (pp. 188–205) in Charles Martindale and A. B. Taylor, eds., *Shakespeare and the Classics*. Cambridge.

Braden, Gordon (2010). 'Translating Procedures in Theory and Practice' (pp. 89–100) in Braden, Cummings and Gillespie.

Braden, Gordon, Cummings, Robert, and Gillespie, Stuart, eds. (2010). *The Oxford History of Literary Translation in English*, Vol. 2: *1550–1660*. Oxford.

Brannigan, John (1998). *New Historicism and Cultural Materialism*. London.

Braund, Susanna (1988). *Beyond Anger: A Study of Juvenal's Third Book of Satires*. Cambridge.

Braund, Susanna, ed. and trans. (2004a). *Juvenal and Persius* (Loeb). Cambridge, MA, and London.

Braund, Susanna (2004b). 'Safe Sex? Dryden's Translation of Juvenal's Sixth Satire' (pp. 139–57) in *John Dryden (1631–1700): His Politics, His Plays, and His Poets*, ed. Claude Rawson and Aaron Santesso. Newark, DE.

Brooks, Harold (1949). 'The "Imitation" in English Poetry, Especially in Formal Satire, before the Age of Pope', *Review of English Studies* 25: 124–40.

Brooks, Harold, ed. (1979). *A Midsummer Night's Dream*. London.

Brower, Reuben A. (1971). *Hero and Saint: Shakespeare and the Graeco-Roman Heroic Tradition*. Oxford.

Brown, Sarah (1994). 'Ovid, Golding, and *The Tempest*', *Translation and Literature* 3: 3–29.

Burgess, John (2005). *The Faber Guide to Greek and Roman Drama*. London.

Burrow, Colin (2002). 'Re-embodying Ovid: Renaissance Afterlives' (pp. 301–19) in *The Cambridge Companion to Ovid*, ed. Philip Hardie. Cambridge.

Butler, Marilyn (1984). 'Satire and the Images of Self in the Romantic Period: The Long Tradition of Hazlitt's *Liber Amoris*' (pp. 209–25) in *English Satire and the Satiric Tradition*, ed. Claude Rawson (*Yearbook of English Studies*, 14). Oxford.

Calabrese, Michael A. (1985). *Chaucer's Ovidian Arts of Love*. Gainesville, FL.

Caldwell, Tanya M. (2008). *Virgil Made English: The Decline of Classical Authority*. New York.

Calvin, Robert (1928). 'Juvenal in England 1750–1802', *Philological Quarterly* 7: 9–16.

Calvino, Italo (1989). *The Literature Machine: Essays*, trans. Patrick Creagh. London.

Cameron, Alan (1970). *Claudian: Poetry and Propaganda at the Court of Honorius*. Oxford.

Cantor, Paul (1997). 'Shakespeare's Parallel Lives: Plutarch and the Roman Plays' (pp. 69–82) in *Shakespeare's Plutarch* (*Poetica*, 48), ed. Mary Ann McGrail. Tokyo.

Carne-Ross, D. S. (1961). 'Translation and Transposition' (pp. 3–21) in *The Craft and Context of Translation: A Symposium*, ed. William Arrowsmith and Roger Shattuck. Austin, TX. Reprinted in Carne-Ross (2010).

Carne-Ross, D. S. (1974). 'On Looking into Fitzgerald's Homer', *New York Review of Books*, 12 December. Reprinted in Carne-Ross (2010).

Carne-Ross, D. S. (1990). 'Jocasta's Divine Head: English with a Foreign Accent', *Arion*, 3rd series, 1: 106–41. Reprinted in Carne-Ross (2010).

Carne-Ross, D. S. (2010). *Classics and Translation: Essays*, ed. Kenneth Haynes. Lewisburg, PA.

Chalmers, Alexander, ed. (1810). *The Works of the English Poets, from Chaucer to Cowper*, 21 vols. London.

Chandler, James (1999). *England in 1819: The Politics of Literary Culture and the Case of Romantic Hellenism*. Chicago.

Chapman, George (1618). *The Georgicks of Hesiod*. London.

Cheney, Patrick (1997). *Marlowe's Counterfeit Profession: Ovid, Spenser, Counter-Nationhood*. Toronto, Buffalo and London.

Clancy, Richard W. (2000). *Wordsworth's Classical Undersong: Education, Rhetoric and Poetic Truth*. Basingstoke.

Clarke, Danielle (2010). 'Translation and the English Language' (pp. 17–23) in Braden, Cummings and Gillespie (2010).

Claudian (1650). *Cl. Claudiani quæ exstant: ex emendatione Nicolai Heinsij*. Lugduni Batavorum.

Claudian (1993). 'Claudian's "Old Man of Verona": An Anthology of English Translations with a New Poem by Edwin Morgan', *Translation and Literature* 2: 87–97.

Clogan, Paul (1967). 'Chaucer's Use of the *Thebaid*', *English Miscellany* 18: 9–31.

Clogan, Paul (1968). *The Medieval Achilleid of Statius*. Leiden.

Clogan, Paul (1991). 'The Renaissance Commentators on Statius' (pp. 237–9) in *Actus Conventus Neo-Latini Torontoensis*, ed. Alexander Dalzell, Charles Fantazzi, and Richard J. Schoeck.

Cobb, Samuel (1710). *Poems on Several Occasions*. London (first published 1707).

Coleridge, Samuel Taylor (1955). *Coleridge on the Seventeenth Century*, ed. Roberta Florence Brinkley. Durham, NC.

Colvin, Sidney (1917). *John Keats: His Life and Poetry, His Friends, Critics and After-Fame*. London.

Commager, Steele (1961). *The Odes of Horace*. London.

Connor, Peter (1987). *Horace's Lyric Poetry: the Force of Humour*. Berwick, Victoria, Australia.

Conte, Gian Biagio (1994). *Latin Literature: A History*, translated by Joseph B. Solodow, revised by Don Fowler and Glenn W. Most. Baltimore, MD.

Costa, C. D. N., ed. (1974). *Seneca*. London and Boston, MA.

Courtney, E. (1980). *A Commentary on the Satires of Juvenal*. London.

Cowley, Abraham (1905). *English Writings*, ed. A. R. Waller, 2 vols. Cambridge.

Crawford, Robert, ed. (1998). *The Scottish Invention of English Literature*. Cambridge.

Creech, Thomas (1700). *Lucretius his Six Books of Epicurean Philosophy*. London (first published 1682).

Crum, Margaret (1969). *First-line Index of English Poetry, 1500–1800, in Manuscripts of the Bodleian Library, Oxford*, 2 vols. Oxford.

Cummings, Robert (1995). ' "To the cart the fift quheill": Gavin Douglas's Humanist Supplement to Virgil', *Translation and Literature* 4: 133–56.

Cummings, Robert (2010). 'Translation and Literary Innovation' (pp. 32–44) in Braden, Cummings and Gillespie.

Cummings, Robert, and Gillespie, Stuart (2009). 'Translations from Greek and Latin Classics 1550–1700: A Revised Bibliography', *Translation and Literature* 18: 1–42.

Curtis, Jared (1997). 'William Wordsworth, Francis Wrangham, and the Imitation of Juvenal's Eighth Satire', *Wordsworth Circle* 28: 103–5.

Curtis, Jared, ed. (1999). *Last Poems, 1821–1850* (The Cornell Wordsworth). New York.

Daalder, Joost (1989). 'Seneca and the Text of Marvell's "Climb at court for me that will" ', *Parergon* 7: 107–10.

Daniel, Samuel (1885–96). *The Complete Works in Verse and Prose*, ed. Alexander B. Grosart, 5 vols. London.

Dawe, R. D. (1993). *The Odyssey: Translation and Analysis*. Lewes.

De Quehen, Hugh, ed. (1996). *Lucy Hutchinson's Translation of Lucretius: De rerum natura*. Ann Arbor, MI.

De Selincourt, Ernest, ed. (1935). *The Letters of William and Dorothy Wordsworth: The Early Years, 1787–1805*. Oxford.

De Selincourt, Ernest, ed. (1937). *The Letters of William and Dorothy Wordsworth: The Middle Years*, Vol. I: *1806–June 1811*. Oxford.

De Selincourt, Ernest, ed. (1978). *The Letters of William and Dorothy Wordsworth: The Later Years*, Part 1, rev. Alan G. Hill. Oxford.

De Selincourt, Ernest, and Darbishire, Helen, eds. (1941–9). *Wordsworth: The Poetical Works*, 5 vols. Oxford.

Denton, John (1997). 'Plutarch, Shakespeare, Roman Politics and Renaissance Translation' (pp. 187–209) in *Shakespeare's Plutarch* (*Poetica*, 48), ed. Mary Ann McGrail.

Dix, Robin C. (2002). 'Wordsworth and Lucretius: The Psychological Impact of Creech's Translation', *English Language Notes* 39: 25–33.

Donno, Elizabeth Story, ed. (1972). *Andrew Marvell: The Complete Poems*. Harmondsworth.

Drayton, Michael (1931–41). *Works*, ed. J. William Hebel, 5 vols. Oxford.

Dryden, John (1808). *Works*, ed. Sir Walter Scott, 18 vols. London.

Dryden, John (1956–2000). *Works*, ed. E. N. Hooker *et al.*, 20 vols. Berkeley, CA.

Dryden, John, *et al.* (1754). *The Satires of Decimus Junius Juvenalis ... Translated into English Verse by Mr. Dryden and several other Hands*. London.

Dryden, John, trans. (1693). *The Satires of Aulus Persius Flaccus*. London.

Duncan-Jones, Katherine (2001). *Ungentle Shakespeare: Scenes from his Life*. London.

Dyce, Alexander, ed. (1887). *Recollections of the Table-Talk of Samuel Rogers*. London.

Dyer, Gary (1997). *British Satire and the Politics of Style, 1789–1832*. Cambridge.

Edden, Valerie (1973). 'The Best of Lyrick Poets' (pp. 135–60) in *Horace*, ed. C. D. N. Costa. London.

Edmonds, J. M. (1928). *The Greek Bucolic Poets with an English Translation* (Loeb). Cambridge, MA (first published 1912).

Eliot, T. S. (1967). 'Euripides and Professor Murray' (pp. 71–7) in *The Sacred Wood: Essays on Poetry and Criticism*. London (first published 1920).

Eliot, T. S., ed. (1928). *Selected Poems of Ezra Pound*. London.

Elwin, Whitwell, and William John Courthope, eds. (1871–89). *The Works of Alexander Pope*, 10 vols. London.

Ewbank, Inga-Stina (1986). 'Transformations of Cleopatra', *University of Leeds Review* 29: 61–78.

Ezell, Margaret J. M. (1993). *Writing Women's Literary History*. Baltimore, MD, and London.

Ezell, Margaret J. M. (1999). *Social Authorship and the Advent of Print*. Baltimore, MD, and London.

Fabian, Bernard (1979) 'Pope and Lucretius: Observations on *An Essay on Man*', *Modern Language Review* 74: 524–37.

Fitzgerald, Robert, translator (1965). *Homer: The Odyssey*. London.

Florio, John (1603). *The Essayes or Morall, Politike and Millitarie Discourses of Lord Michael de Montaigne*. London.

Fraenkel, Eduard (1957). *Horace*. Oxford.

France, Peter, and Haynes, Kenneth, eds. (2006). *The Oxford History of Literary Translation in English*, Vol. 4: *1790–1900*. Oxford.

Frazer, R. M., Jr. (1966). *The Trojan War: The Chronicles of Dictys of Crete and Dares the Phrygian*. Bloomington, IN.

Frost, William (1988). *John Dryden: Dramatist, Satirist, Translator*. New York.

Gifford, William (1802). *The Satires of Decimus Junius Juvenalis, translated into English Verse*. London.

Gill, Stephen (1998). *Wordsworth and the Victorians*. Oxford.

Gillespie, Stuart (1992). 'A Checklist of Restoration English Translations and Adaptations of Classical Greek and Latin Poetry, 1660–1700', *Translation and Literature* 1: 52–67.

Gillespie, Stuart (2001). *Shakespeare's Books: A Dictionary of Shakespeare Sources*. London and New Brunswick, NJ.

Gillespie, Stuart (2002). 'The *Anacreontea* in English: A Checklist of Translations to 1900 with a bibliography of secondary sources and some previously unpublished translations', *Translation and Literature* 11: 149–73.

Gillespie, Stuart (2005). 'The Developing Corpus of Literary Translation, 1660–1790' (pp. 121–46) in Gillespie and Hopkins (2005).

Gillespie, Stuart (2006). 'A New Eighteenth-Century Juvenal Translator: William Popple's Satires VI and X', *Translation and Literature* 15: 47–96.

Gillespie, Stuart (2007a). 'Persius' First Satire Englished: From an Early Eighteenth-Century Manuscript', *Translation and Literature* 16: 76–83.

Gillespie, Stuart (2007b). 'An English Version of Horace's *Odes*, *Satires*, and *Epistles* by William Popple (1700–1764)', *Translation and Literature* 16: 205–35.

Gillespie, Stuart (2009).'Translations from Greek and Latin Classics, Part 2: 1701–1800: A Revised Bibliography', *Translation and Literature* 18: 181–224.

Gillespie, Stuart (2010). 'Literary Afterlives: Metempsychosis from Ennius to Jorge Luis Borges' (pp. 209–25) in *Classical Literary Careers and their Reception*, ed. Philip Hardie and Helen Moore. Cambridge.

Gillespie, Stuart, and Cummings, Robert (2004). 'A Bibliography of Ovidian Translations and Imitations in English', *Translation and Literature* 13: 207–18.

Gillespie, Stuart, and Hardie, Philip, eds. (2007). *The Cambridge Companion to Lucretius*. Cambridge.

Gillespie, Stuart, and Hopkins, David, eds. (2005). *The Oxford History of Literary Translation in English*, Vol. 3: *1660–1790*. Oxford.

Gillespie, Stuart, and Hopkins, David, eds. (2008). *The Dryden–Tonson Miscellanies, 1684–1709*, 6 vols. London, New York and Tokyo.

Gillespie, Stuart, and Mackenzie, Donald (2007). 'Lucretius and the Moderns' (pp. 306–24) in Gillespie and Hardie (2007).

Gillespie, Stuart, and Sowerby, Robin (2005). 'Translation and Literary Innovation' (pp. 21–37) in Gillespie and Hopkins (2005).

Golding, Arthur (1564). *Thabridgment of the Histories of Trogus Pompeius, Collected and wrytten in the Laten Tonge, by the famous Historiographer Justine*. London.

Good, John Mason (1805). *The Nature of Things: A Didactic Poem. Translated*, 2 vols. London.

Goold, G. P., ed. and trans. (1990). *Propertius: Elegies* (Loeb). Cambridge, MA.

Gordon, Cosmo A. (1962). *A Bibliography of Lucretius*. London.

Granville, George, Lord Lansdowne (1736). *The Genuine Works in Verse and Prose*, 3 vols. London.

Graver, Bruce (1986a). 'Wordsworth and the Romantic Art of Translation', *Wordsworth Circle* 17: 169–74.

Graver, Bruce (1986b). 'Wordsworth and the Language of Epic: The Translation of the *Aeneid*', *Studies in Philology* 83: 261–85.

Graver, Bruce (1991). 'Wordsworth's Georgic Beginnings', *Texas Studies in Language and Literature* 33: 137–59.

Graver, Bruce, ed. (1998). *Translations of Chaucer and Virgil* (The Cornell Wordsworth). Ithaca, NY, and London.

Gray, Thomas (1909). *Letters*, ed. Duncan C. Tovey, 3 vols. London.

Gray, Thomas (1966). *Complete Poems*, ed. H. W. Starr and J. R. Hendrickson. Oxford.

Green, Peter, trans. (1994). *Ovid: The Poems of Exile*. London.

Greene, Thomas M. (1982). *The Light in Troy: Imitation and Discovery in Renaissance Poetry*. New Haven, CT, and London.

Gregory, Eileen (1997). *H.D. and Hellenism: Classic Lines*. Cambridge.

Grimald, Nicholas (1550). *Marcus Tullius Ciceroes Thre Bokes of Duties*. London.

H.D. (Hilda Doolittle) (1986). *Collected Poems, 1912–1944*, ed. Louis Martz. New York.

Hall, Edith, Macintosh, Fiona, and Taplin, Oliver, eds. (2000). *Medea in Performance 1500–2000*. Oxford.

Hall, Edith, Macintosh, Fiona, and Wrigley, Amanda, eds. (2004). *Dionysus since 69: Greek Tragedy at the Dawn of the Third Millennium*. Oxford.

Haller, Robert S. (1966). '*The Knight's Tale* and the Epic Tradition', *Chaucer Review* 1: 67–84.

Hammond, Paul (1983). *John Oldham and the Renewal of Classical Culture*. Cambridge.

Hammond, Paul (1985). 'Dryden's Philosophy of Fortune', *Modern Language Review* 80: 769–85.

Hammond, Paul (2002). 'The Restoration Poetic and Dramatic Canon' (pp. 388–409) in *The Cambridge History of the Book in Britain*, Vol. IV: *1557–1695*, ed. John Barnard and D. F. McKenzie. Cambridge.

Hammond, Paul (2006). *The Making of Restoration Poetry*. Cambridge.

Hammond, Paul, and Hopkins, David, eds. (1995–2005). *The Poems of John Dryden*, 5 vols. London.

Hardwick, Lorna (2000). *Translating Words, Translating Cultures*. London.

Hardwick, Lorna (2006). ' "Murmurs in the Cathedral": The Impact of Translations from Greek Poetry and Drama on Modern Work in English by Michael Longley and Seamus Heaney', *Yearbook of English Studies* 36: 204–15.

Harrison, S. J., ed. (2009). *Living Classics: Greece and Rome in Contemporary Poetry in English*. Oxford.

Helms, Lorraine (1997). *Seneca by Candlelight and Other Stories of Renaissance Drama*. Philadelphia, PA.

Henderson, John (1997). *Figuring out Nobility: Juvenal's Eighth 'Satire'*. Exeter.

Henderson, John (1999). *Writing down Rome: Satire, Comedy, and other Offences in Latin Poetry*. Oxford.

Heubeck, Alfred, *et al.* (1988–9). *A Commentary on Homer's Odyssey*, 2 vols. Oxford.

Highet, Gilbert (1954). *Juvenal the Satirist: A Study*. Oxford.

Hoby, Thomas (1588). *The Courtier of Count Baldessar Castilio*. London.

Hodges, Antony (1638). *The Loves of Clitophon and Leucippe ... Englished*. London.

Hodgson, Francis (1807). *The Satires of Juvenal: Translated and Illustrated*. London.

Hoffmann, Michael, and Lasdun, James, eds. (1994). *After Ovid: New Metamorphoses*. London.

Holland, Philemon (1601). *The Historie of the World. Commonly called, the Naturall Historie of C. Plinius Secundus ... The first Tome*. London.

Hollander, John (1959). 'Versions, Interpretations, and Performances' (pp. 205–31) in *On Translation*, ed. Reuben A. Brower. Cambridge, MA.

Holmes, John (2008). 'Lucretius at the Fin de Siècle: Science, Religion, and Poetry', *English Literature in Transition* 51: 266–80.

Honigmann, E. A. J., ed. (1968). *Richard III*. London.

Hooley, Daniel (1988). *The Classics in Paraphrase: Ezra Pound and Modern Translators of Latin Poetry*. London.

Hooley, Daniel (1997). *The Knotted Thong: Structures of Mimesis in Persius*. Ann Arbor, MI.

Hopkins, David (2001). 'Translation, Metempsychosis, and the Flux of Nature: "Of the Pythagorean Philosophy" ' (pp. 145–54) in *Dryden and the World of Neoclassicism*, ed. Holger Klein. Tübingen.

Hopkins, David (2003). Review of Repetzki (2000), *Translation and Literature* 11: 113–18.

Hopkins, David (2004). ' "The English Homer": Shakespeare, Longinus, and English "Neoclassicism" ' (pp. 261–76) in *Shakespeare and the Classics*, ed. Charles Martindale and A. B. Taylor. Cambridge.

Hopkins, David (2007). 'The English Voices of Lucretius from Lucy Hutchinson to John Mason Good' (pp. 254–73) in Gillespie and Hardie.

Hopkins, David (2010). *Conversing with Antiquity: English Poets and the Classics, from Shakespeare to Pope*. Oxford.

Hornsby, R. A. (1958). 'Horace's *Ode* 3.29', *Classical Journal* 54: 119–36.

Howard, Robert (1660). *Poems*. London.

Hughes, Jabez (1737). *Miscellanies in Verse and Prose*. London.

Hurd, Richard (1751). *Q. Horatii Flacci Epistola … to which is added a Discourse Concerning Poetical Imitation*. London.

Hutton, James (1980). 'The Classics in Sixteenth-Century France' (pp. 207–24) in Hutton, *Essays on Renaissance Poetry*, ed. Rita Guerlac. Ithaca, NY.

Jenkins, Thomas E. (2007). 'The "Ultra-Modern" Euripides of Verrall, H.D., and MacLeish', *Classical and Modern Literature* 27: 121–45.

Johnson, Samuel (1905). *The Lives of the English Poets*, ed. George Birkbeck Hill, 3 vols. Oxford.

Johnston, Kenneth (1998). *The Hidden Wordsworth: Poet, Lover, Rebel, Spy*. New York.

Jones, Emrys (1971). *Scenic Form in Shakespeare*. Oxford.

Jones, Emrys (1977). *The Origins of Shakespeare*. Oxford.

Jones, Emrys (1985). 'A "Perpetual Torrent": Dryden's Lucretian Style' (pp. 47–64) in *Augustan Studies: Essays in Honor of Irvin Ehrenpreis*, ed. Douglas Lane Patey and Timothy Keegan. Newark, DE.

Jones, Emrys (2004). 'Dryden's Persius' (pp. 123–38) in *John Dryden: His Politics, His Plays, and His Poets*, ed. Claude Rawson and Aaron Santesso. Newark, DE.

Jones, Emrys, ed. (1964). *Henry Howard, Earl of Surrey: Poems*. Oxford.

Jones, Richard Foster (1953). *The Triumph of the English Language: A Survey of Opinions concerning the Vernacular from the Introduction of Printing to the Renaissance*. London.

Jong, I. J. F. de (2001). *A Narratological Commentary on the Odyssey*. Cambridge.

Jonson, Ben (1975). *Complete Poems*, ed. George Parfitt. Harmondsworth.

Juvenal (1683). *Satura ex doct. virorum emendatione*. The Hague and Rotterdam.

Keegan, Paul, ed. (2000). *The Penguin Book of English Verse*. Harmondsworth.

Keegan, Paul, ed. (2003). *Collected Poems of Ted Hughes*. London.

Kelley, Paul (1983). 'Wordsworth and Lucretius' *De Rerum Natura*', *Notes & Queries* 228: 219–22.

Kelly, Louis (2010). 'Pedagogical Uses of Translation' (pp. 12–16) in Braden, Cummings and Gillespie (2010).

Kenner, Hugh (1972). *The Pound Era*. London.

Kenner, Hugh (1990). 'Ezra Pound and Homer' (pp. 12–23) in Hugh Kenner, *Historical Fictions: Essays*. San Francisco.

Knight, Douglas (1959). 'Translation: The Augustan Mode' (pp. 196–204) in *On Translation*, ed. Reuben A. Brower. Cambridge, MA.

Knight, William, ed. (1882–9). *The Poetical Works of William Wordsworth*, 3 vols. Edinburgh.

Knight, William, ed. (1907). *Letters of the Wordsworth Family from 1787 to 1855*, 2 vols. Boston, MA.

Kragelund, Patrick (2009). '*Octavia* and Renaissance Tragedy from Trissino to Shakespeare', *Classica et Mediaevalia* 60: 237–303.

Lamb, Charles and Mary (1975–8). *The Letters of Charles and Mary Lamb*, ed. E. W. Marrs Jr, 3 vols. Ithaca, NY, and London.

Lamb, Margaret (1980). *Antony and Cleopatra on the English Stage*. London and Toronto.

Landon, Carol, and Curtis, Jared, eds. (1997). *Early Poems and Fragments, 1785–1797* (The Cornell Wordsworth). Ithaca, NY.

Lathrop, Henry Burrowes (1933). *Translations from the Classics into English from Caxton to Chapman 1477–1620*. Madison, WI.

Lefevre, André, ed. (1992). *Translation, History, Culture: A Sourcebook*. London and New York.

Leishman, J. B. (1956). *Translating Horace*. Oxford.

Lewis, C. S. (1938). *The Allegory of Love: A Study in Medieval Tradition* (first published 1936). London.

Lewis, C. S. (1964). *The Discarded Image: An Introduction to Medieval and Renaissance Literature*. Cambridge.

Lewis, C. S. (1966). 'Dante's Statius' (pp. 94–102) in C. S. Lewis, *Studies in Medieval and Renaissance Literature*. Cambridge.

Lindop, Grevil (2001). 'Wordsworth, Pope and the Alps', *Romanticism* 7: 58–72.

Logue, Christopher (1999). *Prince Charming: A Memoir*. London.

Longley, Michael (1995). *The Ghost Orchid*. London.

Longley, Michael (2009). 'Lapsed Classicist' (pp. 97–113) in Harrison.

Lonsdale, Roger, ed. (1969). *Poems of Thomas Gray, William Collins, Oliver Goldsmith*. London.

Love, Harold (1993). *Scribal Publication in Seventeenth-Century England*. Oxford.

Love, Harold (2002). 'Oral and Scribal Texts in Early Modern England' (pp. 97–121) in *The Cambridge History of the Book in Britain*, Vol. IV: *1557–1695*, ed. John Barnard and D. F. McKenzie. Cambridge.

Lyne, Raphael (2001). *Ovid's Changing Worlds: English Metamorphoses 1567–1632*. Oxford.

Lyne, Raphael (2002). 'Ovid in English Translation' (pp. 249–63) in *The Cambridge Companion to Ovid*, ed. Philip Hardie. Cambridge.

Lytton Sells, A. L. (1980). *Thomas Gray: His Life and Works*. London.

Mackenzie, Donald (2005). 'Two Versions of Lucretius: Arnold and Housman', *Translation and Literature* 16: 160–77.

Macleod, Colin (1983). *Collected Essays*. Oxford.

Magoun, F. P., Jr (1955). 'Chaucer's Summary of Statius' *Thebaid* II–XII', *Traditio* 11: 409–20.

Mariotti, Scevola (1952). *Livio Andronico e la traduzione artistica: Saggio critico ed edizione dei frammenti dell' Odyssea*. Urbino.

Marshall, Cynthia (2000). 'Sight and Sound: Two Models of Shakespearean Subjectivity on the British Stage', *Shakespeare Quarterly* 51: 353–61.

Mason, H. A. (1959). *Humanism and Poetry in the Early Tudor Period*. London.

Mason, H. A. (1969). 'Creative Translation: Ezra Pound's *Women of Trachis*', *Cambridge Quarterly* 4: 244–72.

Mason, H. A. (1972). *To Homer through Pope*. London.

Mason, H. A. (1981). 'Living in the Present: Is Dryden's "Horat. Ode 29. Book 3" an Example of "creative translation"?' *Cambridge Quarterly* 10: 91–129.

Mason, Tom (1996). 'Is there a Classical Tradition in English Poetry?' *Translation and Literature* 5: 203–19.

Matthiessen, F. O. (1931). *Translation: An Elizabethan Art*. Cambridge, MA.

Maxwell, J. C. (1964). 'Pope's Statius and Dryden's Ovid', *Notes and Queries* 11: 56.

May, Steven W. (1980). 'Tudor Aristocrats and the Mythical "Stigma of Print"', *Renaissance Papers* 10: 11–18.

Medcalf, Stephen (2008). 'Classical Authors' (pp. 364–89) in *The Oxford History of Literary Translation in English*, Vol. 1: *To 1550*, ed. Roger Ellis. Oxford.

Melville, A. D., trans. (1992). *Statius: Thebaid*. Oxford.

Messing, Gordon M. (1975). 'Pound's Propertius: The Homage and the Damage' (pp. 105–33) in *Poetry and Politics from Ancient Greece to the Renaissance: Studies in Honor of James Hutton*, ed. G. M. Kirkwood. Ithaca, NY, and London.

Minnis, A. J., ed. (1993). *Chaucer's Boece and the Medieval Tradition of Boethius*. Cambridge.

Morini, Massimiliano (2006). *Tudor Translation in Theory and Practice*. Aldershot.

Moss, Joseph William (1837). *A Manual of Classical Bibliography*, 2 vols. London.

Most, Glenn W. (2003). 'Violets in Crucibles: Translating, Traducing, Transmuting', *Transactions of the American Philological Association* 133: 381–90.

Moul, Victoria (2007). 'Versions of Victory: Ben Jonson and the Pindaric Ode', *International Journal of the Classical Tradition* 14: 51–73.

Mozley, J. H., translator (1928). *Statius*, 2 vols. London.

Muir, Kenneth, ed. (1950). *Collected Poems of Sir Thomas Wyatt*. Cambridge, MA.

Munro, H. A. J., ed. and trans. (1928). *T. Lucreti Cari De rerum natura libri sex with Notes and a Translation*, 2 vols. London.

Murray, A. T., trans. (1919). *Homer: The Odyssey*. London.

Nelis, Damien P. (2010). 'Vergil's Library' (pp. 13–25) in *Vergil's 'Aeneid' and its Tradition*, ed. Joseph Farrell and Michael C. J. Putnam. Boston, MA.

Newlands, Carole E. (1988). 'Statius' Villa Poems and Ben Jonson's *To Penshurst*: The Shaping of a Tradition', *Classical and Modern Literature* 8: 291–300.

Nisard, M. D. (1834). *Études de moeurs et de critique sur les poètes Latins de la décadence*. Paris.

Nisbet, R. G. M. (1963). 'Persius' (pp. 39–72) in *Critical Essays on Roman Literature: Satire*, ed. J. P. Sullivan. London.

Norbrook, David (1994). 'Lucan, Thomas May, and the Creation of a Republican Literary Culture' (pp. 45–66) in *Culture and Politics in Early Stuart England*, ed. Kevin Sharpe and Peter Lake. Basingstoke.

Norbrook, David (1999). *Writing the English Republic: Poetry, Rhetoric, and Politics, 1627–1660*. Cambridge.

Nørgaard, H. (1958). 'Translations of the Classics into English before 1600', *Review of English Studies* 9: 164–72.

North, Marcy L. (1982). *The Anonymous Renaissance: Cultures of Discretion in Tudor–Stuart England*. Chicago and London.

North, Thomas, trans. (1579). *The Lives of the Noble Grecians and Romanes Compared*. London.

Nuttall, A. D. (2004). 'Action at a Distance: Shakespeare and the Greeks' (pp. 209–22) in Charles Martindale and A. B. Taylor, eds., *Shakespeare and the Classics*. Cambridge.

Oliver, H. J. (1963). *Sir Robert Howard (1626–1698): A Critical Biography*. Durham, NC.

Osborn, James M. (1965). *John Dryden: Some Biographical Facts and Problems*, revised edition. New Haven, CT.

Ousby, Ian (1993). *The Cambridge Guide to Literature in English*. Cambridge.

Palmer, Henrietta P. (1911). *List of English Editions and Translations of Greek and Latin Classics Printed before 1641*. London.

Patterson, Annabel (2007). 'Too Much Virgil? Too Much Talk? Wordsworth's Anxiety of Influence' (pp. 101–17) in *Pastoral Palimpsests: Essays in the Reception of Theocritus and Virgil*, ed. Michael Paschalis. Heraklion.

Pearcy, Lee T. (1984). *The Mediated Muse: English Versions of Ovid, 1560–1700*. Hamden, CT.

Pelling, Christopher (2002). *Plutarch and History: Eighteen Studies*. London.

Pelling, Christopher (2009). 'Seeing a Roman Tragedy through Greek Eyes: Shakespeare's Julius Caesar' (pp. 264–88) in *Sophocles and the Greek Tragic Tradition*, ed. Simon Goldhill and Edith Hall. New York.

Pelling, Christopher, ed. (1998). *Plutarch: Life of Antony*. Cambridge.

Petrina, Alessandra (2009). *Machiavelli in the British Isles: Two Early Modern Translations of 'The Prince'*. Farnham.

Pigman, G. W. III (1980). 'Versions of Imitation in the Renaissance', *Renaissance Quarterly* 33: 1–32.

Pinder, North, ed. (1869). *Selections from the Less Known Latin Poets.* Oxford.

Pitt, Christopher (1740). *The Aeneid*, 2 vols. London.

Poole, Adrian, and Maule, Jeremy, eds. (1995). *The Oxford Book of Classical Verse in English Translation.* Oxford.

Pope, Alexander (1939–69). *The Twickenham Edition of the Poems of Alexander Pope*, gen. ed. John Butt, 11 vols. London and New Haven, CT.

Portale, Rosario (1991). *Virgilio in Inghilterra: Saggi.* Pisa.

Postgate, J. P., ed. (1881). *Select Elegies of Propertius.* London.

Pound, Ezra (1954). *Literary Essays.* New York.

Pound, Ezra (1975). *Selected Poems 1908–1959.* London.

Priestman, Martin (2007). 'Lucretius in Romantic and Victorian Britain, 1790–1890' (pp. 306–24) in Gillespie and Hardie (2007).

Prior, Matthew (1959). *Literary Works*, ed. H. Bunker Wright and Monroe K. Spears, 2 vols. Oxford.

Prosperi, Valentina (2007). 'Lucretius in the Italian Renaissance' (pp. 214–26) in Gillespie and Hardie.

Pym, Anthony (1995). 'Schliermacher and the Problem of *Blendlinge*', *Translation and Literature* 4: 5–30.

Raab, Felix (1964). *The English Face of Machiavelli: A Changing Interpretation 1500–1700.* London.

Radice, William, and Reynolds, Barbara, eds. (1987). *The Translator's Art: Essays in Honour of Betty Radice.* Harmondsworth.

Ramsay, G. G., trans. (1940). *Juvenal and Persius* (Loeb). London and New York.

Ramsay, Paul (1969). *The Art of John Dryden.* Lexington, KY.

Reading, Peter (1996). *Collected Poems*, 2 vols. Newcastle upon Tyne.

Real, Hermann Josef (1970). *Untersuchungen zur Lukrez-Übersetzung von Thomas Creech.* Zürich.

Rees, Roger, ed. (2009). *Ted Hughes and the Classics.* Oxford.

Rener, Frederick (1989). *Interpretatio: Language and Translation from Cicero to Tytler.* Amsterdam.

Repetzki, Michael M., ed. (2000). *John Evelyn's Translation of Titus Lucretius Carus De Rerum Natura: An Old-Spelling Critical Edition.* Frankfurt.

Revard, Stella (1982). 'Pindar and Jonson's Cary-Morrison Ode' (pp. 17–29) in Claude J. Summers and Ted-Larry Pebworth, eds., *Classic and Cavalier: Essays on Jonson and the Sons of Ben.* Pittsburgh, PA.

Reynolds, Matthew (forthcoming). *The Poetry of Translation.* Oxford.

Rhodes, Neil (2004). *Shakespeare and the Origins of English.* Oxford.

Ricks, David (2006). 'Homer' (pp. 168–77) in France and Haynes (2006).

Ringler, Richard N. (1963). 'Spenser and the *Achilleid*', *Studies in Philology* 60: 174–82.

Robinson, Douglas (1992). 'The Ascetic Foundations of Western Translatology: Jerome and Augustine', *Translation and Literature* 1: 3–25.

Roe, John (2004). '"Character" in Plutarch and Shakespeare: Brutus, Julius Caesar, and Mark Antony' (pp. 173–87) in Charles Martindale and A. B. Taylor, eds., *Shakespeare and the Classics*. Cambridge.

Rogers, Shef (2004). 'William Popple', in *The Oxford Dictionary of National Biography*, ed. H. G. C. Matthew and Brian Harrison, 60 vols. Oxford.

Rosemann, Philipp W. (2008). 'Robert Grosseteste' (pp. 126–36) in Roger Ellis, ed., *The Oxford History of Literary Translation in English*, Vol. 1: *To 1550*. Oxford.

Røstvig, Maren-Sofie (1954–8). *The Happy Man: Studies in the Metamorphosis of a Classical Ideal*, 2 vols. Oslo.

Ruffhead, Owen (1769). *The Life of Alexander Pope*. London.

Ruoff, James (1975). *Crowell's Handbook of Elizabethan and Stuart Literature*. New York.

Russell, Peter, ed. (1950). *Ezra Pound: A Collection of Essays*. London and New York.

Rymer, Thomas (1956), *Critical Works*, ed. Curt A. Zimansky. New Haven, CT.

Schmidt, Gabriela (2010). 'Realigning English Vernacular Poetics Through Metrical Experiment: Sixteenth-Century Translation and the Elizabethan Quantitative Verse Movement', *Literature Compass* 7: 303–17.

Schneider, Ben Ross (1957). *Wordsworth's Cambridge Education*. Cambridge.

Scodel, Joshua (2010). 'Non-Dramatic Verse: Lyric' (pp. 212–47) in Braden, Cummings and Gillespie.

Sellar, W. Y. (1899). *The Roman Poets of the Augustan Age: Horace and the Elegiac Poets*. Oxford.

Serjeantson, Mary S. (1993). *A History of Foreign Words in English*. London.

Shackleton Bailey, D. R., ed. (1985). *Q. Horati Flacci Opera*. Stuttgart.

Silk, Michael (2004). 'Shakespeare and Greek Tragedy' (pp. 241–57) in Charles Martindale and A. B. Taylor, eds., *Shakespeare and the Classics*. Cambridge.

Simonsuuri, Kirsti (1979). *Homer's Original Genius: Eighteenth-Century Notions of the Early Greek Epic (1688–1798)*. Cambridge.

Simpson, James (2002). *The Oxford English Literary History*, Vol. 2: *Reform and Cultural Revolution, 1350–1547*. Oxford.

Smith, Charles George (1963). *Shakespeare's Proverb Lore: His Use of the Sententiae of Leonard Culman and Publilius Syrus*. Cambridge, MA.

Southern, Richard (1952). *Changeable Scenery: Its Origin and Development in the British Theatre*. London.

Sowerby, Robin (1992). 'Chapman's Discovery of Homer', *Translation and Literature* 1: 26–51.

Sowerby, Robin (1994). *The Classical Legacy in Renaissance Poetry*. London.

Sowerby, Robin (2006). *The Augustan Art of Poetry: Augustan Translation of the Classics*. Oxford.

Spence, Joseph (1966). *Observations, Anecdotes and Characters of Books and Men: Collected from Conversation*, ed. James M. Osborn, 2 vols. Oxford.

Spiegelman, Willard (1974). 'Wordsworth's *Aeneid*', *Comparative Literature* 26: 97–109.

Spiegelman, Willard (1985). 'Some Lucretian Elements in Wordsworth', *Comparative Literature* 37: 27–49.

Stack, Frank (1985). *Pope and Horace: Studies in Imitation*. Cambridge.

Steiner, George (1975). *After Babel: Aspects of Language and Translation*. London.

Steiner, George, ed. (1966). *The Penguin Book of Modern Verse Translation*. Harmondsworth.

Steiner, George, ed. (1996). *Homer in English*. Harmondsworth.

Steppat, Michael (1980). *The Critical Reception of Shakespeare's 'Antony and Cleopatra' from 1607 to 1905*. Amsterdam.

Stoneman, Richard, ed. (1982). *Daphne into Laurel: Translations of Classical Poetry from Chaucer to the Present*. London.

Sullivan, J. P. (1965). *Ezra Pound and Sextus Propertius: A Study in Creative Translation*. London.

Sullivan, J. P. (1972). 'In Defence of Persius', *Ramus* 1: 48–62.

T.S. [Thomas Stephens] (1648). *An Essay upon Statius; or, the First Five Books of Publ: Papinius Statius his Thebais. Done into English Verse*. London.

Talbot, John (2006a). '"I Had Set Myself Against Latin": Ted Hughes and the Classics', *Arion* 13/3: 131–61.

Talbot, John (2006b). 'Latin Poetry' (pp. 188–99) in France and Haynes (2006).

Taplin, Oliver (2009). 'The Homeric Convergences and Divergences of Seamus Heaney and Michael Longley', in Harrison.

Taylor, A. B. (1989). 'Golding, Ovid, Shakespeare's "Small Latin", and the Real Object of Mockery in "Pyramus and Thisbe"', *Shakespeare Survey* 42: 53–64.

Taylor, Andrew W. (2010). 'The Bible' (pp. 121–40) in Braden, Cummings and Gillespie.

Terry, Richard (2001). *Poetry and the Making of the English Literary Past 1660–1781*. Oxford.

Thomson, J. A. K. (1952). *Shakespeare and the Classics*. New York.

Tillyard, E. M. W. (1954). *The English Epic and its Background*. London.

Tissol, Garth (2004). 'Lewis, William Lillington', in *The Oxford Dictionary of National Biography*, ed. H. G. C. Matthew and Brian Harrison, 60 vols. Oxford.

Tomlinson, Charles (2003). *Metamorphoses: Poetry and Translation*. Manchester.

Tuck, J. P. (1950). 'The Use of English in Latin Teaching in the Sixteenth Century', *Durham Research Review* 1: 22–30.

Tuckerman, Una Venable (1930). 'Wordsworth's Plan for his Imitation of Juvenal', *Modern Language Notes* 45: 209–15.

Turberville, George, trans. (1567). *The Heroycall Epistles of the learned Poet Publius Ovidius Naso*. London.

Turner, Frank (1973). 'Lucretius among the Victorians', *Victorian Studies* 16: 329–48.

Venuti, Lawrence (1995). *The Translator's Invisibility: A History of Translation*. London.

Vessey, David (1973). *Statius and the Thebaid*. Cambridge.

Vieth, David M. (1972). 'Irony in Dryden's Verses to Sir Robert Howard', *Essays in Criticism* 22: 239–43.

Walker, John, ed. (1914). *A Selection of Curious Articles from the Gentleman's Magazine*, 4 vols. London.

Walker, Keith, ed. (1987). *John Dryden*. Oxford.

Warton, Joseph, ed. (1763). *The Works of Virgil. In English Verse … with Notes on the Whole*, 4 vols. London.

Warton, Joseph, ed. (1822). *The Works of Alexander Pope*, 9 vols. London.

Warton, Thomas (1762). *Observations on the Fairy Queen of Spenser*, 2 vols. London.

Warton, Thomas (1774–81). *The History of English Poetry*, 4 vols. London.

Wasserman, Earl (1947). *Elizabethan Poetry in the Eighteenth Century*. Urbana, IL.

Wasserman, George (1964). *John Dryden*. New York.

Watson, John Selby (1851). *Lucretius of the Nature of Things … literally translated*. London.

Webb, Timothy (1976). *The Violet in the Crucible: Shelley and Translation*. Oxford.

Webb, Timothy (2004). 'Homer and the Romantics' (pp. 287–310) in *The Cambridge Companion to Homer*, ed. Robert Fowler. Cambridge.

Weinbrot, Howard (1993). *Britannia's Issue: The Rise of British Literature from Dryden to Ossian*. Cambridge.

Weissbort, Daniel (2010). 'Ted Hughes and the Translatable', *Comparative Critical Studies* 7: 107–19.

Weissbort, Daniel, and Eysteinsson, Astradur, eds. (2006). *Translation – Theory and Practice: A Reader*. Oxford.

Weissbort, Daniel, ed. (2006). *Selected Translations of Ted Hughes*. London.

Wilcher, Robert, ed. (1986). *Andrew Marvell: Selected Poetry and Prose*. London.

Wilders, John, ed. (1995). *Antony and Cleopatra*. London and New York.

Williams, Gordon, ed. (1969). *The Third Book of Horace's 'Odes'*. Oxford.

Wilson, Thomas (1553). *The Arte of Rhetoricke*. London.

Winn, James A. (2000). 'Past and Present in Dryden's *Fables*', *Huntington Library Quarterly* 63: 157–74.

Winn, James Anderson (1987). *John Dryden and his World*. New Haven, CT.

Wise, B. A. (1911). *The Influence of Statius upon Chaucer*. Baltimore, MD.

Worthington, Jane (1970). *Wordsworth's Reading of Roman Prose*. New Haven, CT.

Woudhuysen, Henry (1996). *Sir Philip Sidney and the Circulation of Manuscripts 1558–1640*. Oxford.

Wu, Duncan (1993–5). *Wordsworth's Reading*, 2 vols. Cambridge.

Yao, Stephen (2002). *Translation and the Languages of Modernism: Gender, Politics, Language*. New York.

Young, Philip H. (2003). *The Printed Homer: A 3000 Year Publishing and Translation History of the 'Iliad' and 'Odyssey'*. Jefferson, NC.

Index of Ancient Authors and Passages

This index does not extend to author names mentioned within lists.

English Translation and Classical Reception: Towards a New Literary History, First Edition.
Stuart Gillespie.
© 2011 Stuart Gillespie. Published 2011 by John Wiley & Sons, Ltd.

General Index

English Translation and Classical Reception: Towards a New Literary History, First Edition.
Stuart Gillespie.
© 2011 Stuart Gillespie. Published 2011 by John Wiley & Sons, Ltd.